The Best of
COUNTRY COOKING
2004

Editors: Jean Steiner, Beth Wittlinger
Art Director: Lori Arndt
Associate Editor: Heidi Reuter Lloyd
Food Editor: Janaan Cunningham
Senior Recipe Editor: Sue A. Jurack
Recipe Editor: Janet Briggs
Food Photography: Dan Roberts, Rob Hagen
Senior Food Photography Artist: Stephanie Marchese
Food Photography Artist: Julie Ferron
Photo Studio Manager: Anne Schimmel
Graphic Art Associates: Ellen Lloyd, Catherine Fletcher
Chairman and Founder: Roy Reiman
President: Russell Denson

©2004 Reiman Media Group, Inc.
5400 S. 60th St., Greendale WI 53129
International Standard Book Number: 0-89821-406-8
International Standard Serial Number: 1097-8321
All rights reserved.
Printed in U.S.A.

For additional copies of this book or information on other books, write *Taste of Home* Books,
P.O. Box 908, Greendale WI 53129, call toll-free 1-800/344-2560 to order with a credit card
or visit our Web site at **www.reimanpub.com**.

PICTURED ON COVER AND ABOVE. From the top: Kiwi Pineapple Cheesecake (p. 114), Penne Pasta Salad (p. 52) and Pinwheel Flank Steaks (p. 13).

Your Comprehensive Collection Of 365 Home-Cooked Favorites

NEW DELIGHTS for every day are found in *The Best of Country Cooking 2004*. It's the seventh in our popular cookbook series, and it's serving up 365 country favorites. So you can find something new every day of the year!

This giant collection includes the very best recipes from recent issues of *Country Woman*, *Country*, *Country EXTRA*, *Reminisce* and *Reminisce EXTRA* magazines. All are hearty, wholesome and proven favorites of a family just like yours.

You see, these recipes weren't developed in some high-tech industrial "kitchen". Instead, they're from the personal recipe files of hundreds of everyday cooks across the country. Each and every dish has been sampled and approved by the toughest critic around—a hungry family!

What's more, every recipe in this book was tested—many of them twice—by us as well. So you can be doubly confident each and every dish is a "keeper".

So go ahead today and take your pick of this beautiful book's 76 Main Dishes, including Pinwheel Flank Steaks from Nancy Tafoya of Fort Collins, Colorado. These elegant-looking steaks are a breeze to make because much of the prep can be done in advance.

There's also a Side Dishes & Condiments chapter filled with 31 country-style complements like Creamy Potato Casserole from Patricia Staudt of Marble Rock, Iowa. This comforting casserole will go well with just about any meal. And turn to Breads & Rolls for fresh-baked treats like Nicholasville, Kentucky cook Andrea Durr's Spicy Pumpkin Bread. The aroma of cinnamon, nutmeg and cloves are sure to have your family gathering in the kitchen for the first warm slices!

Everyone will save room for dessert when any of this book's 84 scrumptious cakes, pies, cookies and more will be the sweet conclusion.

In addition, this tried-and-true treasury contains a savory selection of 36 Soups & Salads, and an appealing assortment of Snacks & Beverages. You'll also enjoy some extra-special features most other cookbooks overlook:

Thirty-Minute Meals—Six complete meals (18 recipes in all) that are ready to eat in less than half an hour.

Memorable Meals—Six complete meals featuring 24 favorite recipes.

Cooking for Two—A separate chapter —with 58 recipes including 6 full meals— properly proportioned to serve two people.

Want more? *The Best of Country Cooking 2004* offers individual sections on cooking quick-and-easy fare that you can whip up with little effort.

As you page through *The Best of Country Cooking 2004*, watch for the special symbol at right. It signifies a "best of the best" recipe— a winner of a coast-to-coast cooking contest one of our magazines sponsored.

Finally, throughout this colorful collection are lots of helpful kitchen tips from everyday cooks plus dozens of "restricted diet" recipes marked with this check ✓ that use less fat, sugar or salt.

See why we call this book "The Best"? Now, wait 'til you and your family taste why!

CONTENTS

PREPARING *for a party or treating your family is a snap with this selection of scrumptious snacks and beverages.*

SNACK SAMPLER. From top: Rhubarb Slush Punch, Vegetable Pizza and Deviled Crab Dip (all recipes on p. 5).

Snacks & Beverages

▰▰▰▰▰▰▰▰▰▰▰
VEGETABLE PIZZA
(Pictured at left)

Pat Walter, Pine Island, Minnesota

Refrigerated crescent rolls shape the crust for this party pleaser that features flavored cream cheese and fresh vegetables. It doesn't take long for it to disappear around here.

    1 tube (8 ounces) refrigerated crescent
        rolls
    1 package (8 ounces) cream cheese,
        softened
    1/2 cup mayonnaise
    1-1/2 teaspoons ranch salad dressing mix
    1-1/2 cups chopped broccoli florets
    1-1/2 cups chopped cauliflowerets
    1/2 cup chopped radishes
    1/4 cup chopped ripe olives
    1/2 cup shredded cheddar cheese

Unroll crescent dough and separate into triangles; arrange to fit on an ungreased 12-in. pizza pan. Press perforations together to seal. Bake at 375° for 8-10 minutes or until golden. Cool.

In a small mixing bowl, beat cream cheese, mayonnaise and salad dressing mix until smooth. Spread over the crust. Sprinkle with the broccoli, cauliflower, radishes, olives and cheese. **Yield:** 12 slices.

▰▰▰▰▰▰▰▰▰▰▰

DEVILED CRAB DIP
(Pictured at left)

Debbie Jones, California, Maryland

Because blue crabs are so plentiful in Maryland, we're always looking for new ways to enjoy them. This recipe is easy, elegant and delicious!

    1 cup mayonnaise
    2 tablespoons *each* finely chopped celery,
        green pepper and onion
    2 to 3 teaspoons lemon juice
    1 teaspoon ground mustard
    1 teaspoon Worcestershire sauce
    1/4 teaspoon salt
    1/8 teaspoon lemon-pepper seasoning
    1/8 to 1/4 teaspoon hot pepper sauce

    1-1/2 cups cooked *or* canned crabmeat,
        drained, flaked and cartilage removed
    Raw vegetables *or* crackers

In a bowl, combine the mayonnaise, celery, green pepper, onion, lemon juice, mustard, Worcestershire sauce, salt, lemon-pepper seasoning and hot pepper sauce. Stir in the crab. Cover and refrigerate for at least 1 hour.

Serve dip with vegetables or crackers. **Yield:** about 2 cups.

▰▰▰▰▰▰▰▰▰▰▰

RHUBARB SLUSH PUNCH
(Pictured at left)

Diane Haug, Neenah, Wisconsin

For years, our family has toasted special occasions with this cool, quenching punch. It's easy to freeze, so we serve it year-round. Usually, we double the recipe and freeze it in a clean, empty ice cream bucket.

    6 cups chopped fresh *or* frozen rhubarb,
        thawed
    7 cups water, *divided*
    2 cups sugar
    3/4 cup orange juice concentrate
    3/4 cup lemonade concentrate
    10 cups club soda, chilled

In a large saucepan, bring rhubarb and 4 cups of water to a boil. Reduce heat; simmer, uncovered, for 5-8 minutes or until the rhubarb is tender. Mash the rhubarb and strain. Reserve juice and discard pulp. Add sugar, concentrates and remaining water to juice. Transfer to a freezer container and freeze.

Remove from the freezer 30-45 minutes before serving, scraping the surface as it thaws. Place equal amounts of slush mixture and club soda in each serving glass. Stir together and serve immediately. **Yield:** 10 servings.

RHUBARB REMINDER

Rhubarb lovers can enjoy it out of season by cutting it into 1-inch chunks and freezing it in a freezer-proof plastic bag for up to 9 months.

1 cup sugar
1/2 cup light corn syrup
1/2 cup honey
1/2 cup peanut butter*
1/4 cup butter, softened
1 teaspoon vanilla extract
1 cup salted sunflower kernels
4 quarts popped popcorn

In a saucepan over medium heat, bring the sugar, corn syrup and honey to a boil, stirring often. Boil for 2 minutes. Remove from the heat; stir in the peanut butter, butter and vanilla until smooth. Add sunflower kernels.

Place popcorn in a large bowl. Add syrup and stir to coat. Press into two greased 13-in. x 9-in. x 2-in. baking pans. Cut into bars. Store in an airtight container. **Yield:** 4 dozen.

*Editor's Note: Reduced-fat or generic brands of peanut butter are not recommended for this recipe.

PEPPERMINT CHOCOLATE MALT
(Pictured above)

Carol Gillespie, Chambersburg, Pennsylvania

I'm a retired teacher and an avid recipe contest entrant. I concocted this recipe, and my family and friends love these thick and minty malts.

3 cups chocolate milk
4 cups vanilla ice cream, *divided*
1/3 cup plus 1-1/2 teaspoons malted milk powder, *divided*
2 tablespoons chocolate syrup
1/2 teaspoon peppermint extract
1/8 teaspoon ground cinnamon
Crushed peppermint candy and variegated mint leaves, optional

In a blender, combine the milk, 2 cups ice cream, 1/3 cup malted milk powder, chocolate syrup, extract and cinnamon. Cover and process until smooth. Pour into five chilled glasses. Top each with a scoop of the remaining ice cream. Sprinkle with remaining malted milk powder. Garnish with candy and mint if desired. **Yield:** 5 servings.

SUNFLOWER POPCORN BARS

Karen Ann Bland, Gove, Kansas

Kansas is called the Sunflower State because of the wild sunflowers that grow abundantly. Cultivated varieties of sunflowers are now becoming an important crop for many Kansas farmers.

THICK FRUIT WHIP

Nancy Zimmerman
Cape May Court House, New Jersey

This refreshing drink combines the great tastes of bananas and strawberries, but it can be adapted with other fruit combinations.

1 can (14 ounces) sweetened condensed milk
1 cup sliced unsweetened strawberries
1 medium firm banana
1/4 cup lemon juice
2 cups ice cubes

In a food processor or blender, combine all of the ingredients. Cover and process until smooth. Pour into glasses; serve immediately. **Yield:** 4 servings.

HEARTY NACHO DIP
(Pictured at right)

V. Eleanor Dargo, Chapel Hill, North Carolina

This hearty dip is very filling! It's packed with fresh ingredients like avocados, tomatoes, onions and more.

1 can (16 ounces) refried beans
1 can (4 ounces) chopped green chilies, drained
1-1/2 teaspoons chili powder, *divided*
2 teaspoons ground cumin, *divided*
2 ripe avocados, peeled and pitted
1/2 cup finely chopped onion, *divided*
2 teaspoons lemon juice
1/2 teaspoon sugar

1/2 teaspoon celery salt
1/8 teaspoon cayenne pepper
 2 cups salsa, *divided*
 1 cup (8 ounces) sour cream
 1 cup mayonnaise
 2 teaspoons paprika
1/2 teaspoon garlic powder
1/2 teaspoon hot pepper sauce
1/4 teaspoon dried oregano
 1 cup (4 ounces) shredded Monterey Jack
   cheese
 1 cup (4 ounces) shredded cheddar cheese
 2 packages (8 ounces *each*) cream cheese,
   softened
Chopped green onions and tomatoes
Tortilla chips *or* raw vegetables

In a bowl, combine the refried beans, chilies, 1 teaspoon chili powder and 1 teaspoon cumin; mix well. Spread over a 14-in. platter. In another bowl, mash the avocados; add 1/4 cup onion, lemon juice, sugar, celery salt and cayenne. Spread over the bean layer.

Combine 1 cup salsa, sour cream, mayonnaise, paprika, garlic powder, pepper sauce, oregano, and remaining onion, cumin and chili powder; mix well. Spread over avocado layer; sprinkle with Monterey Jack and cheddar cheeses.

In a mixing bowl, beat the cream cheese until smooth. Add the remaining salsa. Spread over cheeses. Sprinkle with the green onions and tomatoes. Cover and refrigerate until serving. Serve with chips or vegetables. **Yield:** 20-25 servings.

▪▪▪▪▪▪▪▪▪▪▪▪▪▪
MOLDED SHRIMP SPREAD
(Pictured above)

Mrs. Austin Locke, Prineville, Oregon

I usually make this seafood spread for parties and family gatherings. It never lasts long because folks go straight for it.

 1 can (10-3/4 ounces) condensed cream
   of mushroom soup, undiluted
 1 package (8 ounces) cream cheese,
   cubed
 1 envelope unflavored gelatin
 3 tablespoons cold water
 1 cup finely chopped celery
 1 cup mayonnaise
 3 tablespoons lemon juice
 4 green onions, finely chopped
1/2 pound cooked shrimp, peeled, deveined
   and coarsely chopped
Lettuce leaves and additional shrimp, optional
Assorted crackers

In a saucepan, heat soup and cream cheese over medium heat until cheese is melted, stirring frequently. Remove from the heat; set aside to cool.

In a small microwave-safe bowl, sprinkle gelatin over water; let stand for 1 minute. Microwave on high for 40 seconds; stir. Let stand for 2 minutes or until gelatin is completely dissolved. Stir the gelatin mixture, celery, mayonnaise, lemon juice and onions into soup mixture. Fold in shrimp.

Pour into a 5-cup ring mold coated with nonstick cooking spray. Cover and refrigerate for 8 hours or until set. Invert onto a serving plate. Fill center with lettuce and shrimp if desired. Serve with crackers. **Yield:** 4-1/4 cups.

CHUNKY BLACK BEAN SALSA

Chris Behnke, Fruitland, Iowa

Chock-full of color and lively flavor, this salsa makes a nice appetizer paired with tortilla chips. It's great for parties because it's easy and delicious.

    5 plum tomatoes, seeded and chopped
1/2 cup minced fresh cilantro
    1 jalapeno pepper, chopped*
3/4 cup canned black beans, rinsed and drained
1/2 cup canned diced tomatoes with green chilies, drained
1/4 cup chopped ripe olives
    2 tablespoons chopped red onion
1/2 cup Italian salad dressing
Tortilla chips

In a bowl, combine the first eight ingredients. Toss to coat. Serve with chips. Refrigerate leftovers. **Yield:** 5 cups.

*Editor's Note: When cutting or seeding hot peppers, use rubber or plastic gloves to protect your hands. Avoid touching your face.

STRAWBERRY FRUIT DIP

(Pictured below)

Lydia Graf, Norton, Ohio

I got this recipe from my husband's cousin. It's a refreshing treat during summer months.

    1 cup sliced fresh strawberries
1/4 cup sour cream
    1 tablespoon sugar
1/4 teaspoon vanilla extract
1/2 cup heavy whipping cream
Assorted fresh fruit

In a blender, combine strawberries, sour cream, sugar and vanilla. Cover and process until smooth. In a small mixing bowl, beat cream until stiff peaks form. Fold into strawberry mixture. Cover and refrigerate for at least 1 hour. Serve with fruit. **Yield:** 1-1/2 cups.

CHEESE SPREAD PINECONE

(Pictured above)

Cindy Harrington, Euless, Texas

Folks quickly cluster around this outdoorsy appetizer. I turned my super cheese spread into a pinecone— using sliced almonds, dill sprigs and a cinnamon stick!

    2 packages (8 ounces *each*) cream cheese, softened
1/4 cup milk
    1 cup (4 ounces) crumbled feta cheese
    1 cup (4 ounces) shredded mozzarella cheese
    2 tablespoons dried minced onion
1/4 teaspoon cayenne pepper
2/3 cup sliced almonds, toasted
    1 cinnamon stick
Fresh dill sprigs
Breadsticks, crackers *and/or* raw vegetables

In a mixing bowl, combine the cream cheese and milk; mix well. Add the feta, mozzarella, onion and cayenne; mix well. Cover and refrigerate for 2 hours or until firm.

On a serving platter, form cheese mixture into a pinecone shape. Beginning at the narrow end, arrange almonds in overlapping rows. Add cinnamon stick and dill for the stem and pine needles. Serve with breadsticks, crackers and/or vegetables. **Yield:** 3-1/2 cups.

STRAWBERRY SHAKES

Ruby Williams, Bogalusa, Louisiana

Full of summer fruit, these thick berry blends are the perfect way to savor hot days.

- 2/3 cup milk
- 3 cups strawberry ice cream
- 1 cup fresh strawberries
- 2 tablespoons strawberry syrup

In a blender, combine all ingredients; cover and process until smooth. Pour into glasses. Serve immediately. **Yield:** 4 servings.

PADDY'S REUBEN DIP

Mary Jane Kimmes, Hastings, Minnesota

This spread tastes just like a Reuben sandwich. Even when I double the recipe, I end up with an empty dish.

- 4 packages (2-1/2 ounces *each*) deli corned beef, finely chopped
- 1 package (8 ounces) cream cheese, cubed
- 1 can (8 ounces) sauerkraut, rinsed and drained
- 1 cup (8 ounces) sour cream
- 1 cup (4 ounces) shredded Swiss cheese

Rye bread *or* crackers

In a mini slow cooker, combine the first five ingredients. Cover and cook on low for 2 hours or until cheese is melted; stir until blended. Serve warm with bread or crackers. **Yield:** about 4 cups.

HOT SPICED PUNCH

Ruth Peterson, Jenison, Michigan

My favorite punches, hot or cold, are the ones made with pineapple juice, like this fruity blend.

- 12 cinnamon sticks (3 inches), broken
- 4 teaspoons whole cloves
- 2 teaspoons whole allspice

Peel of 1 lemon, cut into 1-inch strips

- 9 cups white grape juice
- 1 can (46 ounces) unsweetened pineapple juice
- 3/4 cup lemonade concentrate
- 1/2 cup sugar

Additional cinnamon sticks, optional

Place the first four ingredients in a double thickness of cheesecloth; bring up corners of cloth and tie with kitchen string to form a bag.

In a large kettle, combine the grape juice, pineapple juice, lemonade concentrate and sugar; add the spice bag. Bring to a boil. Reduce heat; simmer, uncovered, for 1 hour or until punch reaches desired temperature. Discard spice bag. Serve hot with additional cinnamon sticks if desired. **Yield:** 4 quarts.

ST. PATRICK'S DAY POPCORN

(Pictured below)

Karen Weber, Salem, Missouri

Everyone's eyes will be smilin' when they see this candy corn with an Irish twist. The green color gives the snack instant holiday appeal.

- 4 quarts popped popcorn
- 1 cup sugar
- 1/2 cup packed brown sugar
- 1/2 cup water
- 1/2 cup light corn syrup
- 1 teaspoon white vinegar
- 1/4 teaspoon salt
- 1/2 cup butter
- 8 to 10 drops green food coloring

Place popcorn in a large roasting pan; place in a 250° oven. Meanwhile, in a large heavy saucepan, combine the sugars, water, corn syrup, vinegar and salt. Cook and stir over medium heat until mixture comes to a boil. Cook, stirring occasionally, until a candy thermometer reads 260° (hard-ball stage).

Remove from the heat; stir in butter until blended. Stir in food coloring. Drizzle over warm popcorn and toss to coat. Let stand until cool. Break apart. Store in an airtight container. **Yield:** 6 quarts.

Editor's Note: We recommend that you test your candy thermometer before each use by bringing water to a boil; the thermometer should read 212°. Adjust your recipe temperature up or down based on your test.

CRANBERRY SLUSH
(Pictured below)

Sharen Christensen, Salem, Utah

One taste of this sweet icy treat leads to another…and another. My mother-in-law makes it for family gatherings, and it never lasts long. Often, my husband and twin daughters request it as a snack or dessert.

    1 pound fresh *or* frozen cranberries
2-1/2 cups cold water, *divided*
3-1/2 cups fresh *or* frozen unsweetened
        raspberries
    1 envelope unflavored gelatin
    2 cups sugar
    2 cups ginger ale
1-3/4 cups raspberry ginger ale *or* additional
        ginger ale

In a large saucepan, cook the cranberries and 1-1/2 cups water over medium heat until the berries pop, about 15 minutes. Stir in raspberries. Transfer to a blender or food processor; cover and process until smooth.

Strain and discard seeds, reserving juice. Pour the juice into a 2-qt. freezer-proof container; set aside. In a small saucepan, sprinkle gelatin over remaining water. Let stand for 1 minute. Stir in sugar. Cook and stir over medium heat until gelatin and sugar are dissolved. Add to berry juice. Stir in ginger ale; cover and freeze.

Remove from the freezer 1 hour before serving. For each serving, combine 1 cup cranberry slush with 1/4 cup raspberry ginger ale in a glass; stir well. **Yield:** 7 servings.

PARMESAN CHICKEN WINGS
(Pictured above)

Ellen Montei, Caro, Michigan

Over the many years I've been cooking, I've had my share of flops, but these well-seasoned chicken wings have never failed me.

    16 whole chicken wings
    3/4 cup finely crushed butter-flavored
        crackers
    3/4 cup grated Parmesan cheese
    1 teaspoon dried basil
    3/4 teaspoon garlic salt
    1/4 cup butter, melted

Cut chicken wings into three sections; discard wing tips. In a small bowl, combine cracker crumbs, Parmesan cheese, basil and garlic salt. Dip wings in butter, then roll in crumb mixture. Place in a single layer on greased baking sheets. Bake at 375° for 35-40 minutes or until golden brown and juices run clear. **Yield:** 8-10 servings.

CHEESY BEAN DIP

Jackie Pritchett, Fulton, Missouri

My family and I can't get enough of this bean dip! It's great at any special gathering.

> ✓ **Uses less fat, sugar or salt. Includes Nutritional Analysis and Diabetic Exchanges.**

    1 package (8 ounces) reduced-fat cream
        cheese

1 cup (8 ounces) reduced-fat sour cream
1 can (16 ounces) fat-free refried beans
1 can (4 ounces) chopped green chilies
1 envelope enchilada seasoning
1 cup (4 ounces) shredded reduced-fat
   cheddar *or* Mexican cheese blend
1 green onion, chopped
Baked tortilla chips

In a mixing bowl, beat cream cheese and sour cream until smooth. Add the beans, chilies and seasoning; mix well. Spread into a 13-in. x 9-in. x 2-in. baking dish coated with nonstick cooking spray. Cover and bake at 350° for 15-20 minutes or until heated through. Sprinkle with cheese and onion. Serve with tortilla chips. **Yield:** 15 servings.

Nutritional Analysis: One serving (1/4 cup dip, calculated without chips) equals 106 calories, 5 g fat (3 g saturated fat), 16 mg cholesterol, 636 mg sodium, 8 g carbohydrate, 2 g fiber, 6 g protein. **Diabetic Exchanges:** 1 lean meat, 1/2 starch, 1/2 fat.

CRANBERRY-ORANGE SHAKE

Anna Mae Roth, Milford, Nebraska

This recipe came with a blender our sons gave us for Christmas back in the 1960s. We made a batch that year and every year since!

2 cups vanilla ice cream
2 cups cranberry juice
1/2 cup orange juice
Red liquid food coloring, optional

In a blender, combine the ice cream and juices; cover and process for 50-60 seconds or until smooth. Tint with food coloring if desired. Pour into chilled glasses; serve immediately. **Yield:** 4 servings.

STRAWBERRY COOLER

Judy Robertson, Russell Springs, Kentucky

During the dog days of summer, my family looks for a cold, thirst-quenching drink. I like this one because it's sparkling, refreshing and fast and easy to make.

5 cups sliced fresh strawberries
3 cups water
3/4 to 1 cup sugar
1/4 cup lemon juice
2 teaspoons grated lemon peel
1 cup ginger ale
Crushed ice
Whole strawberries, optional

In a blender, process the strawberries, water, sugar, lemon juice and peel in batches until smooth. Strain the berry seeds if desired. Pour into a pitcher; stir in the ginger ale. Serve over ice. Garnish with whole berries if desired. **Yield:** 8 servings.

CALICO CHEESE DIP
(Pictured below)

Ellen Keck, Granger, Indiana

As soon as my husband tasted this tantalizing dip at a party, he suggested I get the recipe...not knowing I'd already asked the hostess for it! Attractive and zesty, it's one of my most popular appetizers.

4 cups (16 ounces) shredded Monterey
   Jack cheese
1 can (4 ounces) chopped green chilies
1 can (2-1/4 ounces) sliced ripe olives,
   drained
4 green onions, sliced
3 medium tomatoes, seeded and diced
1/2 cup minced fresh parsley
1 envelope Italian salad dressing mix
Tortilla chips

In a mixing bowl, combine the cheese, chilies, olives, onions, tomatoes and parsley. Prepare salad dressing mix according to package directions; pour over cheese mixture and mix well. Serve immediately with tortilla chips. **Yield:** 6 cups.

THINKING *of what to make is sometimes the greatest challenge. These main dishes feature beef, pork, fish, chicken and more to help take the guesswork out of dinner.*

MAIN SQUEEZE. Clockwise from top left: Round Steak with Dumplings (p. 13), Pinwheel Flank Steaks (p. 13) and Grilled Pineapple Pork Chops (p. 15).

Main Dishes

ROUND STEAK WITH DUMPLINGS

(Pictured at left)

Sherrie Odom, Plant City, Florida

My grandma taught me how to make this old-fashioned mouth-watering main dish. I like to serve it for special occasions.

```
3/4 cup all-purpose flour
  1 tablespoon paprika
  3 pounds boneless beef round steak, cut
    into serving-size pieces
  2 to 3 tablespoons vegetable oil
  1 medium onion, chopped
2-2/3 cups water
  2 cans (10-3/4 ounces each) condensed
    cream of chicken soup, undiluted
1/2 teaspoon pepper
```
DUMPLINGS:
```
  3 cups all-purpose flour
1/4 cup dried minced onion
  2 tablespoons baking powder
  1 tablespoon poppy seeds
1-1/2 teaspoons celery salt
1-1/2 teaspoons poultry seasoning
3/4 teaspoon salt
1-1/2 cups milk
  6 tablespoons vegetable oil
  1 cup dry bread crumbs
1/4 cup butter, melted
```

In a large resealable plastic bag, combine flour and paprika. Add beef, a few pieces at a time, and shake to coat. In a Dutch oven over medium-high heat, brown steak in oil on both sides in batches, adding more oil if necessary. Remove and keep warm.

In the drippings, saute onion until tender. Stir in the water, soup and pepper. Bring to a boil. Return meat to pan. Cover and bake at 325° for 1-1/2 hours.

Meanwhile, for dumplings, combine the flour, minced onion, baking powder, poppy seeds, celery salt, poultry seasoning and salt in a bowl. Combine milk and oil; stir into dry ingredients just until moistened.

Increase oven temperature to 425°. In a bowl, combine bread crumbs and butter. Drop dumpling batter by rounded tablespoonfuls into crumb mixture; roll to form dumplings. Place on top of simmering beef mixture.

Cover and bake 20-25 minutes longer or until a toothpick inserted in a dumpling comes out clean (do not lift the cover while baking). **Yield:** 10-12 servings.

PINWHEEL FLANK STEAKS

(Pictured at left and on front cover)

Nancy Tafoya, Fort Collins, Colorado

Here's a yummy, elegant-looking steak dish that's a breeze to make. Much of the preparation can be done in advance.

```
1-1/2 pounds beef flank steak
  1/4 cup olive oil
    2 tablespoons red wine vinegar
    2 teaspoons Worcestershire sauce
    2 teaspoons Italian seasoning
1-1/2 teaspoons garlic powder
1-1/2 teaspoons pepper, divided
    1 teaspoon seasoned salt
    8 bacon strips, cooked and crumbled
    2 garlic cloves, minced
  1/4 cup minced fresh parsley
  1/4 cup finely chopped onion
  1/2 teaspoon salt
```

Flatten steak to 1/4-in. thickness. In a large resealable plastic bag, combine the oil, vinegar, Worcestershire sauce, Italian seasoning, garlic powder, 1 teaspoon pepper and seasoned salt; add the steak. Seal bag and turn to coat; refrigerate for 8 hours or overnight.

Drain and discard marinade. Combine the bacon, garlic, parsley, onion, salt and remaining pepper; sprinkle over steak to within 1 in. of edges. Roll up jelly-roll style, starting with a long side; tie at 1-in. intervals with kitchen string. Cut into 1-1/4-in. rolls.

Coat grill rack with nonstick cooking spray before starting the grill. Grill steak rolls, uncovered, over medium heat for 10-12 minutes on each side or until meat reaches desired doneness (for rare, a meat thermometer should read 140°; medium, 160°; well-done, 170°). Cut and remove string before serving. **Yield:** 4-6 servings.

The Best of Country Cooking 2004   13

end. Wrap two strips of bacon around each roll-up and secure with toothpicks. Place remaining rice mixture in a greased 11-in. x 7-in. x 2-in. baking dish; place roll-ups over rice.

In a microwave-safe bowl, heat honey, uncovered, on high for 30 seconds; spoon over chicken. Bake, uncovered, at 325° for 28-30 minutes or until chicken juices run clear. Discard toothpicks.

In a small saucepan, combine cream and mustard. Cook over medium-low heat until mixture is reduced and begins to thicken, stirring constantly. Serve warm with chicken. **Yield:** 4 servings.

▲▼▲▼▲▼▲▼▲▼▲▼▲▼

CHEESEBURGER PEPPER CUPS

(Pictured below)

Betty Winscher, Royalton, Minnesota

I like to serve my grandkids something special, and this is one of their favorites. They like red or yellow peppers because they're sweeter and look more appetizing.

> 4 medium sweet red, yellow or green peppers
> 1/2 pound ground beef
> 1/4 cup finely chopped onion
> 2 cups cooked brown rice
> 1 can (6 ounces) tomato paste
> 2 tablespoons ketchup
> 1 tablespoon Worcestershire sauce
> 1 tablespoon spicy brown mustard

▲▼▲▼▲▼▲▼▲▼▲▼▲▼

CHICKEN WITH CRANBERRY STUFFING

(Pictured above)

Jo Anne Cloughly, East Worcester, New York

I came up with this dish by combining various elements my family enjoyed from other recipes. It's a very pretty way to dress up plain chicken breast halves.

> 1/4 cup chopped onion
> 2 garlic cloves, minced
> 2 tablespoons butter
> 3-1/2 cups chicken broth
> 1/2 cup uncooked brown rice
> 1/2 cup uncooked wild rice
> 1/2 cup dried cranberries
> 1 tablespoon minced fresh parsley
> 1/4 teaspoon dried thyme
> 1/4 teaspoon pepper
> 8 bacon strips
> 4 boneless skinless chicken breast halves
> 1/4 cup honey

CREAMY MUSTARD SAUCE:
> 1 cup heavy whipping cream
> 3 tablespoons spicy brown or horseradish mustard

In a large saucepan, saute onion and garlic in butter until tender. Add the broth, brown rice and wild rice; bring to a boil. Reduce heat; cover and cook for 55-65 minutes or until rice is tender. Drain excess liquid if necessary. Stir in the cranberries, parsley, thyme and pepper. In a skillet, cook bacon over medium heat until cooked but not crisp; drain on paper towels.

Flatten chicken to 1/4-in. thickness. Top each with 1/4 cup rice mixture; roll up from one

1/2 teaspoon garlic salt
1/4 teaspoon pepper
　1 cup vegetable broth
　1 cup (4 ounces) shredded cheddar cheese

Cut peppers in half lengthwise and remove seeds; set aside. In a skillet, cook beef and onion over medium heat until meat is no longer pink; drain. Stir in the rice, tomato paste, ketchup, Worcestershire sauce, mustard, garlic salt and pepper. Spoon into peppers.

Place in a greased 13-in. x 9-in. x 2-in. baking dish; pour broth around the peppers. Cover and bake at 350° for 30 minutes. Sprinkle with cheese. Bake, uncovered, 5 minutes longer or until heated through. **Yield:** 4 servings.

 ## GRILLED PINEAPPLE PORK CHOPS

(Pictured on page 12)

Debby Cole, Wolf Creek, Oregon

This is my favorite way to grill pork chops because the meat turns out so moist and tender. The pineapple adds just the right amount of sweetness. I'm sure your family will love it as much as mine does.

1/2 cup packed brown sugar
1/2 cup Italian salad dressing
1/4 cup pineapple juice
　3 tablespoons soy sauce
　6 bone-in pork rib chops (1 inch thick)
　1 can (20 ounces) sliced pineapple, drained

In a 2-cup measuring cup, combine the brown sugar, salad dressing, pineapple juice and soy sauce; mix well. Pour 2/3 cup into a large resealable plastic bag; add the pork chops. Seal bag and turn to coat; refrigerate for at least 3 hours or overnight. Cover and refrigerate remaining marinade for basting.

Drain and discard marinade from pork. Grill, uncovered, over medium heat for 8 minutes on each side. Place pineapple slices on grill. Baste pork and pineapple with reserved marinade. Grill 5-8 minutes longer or until meat juices run clear. Place a pineapple slice on each chop. **Yield:** 6 servings.

HERB DUMPLINGS WITH PORK CHOPS

(Pictured above right)

Cheryl Onken, Wilton, Iowa

My husband, Bob, and I grew up on farms. This recipe reminds me of home.

　1 can (10-3/4 ounces) condensed cream of mushroom soup, undiluted
　1 can (4 ounces) mushroom stems and pieces, undrained
1/2 cup water
1/2 teaspoon rubbed sage
　6 bone-in pork loin chops (1/2 inch thick)
　2 tablespoons vegetable oil
　1 medium onion, sliced
DUMPLINGS:
1-1/2 cups all-purpose flour
　2 teaspoons baking powder
3/4 teaspoon salt
1/2 teaspoon celery seed
1/2 teaspoon rubbed sage
　3 tablespoons shortening
3/4 cup milk
　1 tablespoon minced fresh parsley

In a bowl, combine the soup, mushrooms, water and sage; set aside. In a large skillet, brown the pork chops on both sides in oil; top with onion. Pour soup mixture over top. Bring to a boil; reduce heat.

For dumplings, combine the flour, baking powder, salt, celery seed and sage in a bowl. Cut in shortening until mixture resembles coarse crumbs. Stir in milk just until moistened.

Drop by 1/4 cupfuls onto simmering soup mixture; sprinkle with parsley. Simmer, uncovered, for 15 minutes. Cover and simmer 15 minutes longer or until a toothpick inserted in a dumpling comes out clean (do not lift cover while simmering). **Yield:** 6 servings.

BISCUIT-TOPPED CREAMED HAM
(Pictured below)

Linda Coleman, Cedar Rapids, Iowa

Here's a hearty dish that'll satisfy the hungriest appetite. It's a favorite at our house.

- 1/4 cup chopped green pepper
- 3 tablespoons chopped onion
- 2 tablespoons butter
- 3 tablespoons all-purpose flour
- 1-3/4 cups milk
- 1 can (10-3/4 ounces) condensed cream of chicken soup, undiluted
- 2 cups cubed fully cooked ham
- 1 tablespoon lemon juice

BISCUITS:
- 1 cup all-purpose flour
- 1-1/2 teaspoons baking powder
- 1/2 teaspoon salt
- 2 tablespoons shortening
- 3/4 cup shredded cheddar cheese
- 1/3 cup milk
- 1 teaspoon diced pimientos

In a large skillet, saute green pepper and onion in butter until tender. Stir in flour until blended. Gradually add milk. Bring to a boil; cook and stir for 1-2 minutes or until thickened. Whisk in soup until blended. Stir in the ham and lemon juice; heat through. Pour into a greased 9-in. square baking dish. Bake, uncovered, at 375° for 10 minutes.

Meanwhile, in a large bowl, combine the flour, baking powder and salt; cut in shortening until mixture resembles coarse crumbs. Stir in cheese, milk and pimientos just until moistened. Turn onto a lightly floured surface; knead gently 4-5 times. Roll to about 1/2-in. thickness; cut out six biscuits with a 2-1/2-in. biscuit cutter. Arrange biscuits over ham mixture. Bake 18-22 minutes longer or until biscuits are golden brown. Serve in individual dishes. **Yield:** 6 servings.

PENNSYLVANIA-STYLE PORK ROAST
(Pictured above)

Ronda Jay Holcomb, Farmington, New Mexico

Our children wouldn't dream of eating sauerkraut until they tasted it with this tender and juicy pork roast at a family celebration. They devoured it and went back for seconds! Now it's a mainstay in my pork recipe file.

- 1 teaspoon onion powder
- 1 teaspoon garlic powder
- 1 teaspoon celery seed, crushed
- 1 teaspoon Worcestershire sauce
- 1/4 teaspoon pepper
- 1 boneless rolled pork loin roast (4 to 5 pounds)
- 2 cans (14 ounces *each*) sauerkraut, undrained
- 1 teaspoon sugar, optional
- 8 ounces fully cooked kielbasa *or* Polish sausage, cut into 1/2-inch pieces

In a small bowl, combine the first five ingredients; rub over roast. Place roast fat side up in a Dutch oven. Combine sauerkraut and sugar if desired. Spoon sauerkraut and sausage over and around roast. Cover and bake at 350° for 2-1/4 to

2-3/4 hours or until a meat thermometer reads 160°. Let stand for 15 minutes before slicing. **Yield:** 12-16 servings.

MARMALADE-GLAZED HAM LOAF

Janet Fisher, Butler, Pennsylvania

I used to make this delicious entree often for my family. I still make it when I have company.

      2 eggs
      2 cups milk
  1-1/2 cups crushed herb stuffing mix
      1 medium onion, chopped
    1/4 teaspoon salt
  1-1/2 pounds ground pork
  1-1/2 pounds ground fully cooked ham
      1 jar (12 ounces) orange marmalade
      2 tablespoons cider vinegar
      1 teaspoon ground mustard
    1/4 teaspoon ground cinnamon
    1/8 to 1/4 teaspoon ground cloves

In a large bowl, combine eggs, milk and stuffing mix; let stand for 5 minutes. Add onion and salt. Crumble pork and ham over mixture and mix well. Pat into a greased 9-in. square baking dish (pan will be full). Bake, uncovered, at 350° for 30 minutes; drain. Bake 30 minutes longer; drain.

Combine the marmalade, vinegar, mustard, cinnamon and cloves; spread over ham loaf. Bake 10-15 minutes longer or until a meat thermometer reads 160°. Let stand for 5-10 minutes before cutting. **Yield:** 9 servings.

THANKSGIVING SANDWICHES

Robyn Limberg-Child, St. Clair, Michigan

This sandwich tastes like Thanksgiving turkey, stuffing and cranberry sauce rolled into one. I'm always asked for this recipe, and people are surprised at how simple it is!

      2 cups cubed cooked turkey
    3/4 cup dried cranberries
      1 celery rib, chopped
    1/2 cup chopped pecans, toasted
    3/4 cup honey mustard salad dressing
      4 whole wheat pita breads (6 inches),
        halved
Lettuce leaves, optional

In a bowl, combine the turkey, cranberries, celery and pecans. Add dressing and toss to coat. If desired, line pita halves with lettuce; fill with turkey mixture. **Yield:** 4-8 servings.

EASY CHICKEN ENCHILADAS

(Pictured below)

Cheryl Pomrenke, Coffeyville, Kansas

A must for any Mexican meal at my house, these enchiladas tingle taste buds when I serve them. Try them as a main dish or include them as part of a buffet.

      3 cups (12 ounces) shredded cheddar
        cheese, *divided*
      2 cups (8 ounces) shredded Monterey
        Jack cheese
      2 cups chopped cooked chicken
      2 cups (16 ounces) sour cream
      1 can (10-3/4 ounces) condensed cream
        of chicken soup, undiluted
      1 can (4 ounces) chopped green chilies
      2 tablespoons finely chopped onion
    1/4 teaspoon pepper
    1/8 teaspoon salt
     10 flour tortillas (8 inches), warmed

In a large bowl, combine 2 cups cheddar cheese, Monterey Jack cheese, chicken, sour cream, soup, chilies, onion, pepper and salt. Spoon about 1/2 cup off center on each tortilla; roll up. Place seam side down in a greased 13-in. x 9-in. x 2-in. baking dish.

Cover and bake at 350° for 20 minutes. Uncover; sprinkle with remaining cheddar cheese. Bake 5 minutes longer or until cheese is melted. Let stand for 10 minutes before serving. **Yield:** 8 servings.

STRAWBERRY BLISS OMELET

(Pictured above)

Selina Smith, Frostburg, Maryland

Instead of the usual ham and cheese, try dressing up eggs with strawberries and cream cheese. I first tasted this dish while vacationing at the beach. We like it now as a change of pace for dinner.

> 6 eggs
> 2 tablespoons water
> 1/2 teaspoon salt
> Dash pepper
> 2 tablespoons butter
> 2 ounces cream cheese, cut into 1/2-inch cubes
> 3 tablespoons brown sugar
> 1-1/2 cups sliced fresh strawberries, *divided*
> Confectioners' sugar

In a bowl, beat the eggs, water, salt and pepper. Heat butter in a 10-in. nonstick skillet over medium heat; add egg mixture. As the eggs set, lift edges, letting uncooked portion flow underneath.

When the eggs are almost set, sprinkle cream cheese, brown sugar and 1 cup strawberries over one side. Fold omelet in half. Cover and cook for 1-2 minutes or until brown sugar begins to melt. Slide omelet onto a plate; top with remaining strawberries and dust with confectioners' sugar. **Yield:** 2-3 servings.

 ## MARINATED PORK CHOPS

(Pictured on page 20)

Ruth Reazin, Lyons, Kansas

My husband brought home a variation of this recipe from a pork conference. Not only did it win raves at home, it received a blue ribbon at a fair.

> 1 can (12 ounces) cola
> 1/4 cup soy sauce
> 3/4 teaspoon garlic powder
> 3/4 teaspoon ground ginger
> 3/4 teaspoon ground mustard
> 1/2 teaspoon salt
> 1/2 teaspoon pepper
> 6 bone-in pork loin chops (3/4 inch thick)

In a 2-cup measuring cup, combine the first seven ingredients; mix well. Pour 1-1/2 cups into a large resealable plastic bag; add pork chops. Seal bag and turn to coat; refrigerate for 8 hours or overnight. Cover and refrigerate remaining marinade for basting.

Drain and discard marinade from pork. Grill, covered, over medium heat for 5-6 minutes on each side or until meat juices run clear, basting with reserved marinade. **Yield:** 6 servings.

STRAW AND HAY

(Pictured below)

Ardinelle Dover, Yreka, California

Years after I clipped this recipe from a local newspaper, it's still one of my husband's and my favorites. Sometimes I substitute shrimp or scallops for the ham. We can't decide which way we like it more!

> 1 cup milk
> 1/2 cup small-curd cottage cheese
> 1 tablespoon cornstarch
> 1/4 teaspoon salt
> 1/4 teaspoon pepper
> 1/8 teaspoon ground nutmeg
> 1/2 cup shredded Parmesan cheese, *divided*

4 ounces uncooked fettuccine
4 ounces uncooked spinach fettuccine
1/2 cup cubed fully cooked ham (4 ounces)
1 garlic clove, minced
1/2 cup frozen peas, thawed

In a blender or food processor, combine the milk, cottage cheese and cornstarch; cover and process until smooth. Transfer to a saucepan; add salt, pepper and nutmeg. Cook and stir over medium heat until mixture comes to a boil. Remove from the heat; stir in 1/4 cup Parmesan cheese until melted.

Cook fettuccine according to package directions. Meanwhile, in a large nonstick skillet coated with nonstick cooking spray, heat ham and garlic for 2 minutes. Add peas; heat through. Remove from the heat; stir in cheese sauce. Drain fettuccine; toss with sauce. Sprinkle with remaining Parmesan. **Yield:** 6 servings.

TERIYAKI SIRLOIN STEAK
(Pictured on page 20)

Nilah Lewis, Calgary, Alberta

Since a co-worker shared this recipe with me a number of years ago, I seldom make steak any other way. It's an excellent entree for folks like my husband who really savor tasty meat, and it's earned me many compliments on my cooking.

1/2 cup soy sauce
1/4 cup vegetable oil
1/4 cup packed brown sugar
2 teaspoons ground mustard
2 teaspoons ground ginger
1 teaspoon garlic powder
1 to 1-1/2 pounds boneless beef sirloin steak (3/4 inch thick)

In a large resealable plastic bag, combine the first six ingredients; add the steak. Seal bag and turn to coat; refrigerate for 8 hours or overnight.

Drain and discard marinade. Grill steak, covered, over medium heat for 5-8 minutes on each side or until meat reaches desired doneness (for rare, a meat thermometer should read 140°; medium, 160°; well-done, 170°). **Yield:** 4-6 servings.

CHICKEN WITH CHEESE SAUCE
(Pictured above right)

Joyce Breeding, Falkville, Alabama

Dinner guests are always impressed when I serve this appetizing main dish. It's a delicious and pretty way to dress up plain chicken breasts.

4 boneless skinless chicken breast halves
1/2 cup Italian salad dressing, *divided*
1/4 cup chopped onion
1 cup crushed saltines (about 30 crackers), *divided*
1 package (10 ounces) frozen chopped spinach, thawed and drained
2 tablespoons minced fresh parsley
2 tablespoons butter
1 envelope white sauce mix
2 cups milk
2/3 cup shredded Swiss cheese
Ground nutmeg, optional

Flatten chicken to 1/8-in. thickness. Place in a resealable plastic bag; add 1/4 cup salad dressing. Seal bag and turn to coat; refrigerate for 2 hours.

In a skillet, saute onion in remaining salad dressing. Add 1/2 cup cracker crumbs, spinach and parsley. Cook for 5 minutes or until heated through. Remove from the heat.

Drain and discard marinade from chicken. Spoon about 1/2 cup spinach mixture on each chicken breast; roll up and overlap ends. Secure with a toothpick. Roll in remaining crumbs. Place in a greased 9-in. square baking dish. Bake, uncovered, at 375° for 35 minutes or until chicken juices run clear.

Meanwhile, melt butter in a saucepan. Stir in the white sauce mix until smooth; gradually stir in milk. Bring to a boil; cook and stir for 2 minutes or until thickened. Reduce heat; stir in cheese until melted. Serve over chicken. Sprinkle with nutmeg if desired. **Yield:** 4 servings.

SATISFY HUNGRY APPETITES *with a tender and flavorful meal of pork or beef. Your family will savor every mouthful!*

CUT-ABOVE FARE. Clockwise from top left: Marinated Pork Chops (p. 18), Italian Swiss Steak (p. 23), Pork Chops Creole (p. 22), Teriyaki Sirloin Steak (p. 19) and Mexican Beef and Mushrooms (p. 22).

ITALIAN CHEESE LOAF
(Pictured below)

Mary Ann Marino, West Pittsburg, Pennsylvania

Here's a deliciously different sandwich. It's yummy warm from the oven or off the grill at a cookout. The cheesy filling is complemented by a mix of garden-fresh ingredients and crusty bread. I usually serve it with a salad and onion rings.

> 1 loaf (1 pound) French bread
> 2 cups diced fresh tomatoes
> 1 cup (4 ounces) shredded mozzarella cheese
> 1 cup (4 ounces) shredded cheddar cheese
> 1 medium onion, finely chopped
> 1/4 cup grated Romano cheese
> 1/4 cup chopped ripe olives
> 1/4 cup Italian salad dressing
> 1 teaspoon chopped fresh basil
> 1 teaspoon chopped fresh oregano

Cut top half off loaf of bread; set aside. Carefully hollow out bottom of loaf, leaving a 1/2-in. shell (discard removed bread or save for another use).

In a bowl, combine the remaining ingredients; mix well. Spoon into bread shell; replace top. Wrap in foil. Bake at 350° for 25 minutes or until cheese is melted. Slice and serve warm. **Yield:** 12 servings.

PORK CHOPS CREOLE
(Pictured on page 21)

Josephine Baker, Litchfield, Illinois

A sure way to perk up pork chops is with this herbed creole sauce. You can adjust the range of seasonings to suit your tastes. The red sauce with a sprinkle of green parsley makes a pretty presentation on the dinner plate.

> 1/4 cup all-purpose flour
> 4 boneless pork loin chops (3/4 inch thick)
> 5 tablespoons olive oil
> 1 large onion, thinly sliced
> 1/2 cup finely chopped green pepper
> 1 celery rib, finely chopped
> 2 garlic cloves, minced
> 2 cups stewed tomatoes
> 1/2 teaspoon salt
> 1/2 teaspoon sugar
> 1 to 1-1/2 teaspoons dried thyme
> 1/4 to 1/2 teaspoon pepper
> 1/4 to 1/2 teaspoon hot pepper sauce
> Minced fresh parsley

Place flour in a large resealable plastic bag. Add the pork chops, one at a time, and shake to coat. In a large skillet over medium-high heat, brown pork chops on both sides in oil. Remove chops and keep warm. In the drippings, saute onion, green pepper, celery and garlic until vegetables are tender. Stir in the tomatoes, salt, sugar, thyme, pepper and hot pepper sauce.

Return pork chops to the pan. Bring to a boil. Reduce heat; cover and simmer for 10-15 minutes or until meat juices run clear. Serve sauce over pork chops; sprinkle with parsley. **Yield:** 4 servings.

MEXICAN BEEF AND MUSHROOMS
(Pictured on page 20)

Sharon De Motts, Waupun, Wisconsin

This main dish made an impression on our children. Now grown, every one of them has requested the recipe. Often, I stir my home-canned salsa into the mix.

> 2-1/2 pounds boneless beef round steak, cut into 1-inch cubes
> 1 large onion, chopped
> 1 garlic clove, minced
> 2 tablespoons butter
> 2 jars (6 ounces *each*) sliced mushrooms, drained

1 jar (16 ounces) salsa
1 cup water
1/2 teaspoon salt
1/4 teaspoon chili powder
3 cups hot cooked rice
1 cup (8 ounces) sour cream
1 cup (4 ounces) shredded cheddar cheese

In a Dutch oven over medium-high heat, cook beef, onion and garlic in butter for 4-6 minutes or until meat is browned. Stir in the mushrooms, salsa, water, salt and chili powder. Reduce heat; cover and simmer for 1-1/2 to 2 hours or until the meat is tender. Serve over rice and top with sour cream and cheese. **Yield:** 6-8 servings.

ORIENTAL PORK BURGERS
(Pictured at right)

Deborah Messerly, Steamboat Rock, Iowa

My home state of Iowa is a leader in pork production. This recipe is a truly delicious and nutritious way to use ground pork.

1 cup soft bread crumbs
1/3 cup finely chopped green onions
1/3 cup finely chopped green pepper
1 can (8 ounces) water chestnuts, drained and chopped
1 egg, lightly beaten
2 tablespoons soy sauce
1 garlic clove, minced
1 teaspoon salt
1/8 teaspoon ground ginger
2 pounds ground pork
SAUCE:
1 can (8 ounces) crushed pineapple, drained
2/3 cup ketchup
1/4 cup white vinegar
1/4 cup orange marmalade
2 tablespoons prepared mustard
8 hamburger buns, split and toasted

In a large bowl, combine the first nine ingredients. Crumble pork over mixture and mix well. Shape into eight patties. Cover and refrigerate for 1 hour. Meanwhile, in a saucepan, combine the pineapple, ketchup, vinegar, marmalade and mustard. Cook and stir for 5 minutes or until marmalade is melted. Remove from the heat; set aside.

Grill patties, covered, over medium heat for 4-6 minutes on each side or until a meat thermometer reads 160°. Spoon 1 tablespoon of sauce onto each burger during the last 2 minutes of grilling. Serve on buns with remaining sauce. **Yield:** 8 servings.

ITALIAN SWISS STEAK
(Pictured on page 21)

Janice Lyhane, Marysville, Kansas

This Swiss steak supper combines tender beef and vegetables in a tangy sauce that melds tomato and basil under a cheesy topping. It's quick to put together. Add a salad and warm bread, and you have a complete meal.

3 tablespoons all-purpose flour
2 pounds boneless beef round steak, cut into serving-size pieces
1/4 cup butter
1 can (14-1/2 ounces) diced tomatoes, undrained
1-1/2 teaspoons salt
1/4 teaspoon dried basil
1/8 teaspoon pepper
1/2 cup chopped green pepper
1/2 cup chopped onion
1 cup (4 ounces) shredded mozzarella cheese

Place flour in a large resealable plastic bag. Add beef, a few pieces at a time, and shake to coat. Remove meat from bag; pound to flatten. In a large skillet over medium-high heat, brown steak on both sides in butter. Add the tomatoes, salt, basil and pepper; bring to a boil. Reduce heat; cover and simmer for 1 hour.

Add green pepper and onion. Cover and simmer for 25-30 minutes or until vegetables are tender. Sprinkle with cheese; cook 2 minutes longer or until cheese is melted. **Yield:** 6-8 servings.

CRANBERRY MEAT LOAF
(Pictured below)

Marcia Harris, Stevensville, Michigan

Everyone in my family loves this unusual recipe. It's especially fun to serve in the fall and around the holidays when fresh cranberries are available.

> 2 eggs
> 3/4 cup crushed saltines (about 22 crackers)
> 1/2 cup whole-berry cranberry sauce
> 1/4 cup fresh or frozen cranberries, thawed
> 1/4 cup packed brown sugar
> 2 tablespoons chopped onion
> 1-1/2 teaspoons salt
> 1/8 teaspoon pepper
> 1-1/2 pounds ground beef
> 1/2 pound ground ham
> 1/2 cup barbecue sauce, optional
> **Bay leaves and fresh cranberries, optional**

In a large bowl, combine the first eight ingredients. Crumble beef and ham over mixture and mix well. Pat into a greased 9-in. x 5-in. x 3-in. loaf pan. Bake, uncovered, at 350° for 1-1/4 hours or until a meat thermometer reads 160°.

During the last 15 minutes of baking, baste meat loaf with barbecue sauce if desired. Garnish with bay leaves and cranberries if desired. Discard bay leaves before slicing. **Yield:** 4-5 servings.

CITRUS GRILLED SALMON
(Pictured above)

Margaret Pache, Mesa, Arizona

The citrus flavor really comes through in this delicious grilled salmon. It's definitely one of our favorite recipes.

> 1/2 cup orange juice
> 1/2 cup honey
> 2 teaspoons prepared horseradish
> 2 teaspoons teriyaki sauce
> 1 teaspoon grated orange peel
> 1 salmon fillet (about 2-1/2 pounds)

In a small bowl, combine the first five ingredients; mix well. Pour 2/3 cup into a large resealable plastic bag; add salmon. Seal bag and turn to coat; refrigerate for at least 2 hours. Cover and refrigerate remaining marinade.

Coat grill rack with nonstick cooking spray before starting the grill. Drain and discard marinade from salmon. Place salmon skin side down on grill rack. Grill, covered, over medium heat for 5 minutes. Brush with some of the reserved marinade. Grill 10-15 minutes longer or until fish flakes easily with a fork, basting occasionally with remaining marinade. **Yield:** 6-8 servings.

GRILLED BREADED CHICKEN

Kristy McClellan, Morgan, Utah

When I got married, my husband's aunt gave us all of her favorite recipes. This chicken dish was one of them that we really enjoy.

> ☑ **Uses less fat, sugar or salt. Includes Nutritional Analysis and Diabetic Exchanges.**

> 1 cup (8 ounces) reduced-fat sour cream
> 1/4 cup lemon juice

4 teaspoons Worcestershire sauce
2 teaspoons paprika
1 teaspoon celery salt
1/8 teaspoon garlic powder
8 boneless skinless chicken breast halves
2 cups crushed herb-seasoned stuffing
Refrigerated butter-flavored spray*

In a large resealable plastic bag, combine the first six ingredients; add chicken. Seal bag and turn to coat; refrigerate for at least 8 hours or overnight.

Coat grill rack with nonstick cooking spray before starting the grill. Drain and discard marinade. Coat both sides of chicken with stuffing crumbs; spritz with butter-flavored spray. Grill, covered, over medium heat for 4 minutes on each side or until the juices run clear. **Yield:** 8 servings.

Nutritional Analysis: One serving (1 chicken breast half) equals 224 calories, 5 g fat (2 g saturated fat), 75 mg cholesterol, 419 mg sodium, 12 g carbohydrate, trace fiber, 30 g protein. **Diabetic Exchanges:** 3 lean meat, 1 starch.

*Editor's Note: This recipe was tested with I Can't Believe It's Not Butter Spray.

WAGON WHEEL CASSEROLE

Barbara Hopkins, Lusby, Maryland

My ground beef hot dish is a family pleaser. We love the combination of ingredients.

> ✓ Uses less fat, sugar or salt. Includes Nutritional Analysis and Diabetic Exchanges.

1 pound lean ground beef
1 pound fresh mushrooms, thinly sliced
1 large onion, chopped
8 ounces wagon wheel pasta, cooked and drained
1/3 cup grated Parmesan cheese
3/4 cup thinly sliced green pepper
1 jar (26 ounces) meatless spaghetti sauce
1 cup (4 ounces) shredded part-skim mozzarella cheese

In a large nonstick skillet, cook the beef, mushrooms and onion over medium heat until meat is no longer pink; drain. In a shallow 3-qt. baking dish coated with nonstick cooking spray, layer the pasta, Parmesan cheese, green pepper, beef mixture and spaghetti sauce.

Cover and bake at 350° for 30 minutes. Uncover; sprinkle with mozzarella cheese. Bake 10 minutes longer or until cheese is melted. Let stand for 10 minutes before serving. **Yield:** 8 servings.
Nutritional Analysis: One serving equals 257 calories, 9 g fat (5 g saturated fat), 32 mg cholesterol, 576 mg sodium, 23 g carbohydrate, 3 g

fiber, 22 g protein. **Diabetic Exchanges:** 2 lean meat, 1 starch, 1 vegetable, 1 fat.

CABBAGE BUNDLES WITH KRAUT
(Pictured below)

Jean Kubley, Glidden, Wisconsin

In our area, cabbage rolls are a popular dish at potluck dinners. My family loves them.

1 large head cabbage
2 eggs
1 medium onion, chopped
1/2 cup uncooked long grain rice
2 teaspoons salt
1/4 teaspoon pepper
2 pounds ground beef
1 can (27 ounces) sauerkraut, drained
2 cups water

In a large saucepan, cook cabbage in boiling water just until leaves fall off the head. Set aside 10 large leaves for bundles (refrigerate remaining cabbage for another use). Cut out the thick vein from each reserved leaf, making a V-shaped cut; set aside.

In a bowl, combine eggs, onion, rice, salt and pepper. Crumble beef over mixture; mix well. Place 1/2 cup meat mixture on each cabbage leaf; overlap cut ends of leaf. Fold in sides, beginning from cut end. Roll up to enclose filling.

Place five bundles in a Dutch oven. Top with sauerkraut and remaining bundles. Pour water over all. Bring to a boil over medium heat. Reduce heat; cover and simmer for 1-1/4 to 1-1/2 hours or until meat is no longer pink and cabbage is tender. **Yield:** 5 servings.

SLOPPY JOE PIZZA

Brenda Rohlman, Kingman, Kansas

If your kids like sloppy joes, they'll love this pizza. The six-ingredient recipe is easy to assemble.

- 2 tubes (10 ounces *each*) refrigerated pizza crust
- 1 pound ground beef
- 1 can (15-1/2 ounces) sloppy joe sauce
- 2 cups (8 ounces) shredded mozzarella cheese
- 1 cup (4 ounces) shredded cheddar cheese
- 1/2 cup grated Parmesan cheese

Unroll pizza dough; place on two greased 12-in. pizza pans. Bake at 425° for 6-7 minutes or until golden brown. In a skillet, cook beef over medium heat until no longer pink; drain. Add sloppy joe sauce. Spread over crusts. Sprinkle with cheeses. Bake at 425° for 6-8 minutes or until cheese is melted. **Yield:** 2 pizzas (8 slices each).

STUFFED WALLEYE

(Pictured above)

Kim Leonard, Kalamazoo, Michigan

Walleye is the No. 1 game fish in the Midwest. It's a thrill to catch and tastes great, too. This recipe, created by my husband, is a favorite of my family.

- 4 bacon strips, halved
- 1/4 cup chopped onion
- 2 celery ribs, finely chopped
- 1 can (6 ounces) crabmeat, drained, flaked and cartilage removed *or* 1 cup imitation crabmeat, flaked
- 1/4 cup butter
- 4 cups crushed seasoned stuffing
- 1-1/2 cups boiling water
- 1/2 teaspoon salt
- 1/8 teaspoon pepper
- 1/8 teaspoon cayenne pepper
- 4 walleye fillets (about 8 ounces *each*)

In a skillet, cook the bacon over medium heat for 3-5 minutes or until it begins to crisp; drain on paper towels. In the same skillet, saute onion, celery and crab in butter until vegetables are tender. Transfer to a large bowl; add the stuffing, water, salt, pepper and cayenne; toss to moisten.

Place fillets in a greased 15-in. x 10-in. x 1-in. baking pan. Spoon stuffing mixture over fillets; top each with two pieces of bacon. Bake, uncovered, at 425° for 20-25 minutes or until fish flakes easily with a fork and bacon is cooked. **Yield:** 4 servings.

CHICKEN AND ASPARAGUS BAKE

(Pictured below)

Ramona Ruskell, Columbia, Missouri

You can greet guests with a taste of springtime when this chicken and asparagus casserole is on the menu. It bakes in just half an hour. People savor the rich cheesy sauce, and it freezes well, too.

- 1 medium onion, chopped
- 1/4 cup butter
- 1 can (10-3/4 ounces) condensed cream of mushroom soup, undiluted

1 can (8 ounces) mushroom stems and
   pieces, drained
1 can (5 ounces) evaporated milk
2 tablespoons chopped pimientos
2 teaspoons soy sauce
1/2 teaspoon pepper
1/4 teaspoon hot pepper sauce
2 cups (8 ounces) shredded cheddar
   cheese
5 to 5-1/2 cups cubed cooked chicken
1 package (10 ounces) frozen cut
   asparagus, thawed
3 tablespoons chopped almonds

In a large saucepan, saute onion in butter until
tender. Stir in the soup, mushrooms, milk,
pimientos, soy sauce, pepper and pepper sauce.
Stir in cheese until melted.

In a greased shallow 2-1/2-qt. baking dish, layer half of the chicken, asparagus and cheese
sauce. Repeat layers. Sprinkle with almonds.
Bake, uncovered, at 350° for 25-30 minutes or
until bubbly. **Yield:** 8-10 servings.

SPICED POT ROAST

(Pictured above right)

Loren Martin, Big Cabin, Oklahoma

*Just pour these ingredients over your pot roast and let
the slow cooker do the work. Herbs and spices give the
beef an excellent taste. I often serve this roast over
noodles or with mashed potatoes.*

1 boneless beef chuck roast (2-1/2 pounds)
1 medium onion, chopped
1 can (14-1/2 ounces) diced tomatoes,
   undrained
1/4 cup white vinegar
3 tablespoons tomato puree
2 teaspoons Dijon mustard
1/2 teaspoon lemon juice
4-1/2 teaspoons poppy seeds
2 garlic cloves, minced
2-1/4 teaspoons sugar
1/2 teaspoon ground ginger
1/2 teaspoon salt
1/2 teaspoon dried rosemary, crushed
1/4 teaspoon ground turmeric
1/4 teaspoon ground cumin
1/4 teaspoon crushed red pepper flakes
1/8 teaspoon ground cloves
1 bay leaf
Hot cooked noodles

Place roast in a slow cooker. In a large bowl,
combine the onion, tomatoes, vinegar, tomato
puree, mustard, lemon juice and seasonings; pour
over roast. Cover and cook on low for 8-9 hours

or until meat is tender. Discard bay leaf. Thicken
cooking juices if desired. Serve over noodles.
Yield: 6-8 servings.

GOUDA SPINACH QUICHE

Mary Rose Mattingly, Austin, Kentucky

*My husband and I have run a dairy for over 30 years
and began making cheese 5 years ago. Gouda's distinctive, buttery taste is sensational in this quiche.*

Pastry for a single-crust deep-dish pie (9 inches)
1 medium onion, chopped
1 tablespoon butter
8 cups torn fresh spinach
1 cup (4 ounces) shredded Gouda cheese
6 bacon strips, cooked and crumbled
4 eggs
2 cups half-and-half cream
1/2 teaspoon salt
1/2 teaspoon pepper

Line a deep-dish 9-in. pie plate with pastry. Trim
and flute edge. Line unpricked pastry shell with
a double thickness of heavy-duty foil. Bake at
450° for 5 minutes. Remove foil; bake 5 minutes
longer. Place on a wire rack. Reduce heat to 350°.

In a skillet, saute the onion in butter until tender. Stir in spinach. Remove from the heat. Sprinkle cheese and bacon into crust; top with spinach
mixture. In a bowl, beat eggs. Add the cream, salt
and pepper; mix well. Carefully pour into crust.
Bake at 350° for 45-50 minutes or until a knife
inserted near the center comes out clean. Let stand
for 10 minutes before cutting. **Yield:** 6-8 servings.

STUFFED-TO-THE-GILLS PIZZA
(Pictured below)

Dyann Schieltz, Parker, Colorado

I use my bread machine to make dough for this filling pizza. We used to pick one up from a local pizza parlor, until I dreamed up this recipe.

1-1/2 cups water (70° to 80°)
   2 teaspoons salt
   2 teaspoons sugar
   2 teaspoons olive oil
   5 cups all-purpose flour
   4 teaspoons active dry yeast
   1 can (8 ounces) tomato sauce
   3 tablespoons tomato paste
   1 garlic clove, minced
   1 teaspoon Italian seasoning
Dash crushed red pepper flakes
 1/2 pound Italian sausage, cooked and
     crumbled
 1/4 pound hard salami, diced
  30 slices pepperoni
 1/2 cup chopped red onion
   1 cup (4 ounces) shredded cheddar
     cheese, *divided*
   1 cup (4 ounces) shredded mozzarella
     cheese, *divided*
   1 plum tomato, diced

In bread machine pan, place the first six ingredients in order suggested by manufacturer. Select dough setting (check dough after 5 minutes of mixing; add 1 to 2 tablespoons of water or flour if needed). When cycle is completed, turn dough onto a lightly floured surface and punch down; divide

in half. Roll one portion into a 13-in. circle. Place on a greased 14-in. pizza pan.

In a bowl, combine the tomato sauce, tomato paste, garlic, Italian seasoning and pepper flakes. Spread 3/4 cup over dough to within 1 in. of edge. Sprinkle with sausage, salami, pepperoni, onion, 1/2 cup cheddar cheese and 1/2 cup mozzarella cheese.

Roll the remaining dough into a 12-1/2-in. circle. Place over the pizza; seal edges. Cut four slits in top. Spread with the remaining sauce. Bake at 375° for 35 minutes. Sprinkle with diced tomato and remaining cheeses. Bake 5-10 minutes longer or until golden brown. **Yield:** 8 slices.

ITALIAN POT ROAST
(Pictured above)

Marilyn Riel, Swansea, Massachusetts

This recipe was given to me by my mother's friend when I was a newlywed. I was in a panic over what to serve to guests, and she suggested this. It was a big hit, and I've continued serving it for the past 40 years.

   1 boneless beef rump roast (3 to 3-1/2
     pounds)
   2 tablespoons vegetable oil
   1 can (14-1/2 ounces) beef broth
   1 can (6 ounces) tomato paste
   1 can (4 ounces) mushroom stems and
     pieces, drained
   1 medium onion, chopped
   1 large carrot, chopped
   1 celery rib, chopped
   3 garlic cloves, minced

2 teaspoons Italian seasoning
2 teaspoons salt
1/8 teaspoon pepper
2 tablespoons all-purpose flour
1/4 cup cold water

In a Dutch oven, brown roast in oil on all sides over medium-high heat; drain. Combine the broth, tomato paste, mushrooms, onion, carrot, celery, garlic, Italian seasoning, salt and pepper; pour over roast. Bring to a boil. Reduce heat; cover and simmer for 3 to 3-1/4 hours or until the meat is tender.

Remove roast; keep warm. Pour pan drippings and loosened browned bits into a measuring cup. Skim fat; pour drippings into a saucepan. Combine flour and water until smooth; gradually stir into drippings.

Bring to a boil; cook and stir for 2 minutes or until thickened. Slice roast and serve with gravy. **Yield:** 6-8 servings.

GRILLED TURKEY SANDWICHES

Mary Detweiler, West Farmington, Ohio

These sandwiches are my favorite way to prepare turkey for a nice lunch or light supper.

✓ **Uses less fat, sugar or salt. Includes Nutritional Analysis and Diabetic Exchanges.**

1/2 cup chicken broth
1/4 cup olive oil
4-1/2 teaspoons finely chopped onion
1 tablespoon white wine vinegar
2 teaspoons dried parsley flakes
1/2 teaspoon salt
1/2 teaspoon rubbed sage
1/8 teaspoon pepper
6 turkey breast slices (1 pound)
6 whole wheat hamburger buns, split
6 lettuce leaves
6 tomato slices

In a large resealable plastic bag, combine the first eight ingredients. Add turkey; turn to coat. Seal bag and refrigerate for 12 hours or overnight, turning occasionally.

If grilling the turkey, coat grill rack with nonstick cooking spray before starting the grill. Drain and discard marinade. Grill turkey, covered, over indirect medium heat or broil 6 in. from the heat for 3-4 minutes on each side or until juices run clear. Serve on buns with lettuce and tomato. **Yield:** 6 servings.
Nutritional Analysis: One sandwich equals 320 calories, 7 g fat (3 g saturated fat), 47 mg cholesterol, 447 mg sodium, 37 g carbohydrate, 2 g fiber, 26 g protein. **Diabetic Exchanges:** 3 lean meat, 2 starch.

GIANT MEATBALL SUB

(Pictured below)

Deana Paul, San Dimas, California

As either a hearty party sandwich or a filling lunch or dinner, this sub will rise to the top of your list of favorites. It's also a perfect contribution to a potluck...but don't expect to have any leftovers!

2 eggs, beaten
1/3 cup milk
1 medium onion, chopped
2 garlic cloves, minced
1 cup soft bread crumbs
1/2 teaspoon salt
1/2 teaspoon Italian seasoning
1-1/4 pounds bulk Italian sausage
3/4 pound ground beef
2 jars (26 ounces *each*) spaghetti sauce
1 loaf (1 pound) unsliced French bread, halved lengthwise
8 ounces sliced mozzarella cheese
Shredded Parmesan cheese, optional

In a large bowl, combine the eggs, milk, onion, garlic, bread crumbs, salt and Italian seasoning. Crumble sausage and beef over mixture; mix well. Shape into 1-in. balls. Place in a greased 13-in. x 9-in. x 2-in. baking dish. Bake at 425° for 15 minutes or until meat is no longer pink.

In a Dutch oven, heat the spaghetti sauce over medium heat. Add meatballs; simmer for 15 minutes. Meanwhile, bake bread at 325° for 10 minutes or until heated through. Place mozzarella cheese on bottom half of bread; spoon meatballs onto cheese. Replace top. Slice sandwich into serving-size portions; serve with extra spaghetti sauce and Parmesan cheese if desired. **Yield:** 8 servings.

and let rise for 15 minutes. Brush with egg. Bake at 375° for 30-35 minutes or until golden brown. Serve warm. **Yield:** 8 servings.

ONION PIE
(Pictured below)

Marian Benthin, Apalachin, New York

Our area has the soil for growing beautiful onions, so we always have plenty to enjoy. My mother got this recipe over 30 years ago and said it originated in a Pennsylvania Dutch kitchen.

  1-1/3 **cups biscuit/baking mix**
      1 **teaspoon rubbed sage**
   1/2 **teaspoon salt**
    4 to 5 **tablespoons milk**
FILLING:
      5 **cups thinly sliced onions (about 5 medium)**
      2 **tablespoons vegetable oil**
   1/2 **teaspoon salt**
      1 **egg**
      1 **cup half-and-half cream**

In a bowl, combine the biscuit mix, sage and salt. Add enough milk until mixture holds together. Press onto the bottom and up the sides of a 9-in. pie plate; set aside. In a large skillet, saute

HAM AND SWISS BRAID
(Pictured above)

Rose Randall, Derry, Pennsylvania

This is a family favorite I've made many times through the years. I'm creating a cookbook for my children and relatives, and this recipe will definitely be in it.

    4 **cups all-purpose flour**
    2 **tablespoons sugar**
    2 **packages (1/4 ounce *each*) quick-rise yeast**
 1/2 **teaspoon salt**
    1 **cup water**
 1/4 **cup Dijon mustard**
    2 **tablespoons butter**
    1 **pound thinly sliced deli ham**
    1 **cup (4 ounces) shredded Swiss cheese**
 1/2 **cup chopped dill pickles**
    1 **egg, lightly beaten**

In a mixing bowl, combine 3 cups flour, sugar, yeast and salt. In a small saucepan, heat water, mustard and butter to 120°-130°. Add to flour mixture. Stir in enough remaining flour to form a soft dough (dough will be stiff). Turn onto a lightly floured surface; knead until smooth and elastic, about 6-8 minutes.

Roll dough into a 14-in. x 12-in. rectangle on a greased baking sheet. Arrange half of the ham over dough. Top with cheese, pickles and remaining ham. On each long side, cut 3/4-in.-wide strips about 2-1/2 in. into center.

Starting at one end, fold alternating strips at an angle across filling. Pinch ends to seal. Cover

onions in oil until tender. Sprinkle with salt. Spoon into crust. In a bowl, beat egg and cream; pour over onions.

Bake, uncovered, at 375° for 15 minutes. Reduce heat to 325°. Bake 25-30 minutes longer or until a knife inserted near the center comes out clean. **Yield:** 6-8 servings.

NO-FUSS HAM PATTIES

Mrs. Ernest Schoeff, Huntington, Indiana

Folks always want more whenever I make these ham patties. They're fast and easy to make, too.

- 1 egg, lightly beaten
- 1/4 cup milk
- 3 tablespoons sweet pickle relish
- 8 tablespoons dry bread crumbs, *divided*
- 1-1/2 teaspoons ground mustard
- 10 ounces ground fully cooked ham
- 3 tablespoons butter

In a bowl, combine the egg, milk, pickle relish, 6 tablespoons bread crumbs and mustard. Crumble ham over mixture and mix well. Shape into four patties. Sprinkle each side with remaining bread crumbs.

In a large skillet, cook patties in butter over medium heat for 4 to 4-1/2 minutes on each side or until lightly browned. **Yield:** 4 servings.

PORK FAJITA PASTA

Janice Thompson, Lansing, Michigan

My husband and I started making fajitas before we realized we didn't have any tortillas. We improvised and served the pork mixture over noodles instead. It's become a family favorite.

- 1 package (7 ounces) angel hair pasta
- 4 boneless pork loin chops (1/2 inch thick), cut into thin strips
- 1 medium green pepper, julienned
- 1 medium onion, sliced and separated into rings
- 1 envelope (1.4 ounces) fajita seasoning
- 1/3 cup water
- 1 cup (4 ounces) shredded cheddar cheese
- 1 medium tomato, seeded and chopped

Cook pasta according to package directions. Meanwhile, in a large skillet, brown pork over medium heat until juices run clear. Add green pepper and onion; cook and stir for 1-2 minutes. Stir in fajita seasoning and water; heat 1 minute longer.

Drain pasta. In a large bowl, layer pasta, pork mixture, cheese and tomato. **Yield:** 4 servings.

NEW ENGLAND BOILED DINNER
(Pictured above)

Natalie Cook, Scarborough, Maine

This has long been a popular dinner in our family. When we moved to California in 1960, I'd make it often to remind us of New England. We're back home now and continue to enjoy this scrumptious dish.

- 1 smoked boneless pork shoulder butt roast (2 to 2-1/2 pounds)
- 1 pound carrots, sliced lengthwise and halved
- 8 medium red potatoes, peeled and halved
- 2 medium onions, cut into quarters
- 1 large cabbage, cut into quarters
- 1 large turnip, peeled and cut into quarters
- 1 large rutabaga, peeled, halved and sliced

Place pork roast in a Dutch oven or soup kettle; cover with water. Bring to a boil. Reduce heat; cover and simmer for 1 hour. Add the remaining ingredients; return to a boil. Reduce heat; cover and simmer for 1 hour or until the vegetables are tender. Drain. **Yield:** 8-10 servings.

MARINATED TURKEY TENDERLOINS
(Pictured below)

Beth Wynne, Kill Devil Hills, North Carolina

Turkey is a great alternative for those of us who have to watch our cholesterol. This recipe featuring turkey tenderloins is a favorite. I simply marinate the meat overnight, then grill it until it's golden.

  1 cup lemon-lime soda
1/4 cup soy sauce
  2 tablespoons lemon juice
  2 garlic cloves, minced
  1 teaspoon prepared horseradish
1/2 teaspoon lemon-pepper seasoning
1/4 teaspoon curry powder
1/4 teaspoon ground ginger
1/4 teaspoon paprika
1/4 teaspoon crushed red pepper flakes
  2 pounds turkey tenderloins

In a bowl, combine the first 10 ingredients; mix well. Pour 1 cup into a large resealable plastic bag; add the turkey. Seal the bag and turn to coat; refrigerate 8 hours or overnight, turning occasionally. Cover and refrigerate the remaining marinade for serving.

Drain and discard marinade from turkey. Grill, covered, over medium-hot heat for 20-25 minutes or until a meat thermometer reads 170°, turning every 6 minutes. Serve with reserved marinade. **Yield:** 8 servings.

FANCY JOES
(Pictured above)

Linda Emery, Tuckerman, Arkansas

This recipe is a new twist on an old favorite. It uses ground chicken or turkey and English muffins instead of the usual sloppy joe fixings.

  1 pound ground chicken *or* turkey
  1 large onion, chopped
  1 medium green pepper, chopped
  2 cans (15-1/2 ounces *each*) sloppy joe sauce
  3 cups cooked rice
  8 English muffins, split and toasted

In a large skillet, cook the chicken, onion and green pepper over medium heat until chicken is no longer pink; drain. Stir in the sloppy joe sauce. Bring to a boil. Reduce heat; cover and simmer for 10 minutes. Stir in rice; cook 5 minutes longer or until heated through. Spoon 1 cup onto each English muffin. **Yield:** 8 servings.

SLOW-COOKED PORK ROAST

Marion Lowery, Medford, Oregon

This pork roast makes a wonderful summer meal, as the oven never needs heating. It's so tender, it just falls apart when served.

> ✓ **Uses less fat, sugar or salt. Includes Nutritional Analysis and Diabetic Exchanges.**

  2 cans (8 ounces *each*) unsweetened crushed pineapple, undrained
  1 cup barbecue sauce

2 tablespoons unsweetened apple juice
1 tablespoon minced fresh rosemary *or* 1
teaspoon dried rosemary, crushed
2 teaspoons grated lemon peel
1 teaspoon minced garlic
1 teaspoon Liquid Smoke, optional
1/2 teaspoon salt
1/4 teaspoon pepper
1 boneless pork top loin roast (3 pounds)

In a saucepan, combine the first nine ingredients. Bring to a boil. Reduce heat, simmer, uncovered, for 3 minutes. Meanwhile, in a nonstick skillet coated with nonstick cooking spray, brown the pork roast. Place the roast in a 5-qt. slow cooker. Pour sauce over roast and turn to coat. Cook on high for 4 hours or on low for 6-7 hours. Let stand for 15 minutes before carving. **Yield:** 12 servings.

Nutritional Analysis: One serving (3 ounces cooked pork with 1/4 cup sauce) equals 202 calories, 7 g fat (2 g saturated fat), 66 mg cholesterol, 306 mg sodium, 8 g carbohydrate, 1 g fiber, 26 g protein. **Diabetic Exchanges:** 3 lean meat, 1/2 starch.

SKILLET CHICKEN AND VEGETABLES

Sarah McClanahan, Mansfield, Ohio

I regularly make this dish for my family. They love the flavor. Various vegetables can be substituted for the peppers, mushrooms and zucchini, depending on what you have on hand.

1 pound boneless skinless chicken
breasts, cut into 1/2-inch strips
1 teaspoon garlic powder
1 teaspoon dried basil
1 tablespoon vegetable oil
1/2 pound fresh mushrooms, sliced
1 large zucchini, julienned
1 medium onion, chopped
1 medium green pepper, chopped
1 medium sweet red pepper, chopped
1 package (7 ounces) spaghetti
3/4 cup mayonnaise *or* salad dressing*
4 tablespoons grated Parmesan cheese,
divided

In a large skillet, saute the chicken, garlic and basil in oil for 4 minutes. Add the mushrooms, zucchini, onion and peppers. Cook and stir for 5-7 minutes or until chicken juices run clear and vegetables are crisp-tender. Meanwhile, cook the spaghetti according to the package directions.

Stir the mayonnaise and 3 tablespoons cheese into chicken mixture. Drain spaghetti; top with chicken mixture. Sprinkle with remaining cheese. **Yield:** 4 servings.

*Editor's Note: Reduced-fat or fat-free mayonnaise or salad dressing may not be substituted for regular mayonnaise or salad dressing in this recipe.

PORK 'N' GREEN CHILI TORTILLAS
(Pictured below)

Bobbi Jones, Claypool, Arizona

This tortilla recipe is a big hit with my family. I'm often asked to make it for special occasions.

1/3 cup all-purpose flour
1 teaspoon salt
1/2 teaspoon pepper
2 pounds pork tenderloin, cubed
1/4 cup vegetable oil
6 cans (4 ounces *each*) chopped green
chilies
1/2 cup salsa
12 flour tortillas (8 inches)
Shredded cheddar cheese

In a large resealable plastic bag, combine the flour, salt and pepper. Add pork cubes and shake to coat. In a large saucepan or skillet, cook pork in oil over medium heat until no longer pink. Add the chilies and salsa. Bring to a boil. Reduce heat; cover and simmer for 30 minutes or until meat is tender. Spoon 1/2 cup onto each tortilla; sprinkle with cheese and roll up. **Yield:** 6 servings.

EASTER HAM

Jessica Eymann, Watsonville, California

This is what I serve each Easter. The sweet spicy glaze turns a plain ham into a mouth-watering sensation.

    3/4 cup packed brown sugar
    3/4 cup orange marmalade
    1/2 cup Dijon mustard
    1/2 fully cooked bone-in ham (6 to 8
        pounds)
  1-1/2 teaspoons whole cloves

In a small bowl, combine the brown sugar, marmalade and mustard; set aside. Score the surface of the ham, making diamond shapes 1/2 in. deep; insert a whole clove in the center of each diamond. Place ham cut side down on a rack in a shallow roasting pan. Bake, uncovered, at 325° for 2 hours or until a meat thermometer reads 140°.

Brush ham with glaze. Bake 45 minutes longer, brushing with glaze every 15 minutes. Serve remaining glaze with sliced ham. **Yield:** 16-18 servings (2 cups glaze).

GARLIC SHRIMP SPAGHETTI

(Pictured above)

June Foote, Spring Hill, Florida

Served with a salad and garlic bread toast, this recipe makes a tasty dinner.

    1 package (8 ounces) spaghetti
    2 tablespoons cornstarch
  1/2 cup water
    1 can (14-1/2 ounces) chicken broth
    4 garlic cloves, minced
  1/8 teaspoon cayenne pepper
    2 tablespoons olive oil
  1-1/2 pounds cooked shrimp, peeled and
        deveined
    2 tablespoons lemon juice
  1/4 teaspoon grated lemon peel
  1/4 cup minced fresh parsley

Cook spaghetti according to package directions. Meanwhile, in a bowl, combine the cornstarch, water and broth until smooth; set aside. In a large skillet, saute garlic and cayenne in oil until tender. Stir broth mixture and add to the pan. Bring to a boil; cook and stir for 2 minutes or until thickened.

Reduce heat; add shrimp, lemon juice, peel and parsley. Cook for 2-4 minutes or until heated through. Drain spaghetti and place in a large bowl. Add shrimp mixture and toss to coat. **Yield:** 6 servings.

SOUTHERN SCRAPPLE

(Pictured below)

Rusty Lovin, Greensboro, North Carolina

When it comes to regional recipes, this certainly fits the bill. Scrapple is a breakfast staple in this area.

    1/2 pound bulk pork sausage
      4 cups water
      1 cup grits

1 teaspoon salt
1 teaspoon pepper
Dash cayenne pepper
1/4 cup butter, cubed
1 cup (4 ounces) shredded cheddar cheese
Additional butter and maple syrup

In a large skillet, cook sausage over medium heat until no longer pink; drain and set aside. In a saucepan, bring water to a boil. Gradually add grits, salt, pepper and cayenne, stirring constantly until thickened. Stir in butter and cheese until melted. Stir in sausage. Press into a greased 9-in. x 5-in. x 3-in. loaf pan. Cover; refrigerate for 1 hour or until cool.

Remove scrapple from pan; cut into 1/2-in. slices. Fry in a skillet in butter until browned on both sides, adding more butter as needed. Serve warm with syrup. **Yield:** 8-10 servings.

UPSIDE-DOWN MEATLESS PIZZA

Marie Figueroa, Wauwatosa, Wisconsin

I experimented with a recipe for upside-down pizza and made it into a meatless dish. It turned out to be very tasty.

1 small onion, chopped
1/4 cup chopped green pepper
3 tablespoons vegetable oil, *divided*
2 tablespoons plus 1 cup all-purpose flour, *divided*
1/2 teaspoon dried basil
1/2 teaspoon fennel seed
1 package (10 ounces) frozen chopped spinach, thawed and squeezed dry
1 cup sliced fresh mushrooms
1 can (15 ounces) tomato sauce
2 cups (8 ounces) shredded cheddar cheese
2 eggs
3/4 cup milk
1/2 teaspoon salt
2 tablespoons grated Parmesan cheese

In a large skillet, saute the onion and green pepper in 2 tablespoons oil until tender. Stir in 2 tablespoons flour, basil and fennel seed until blended. Add the spinach, mushrooms and tomato sauce. Bring to a boil; cook and stir for 2 minutes or until thickened.

Pour into a greased 11-in. x 7-in. x 2-in. baking dish. Sprinkle with cheddar cheese.

Place the remaining flour in a mixing bowl. Add eggs, milk, salt and remaining oil; beat until smooth. Stir in Parmesan. Pour over vegetable mixture. Bake, uncovered, at 425° for 20-25 minutes or until lightly browned. **Yield:** 8 servings.

PEANUT CHICKEN STIR-FRY

(Pictured above)

Diane Kelly, Puyallup, Washington

Peanut butter is one of my husband's favorite foods. I love that I can use it to make a delicious meal.

1/2 cup plus 1 tablespoon water, *divided*
1/4 cup peanut butter*
3 tablespoons soy sauce
1 tablespoon brown sugar
2 to 3 garlic cloves, minced
2 tablespoons vegetable oil
1 pound boneless skinless chicken breasts, cubed
3 cups broccoli florets
1 tablespoon cornstarch
Hot cooked rice *or* noodles

In a small bowl, combine 1/2 cup water, peanut butter, soy sauce and brown sugar until smooth; set aside. In a skillet or wok, stir-fry garlic in oil for 30 seconds. Add the chicken; stir-fry for 5 minutes or until chicken juices run clear. Add broccoli; stir-fry for 5 minutes.

Stir in the peanut butter mixture; cook and stir until sauce is smooth and broccoli is crisp-tender, about 3 minutes. Combine cornstarch and remaining water until smooth; add to skillet. Bring to a boil; cook and stir for 2 minutes or until thickened. Serve over rice or noodles. **Yield:** 4 servings.

***Editor's Note:** Reduced-fat or generic brands of peanut butter may not be substituted for regular peanut butter in this recipe.

STUFFED FLANK STEAK
(Pictured below)

Kathy Clark, Byron, Minnesota

This recipe came with my first slow cooker. Now I'm on my fourth slow cooker and still use this recipe.

✓ **Uses less fat, sugar or salt. Includes Nutritional Analysis and Diabetic Exchanges.**

- 1 beef flank steak (2 pounds)
- 1 medium onion, chopped
- 1 garlic clove, minced
- 1 tablespoon butter
- 1-1/2 cups soft bread crumbs (about 3 slices)
- 1/2 cup chopped fresh mushrooms
- 1/4 cup minced fresh parsley
- 1/4 cup egg substitute
- 3/4 teaspoon poultry seasoning
- 1/2 teaspoon salt
- 1/8 teaspoon pepper
- 1/2 cup beef broth
- 2 teaspoons cornstarch
- 4 teaspoons water

Flatten steak to 1/2-in. thickness; set aside. In a nonstick skillet, saute onion and garlic in butter until tender. Add the bread crumbs, mushrooms, parsley, egg substitute, poultry seasoning, salt and pepper; mix well. Spread over steak to within 1 in. of edge. Roll up jelly-roll style, starting with a long side; tie with kitchen string. Place in a 5-qt. slow cooker; add broth. Cover and cook on low for 8-10 hours.

Remove meat to a serving platter and keep

warm. Skim fat from cooking juices; pour juices into a small saucepan. Combine cornstarch and water until smooth; stir into juices. Bring to a boil; cook and stir for 1-2 minutes or until thickened. Remove string before slicing steak; serve with gravy. **Yield:** 8 servings.

Nutritional Analysis: One serving equals 230 calories, 11 g fat (5 g saturated fat), 62 mg cholesterol, 348 mg sodium, 6 g carbohydrate, trace fiber, 26 g protein. **Diabetic Exchanges:** 3 lean meat, 1/2 starch, 1/2 fat.

SHRIMP FRIED RICE
(Pictured above)

Sandra Thompson, White Hall, Arkansas

This delectable dish is filled with color and taste that makes it vanish fast. Our family of four can't get enough of it. Bacon adds crispness and a hint of heartiness.

- 4 tablespoons butter, *divided*
- 4 eggs, lightly beaten
- 3 cups cold cooked rice
- 1 package (16 ounces) frozen mixed vegetables
- 1 pound uncooked medium shrimp, peeled and deveined
- 1/2 teaspoon salt
- 1/4 teaspoon pepper
- 8 bacon strips, cooked and crumbled, optional

In a large skillet, melt 1 tablespoon butter over medium-high heat. Pour eggs into skillet. As eggs set, lift edges, letting uncooked portion flow underneath. Remove eggs and keep warm.

Melt remaining butter in the skillet. Add rice, vegetables and shrimp; cook and stir for 5 minutes or until shrimp turn pink. Return eggs to the pan; sprinkle with salt and pepper. Cook until heated through. Sprinkle with bacon if desired. **Yield:** 8 servings.

ONION MEATBALL STEW

Valerie Warner, North Manchester, Indiana

When fall comes calling, it's time to cook up comforting fare like this stew. Complete with meatballs and veggies, this old-fashioned dish will satisfy even the heartiest appetite.

      1 egg, lightly beaten
  1/2 cup soft bread crumbs
      1 garlic clove, minced
  1/2 teaspoon salt
  1/2 teaspoon dried savory
      1 pound ground beef
      1 tablespoon vegetable oil
      1 can (10-1/2 ounces) condensed French
         onion soup, undiluted
  2/3 cup water
      3 medium carrots, cut into 3/4-inch chunks
      2 medium potatoes, peeled and cut
         into 1-inch chunks
      1 medium onion, cut into thin wedges
      1 tablespoon minced fresh parsley

In a bowl, combine the egg, bread crumbs, garlic, salt and savory. Crumble beef over mixture and mix well. Shape into 1-1/4-in. balls.

In a large skillet, brown meatballs in oil over medium heat; drain. Stir in the soup, water, carrots, potatoes and onion. Bring to a boil. Reduce heat; cover and simmer for 25-30 minutes or until vegetables are tender. Sprinkle with parsley. **Yield:** 4 servings.

THREE-CHEESE PESTO PIZZA
(Pictured at right)

Ann Bridges, Albuquerque, New Mexico

Creamy pesto adds flair to this thick-crust pizza. The homemade crust is so simple. It also freezes nicely.

      1 package (1/4 ounce) active dry yeast
      1 cup warm water (110° to 115°)
      2 teaspoons sugar
      4 tablespoons olive oil, *divided*
  1-1/2 teaspoons salt
  3-1/2 to 4 cups all-purpose flour
      1 cup fresh basil

      2 garlic cloves, minced
      1 package (8 ounces) cream cheese, cubed
  1/2 pound bulk Italian sausage
      1 cup chopped onion
      1 cup spaghetti sauce
  1/3 cup grated Parmesan cheese
      2 cups sliced fresh mushrooms
      1 can (2-1/4 ounces) sliced ripe olives,
         drained
  1-1/2 cups (6 ounces) shredded Monterey
         Jack cheese

In a mixing bowl, dissolve yeast in warm water. Add sugar; let stand for 5 minutes. Add 3 tablespoons oil, salt and 2 cups flour. Beat until smooth. Stir in enough remaining flour to form a firm dough. Turn onto a lightly floured surface; knead until smooth and elastic, about 6-8 minutes. Place in a greased bowl, turning once to grease top. Cover and let rise in a warm place until doubled, about 1 hour.

Meanwhile, for pesto, place basil and garlic in a blender or food processor; cover and process until smooth. Transfer to a mixing bowl. Add cream cheese and remaining oil; beat until smooth. Set aside. In a skillet, cook sausage and onion over medium heat until meat is no longer pink; drain. Set aside.

Punch dough down. On a lightly floured surface, roll into a 15-in. x 10-in. rectangle. Transfer to a greased 15-in. x 10-in. x 1-in. baking pan. Build up edges slightly. Spread with pesto. Layer with the spaghetti sauce, Parmesan cheese, sausage mixture, mushrooms, olives and Monterey Jack cheese. Bake at 400° for 30-35 minutes or until crust is golden brown and cheese is melted. **Yield:** 12 slices.

fat from cooking juices; pour juices into a saucepan. Combine flour, water and browning sauce if desired until smooth; stir into cooking juices. Bring to a boil; cook and stir for 2 minutes or until thickened. Cover and refrigerate.

Place beef slices in a shallow baking dish; top with mushrooms, cranberries and gravy. Cover and bake at 325° for 60-65 minutes or until heated through and mushrooms are tender. **Yield:** 10-12 servings.

*Editor's Note: This is a fresh beef brisket, not corned beef.

CRANBERRY-MUSHROOM BEEF BRISKET
(Pictured above)
Margaret Welder, Madrid, Iowa

I quickly fell for this fantastic sweet-and-sour brisket when I had it at a family wedding reception. Since the meat needs to be refrigerated overnight after it bakes, it is a great make-ahead entree.

      2 cups beef broth
  1/2 cup cranberry juice concentrate
  1/4 cup red wine vinegar
4-1/2 teaspoons chopped fresh rosemary
        or 1-1/2 teaspoons dried rosemary,
        crushed
      4 garlic cloves, minced
      1 large onion, thinly sliced
      1 fresh beef brisket* (4 pounds)
  1/2 teaspoon salt
  1/4 teaspoon pepper
  1/4 cup all-purpose flour
  1/4 cup cold water
  1/4 to 1/2 teaspoon browning sauce,
        optional
      1 pound fresh mushrooms, sliced
1-1/2 cups dried cranberries

In a bowl, combine the broth, cranberry juice concentrate, vinegar, rosemary and garlic; pour into a large roasting pan. Top with onion slices. Season beef with salt and pepper; place fat side up in the pan. Cover and bake at 325° for 3 to 3-1/2 hours or until meat is tender.

Remove meat and thinly slice across the grain. Cover and refrigerate overnight. For gravy, skim

ALMOND CHICKEN STIR-FRY
(Pictured below)
Darlene Markel, Sublimity, Oregon

I make this dish often because it is so quick and easy to prepare. My family likes the flavor the sugar snap peas and almonds add. Sometimes I top it with chow mein noodles for extra crunch.

      1 cup whole unblanched almonds
  1/4 cup vegetable oil
      1 pound boneless skinless chicken
        breasts, cut into cubes
      1 tablespoon cornstarch
  1/2 cup chicken broth
      3 tablespoons soy sauce
      2 teaspoons honey
      1 teaspoon ground ginger

Clues for Steaks and Chops

• Swiss steak is fabulous made with venison instead of beef round steak.
—*Judee Oris*
Endicott, New York

• I make extra when I prepare Swiss steak. I find it freezes very well, and it's great to have an already prepared dish on hand to take to family gatherings or potlucks.
—*Olive Rumage, Jacksboro, Texas*

• I find that 1/2-inch- to 1-inch-thick pork loin chops are ideal for most pork chop recipes.
—*Josephine Baker*
Litchfield, Illinois

• I often put potatoes, apples, cabbage or carrots in the oven when I make my baked round steak with creamy mushroom gravy. After an hour, everything is done. It's an easy way to make a complete, satisfying meal.
—*Jane O'Tool, Ida Grove, Iowa*

• To add a subtle yet distinctive flavor to grilled steaks and chops, sprinkle soaked fresh herbs like tarragon, basil, rosemary and bay leaves on the coals before adding the meat. To soak the herbs, just cover with water and let stand for 1 hour before using.
—*Marlene Wiczek*
Little Falls, Minnesota

• My hearty broiled steak sandwiches, which I serve in pitas, make a great weeknight supper when accompanied by soup.
—*Betty Jean Nichols*
Eugene, Oregon

• I jazz up my Italian salad dressing marinade with pineapple juice, soy sauce and brown sugar and use it to marinate pork chops. If you like to have a fuss-free dinner at your fingertips, double the marinade and use half for tonight's dinner, then add pork chops to the remaining marinade and freeze together in a freezer bag—just thaw in the fridge before grilling or broiling.
—*Debby Cole, Wolf Creek, Oregon*

• Bottled chili sauce makes a great base for homemade barbecue sauces. I find that different brands vary in flavor, so I sometimes add tomato paste for a more pungent tomato flavor and horseradish for a little added zip.
—*Edie DeSpain, Logan, Utah*

• I marinate less tender cuts of meat, such as round steak, for better flavor and tenderness. For variety, I'll cube the steak before marinating, then skewer and grill for shish kabobs. —*Melissa Mowrey*
Martinton, Illinois

---

1 package (14 ounces) frozen sugar
   snap peas
Hot cooked pasta *or* rice

In a large skillet over medium heat, cook almonds in oil for 3 minutes. Add chicken; stir-fry until lightly browned. In a bowl, combine the cornstarch, broth, soy sauce, honey and ginger until smooth; add to the chicken mixture. Bring to a boil; cook and stir for 2 minutes or until thickened. Reduce heat. Stir in the peas; heat through. Serve over pasta. **Yield:** 4 servings.

BARBECUED CHICKEN

Mildred Dieffenbach, Womelsdorf, Pennsylvania

My husband is a diabetic, so I'm always looking for great-tasting recipes that are low in sugar and carbohydrates. To reduce the sugar content of this recipe even further, I use diet cola.

1 can (12 ounces) cola
1 can (6 ounces) tomato paste
2 tablespoons finely chopped onion
1 tablespoon red wine vinegar
1 tablespoon Worcestershire sauce
1/4 teaspoon salt
2 broiler/fryer chickens (3 pounds *each*),
   cut in half

In a saucepan, combine the cola, tomato paste, onion, vinegar, Worcestershire sauce and salt. Bring to a boil. Reduce heat; simmer, uncovered, for 15 minutes. Set aside 1/2 cup for basting; cover and refrigerate.

Carefully loosen the skin of the chicken; brush remaining sauce under skin. Cover and refrigerate for 30 minutes.

Place chicken on grill rack. Grill, uncovered, over indirect medium heat for 20 minutes. Turn; grill 20-30 minutes longer or until chicken juices run clear, basting occasionally with reserved sauce. **Yield:** 8 servings.

CHICAGO-STYLE DEEP-DISH PIZZA
(Pictured below)

Lynn Hamilton, Naperville, Illinois

My husband and I tried to duplicate the pizza from a popular Chicago restaurant, and I think our recipe turned out even better. The secret is baking it in a cast-iron skillet.

3-1/2 cups all-purpose flour
1/4 cup cornmeal
1 package (1/4 ounce) quick-rise yeast
1-1/2 teaspoons sugar
1/2 teaspoon salt
1 cup water
1/3 cup olive oil
TOPPINGS:
6 cups (24 ounces) shredded mozzarella cheese, *divided*
1 can (28 ounces) diced tomatoes, well drained
1 can (8 ounces) tomato sauce
1 can (6 ounces) tomato paste
1/2 teaspoon salt
1/4 teaspoon *each* garlic powder, dried oregano, dried basil and pepper
1 pound bulk Italian sausage, cooked and crumbled
48 slices pepperoni
1/2 pound sliced fresh mushrooms
1/4 cup grated Parmesan cheese

In a mixing bowl, combine 1-1/2 cups flour, cornmeal, yeast, sugar and salt. In a saucepan, heat water and oil to 120°-130°. Add to dry ingredients; beat just until moistened. Add remaining flour to form a stiff dough. Turn onto a floured surface; knead until smooth and elastic, about 6-8 minutes. Place in a greased bowl, turning once to grease top. Cover and let rise in a warm place until doubled, about 30 minutes.

Punch dough down; divide in half. Roll each portion into an 11-in. circle. Press onto bottom and up sides of two greased 10-in. ovenproof skillets. Sprinkle each with 2 cups mozzarella cheese.

In a bowl, combine the tomatoes, tomato sauce, tomato paste and seasonings. Spoon 1-1/2 cups over each pizza. Layer each with half of the sausage, pepperoni, mushrooms, 1 cup mozzarella and 2 tablespoons Parmesan cheese. Cover and bake at 450° for 35 minutes. Uncover; bake 5 minutes longer or until lightly browned. **Yield:** 2 pizzas (8 slices each).

Editor's Note: Two 9-in. springform pans may be used in place of the skillet. Place pans on baking sheets. Run knife around edge of pan to loosen crust before removing sides.

PINEAPPLE BEEF STIR-FRY
(Pictured above)

Connie Braisted, Oceanside, California

This tasty sweet-sour combination features sirloin instead of chicken for a fun change of pace. Pineapple, red pepper and slices of celery and green onion create a colorful feast for the eyes.

1/2 cup soy sauce
2 garlic cloves, minced
1 teaspoon ground ginger

1 pound boneless beef sirloin steak, cut into 1/4-inch thin strips
1 tablespoon vegetable oil
2 celery ribs, thinly sliced
1 cup cubed sweet red pepper
1 cup sliced green onions
1 cup sliced fresh mushrooms
1 can (20 ounces) pineapple chunks
1 can (8 ounces) sliced water chestnuts, drained
2 to 3 tablespoons cornstarch
1/2 cup water
Hot cooked rice

In a bowl, combine the soy sauce, garlic and ginger. Add beef; toss to coat. Let stand for 15 minutes. In a large skillet, stir-fry beef mixture in oil for 2 minutes. Add celery and red pepper; stir-fry for 2 minutes. Add onions and mushrooms; cook 2 minutes longer.

Drain pineapple, reserving juice. Stir pineapple and water chestnuts into skillet. In a bowl, combine cornstarch, water and reserved pineapple juice until smooth. Gradually stir into beef and vegetables. Bring to a boil; cook and stir for 1-2 minutes or until thickened. Serve over rice. **Yield:** 4 servings.

STEAK FAJITAS

Jackie Hannahs, Fountain, Michigan

I found this recipe and changed a few things to our liking. It's quick and easy to make.

✓ Uses less fat, sugar or salt. Includes Nutritional Analysis and Diabetic Exchanges.

1 pound boneless beef sirloin steak, cut into thin 3-inch strips
2 teaspoons canola oil
1 medium green pepper, cut into thin strips
1 medium onion, quartered and thinly sliced
3 garlic cloves, minced
1/2 teaspoon chili powder
1/4 teaspoon dried oregano
1/4 teaspoon pepper
1 cup salsa or picante sauce
5 flour tortillas (8 inches), warmed

In a nonstick skillet, brown beef in oil; drain. Add the green pepper, onion, garlic, chili powder, oregano and pepper. Cook and stir for 5 minutes or until vegetables are crisp-tender. Add salsa; cook 3 minutes longer or until heated through. Spoon 3/4 cup beef mixture down the center of each tortilla. Fold one side over filling and roll up. Serve immediately. **Yield:** 5 servings.

Nutritional Analysis: One fajita equals 331 calories, 10 g fat (2 g saturated fat), 60 mg cholesterol, 522 mg sodium, 34 g carbohydrate, 2 g fiber, 26 g protein. **Diabetic Exchanges:** 3 lean meat, 2 vegetable, 1-1/2 starch.

BROCCOLI SAUSAGE BREAKFAST BAKE

(Pictured below)

Kara Cash, Dumont, Texas

I'm very involved in 4-H and raise hogs to show at our county fair. I like to share tasty recipes that help promote the pork industry.

1/2 pound bulk pork sausage
1 cup chopped fresh broccoli
2 cups (8 ounces) shredded cheddar cheese
3 eggs
1-1/4 cups milk
1/2 cup biscuit/baking mix

In a skillet, cook sausage over medium heat until no longer pink; drain and set aside. Add 1 in. of water and broccoli to a saucepan; bring to a boil. Reduce heat. Cover and simmer for 5-8 minutes or until crisp-tender; drain.

In a greased 9-in. pie plate, layer the sausage, cheese and broccoli. In a bowl, combine the eggs, milk and biscuit mix. Pour over broccoli. Bake at 350° for 25-30 minutes or until a knife inserted near the center comes out clean. **Yield:** 6-8 servings.

HERBED PORK RIB ROAST

Joyce Kramer, Donalsonville, Georgia

My husband, Dale, created this recipe, and it's become the specialty of the house. The seasoning also works well on pork chops, beef roast and chicken.

- 1 tablespoon garlic powder
- 1 tablespoon onion powder
- 1 tablespoon dried marjoram
- 1 tablespoon dried parsley flakes
- 1 to 2 teaspoons cayenne pepper
- 1 bone-in pork rib roast (about 4 pounds)

In a small bowl, combine the garlic powder, onion powder, marjoram, parsley and cayenne. Rub over roast. Cover and refrigerate overnight. Place roast on a rack in a shallow roasting pan. Bake, uncovered, at 350° for 2-1/2 to 3 hours or until a meat thermometer reads 160°. Let stand for 10 minutes before carving. **Yield:** 8 servings.

COFFEE MARINATED STEAK
(Pictured above)

Julie Walk, Tyrone, Pennsylvania

My dad—a big steak lover—got this recipe from a friend, and now we never eat steak without using this marinade. It makes the meat so juicy and adds a great flavor.

- 2 tablespoons sesame seeds
- 6 tablespoons butter
- 1 medium onion, chopped
- 4 garlic cloves, minced
- 1 cup strong brewed coffee
- 1 cup soy sauce
- 2 tablespoons white vinegar
- 2 tablespoons Worcestershire sauce
- 2 pounds boneless beef top sirloin steak (1 inch thick)

In a skillet, toast sesame seeds in butter. Add onion and garlic; saute until tender. In a bowl, combine the coffee, soy sauce, vinegar, Worcestershire sauce and sesame seed mixture. Pour half into a large resealable plastic bag; add steak. Seal bag and turn to coat; refrigerate for 8 hours or overnight, turning occasionally. Cover and refrigerate remaining marinade.

Drain and discard marinade from steak. Grill steak, covered, over medium-hot heat for 6-10 minutes on each side or until meat reaches desired doneness (for rare, a meat thermometer should read 140°; medium, 160°; well-done, 170°). Warm reserved marinade and serve with steak. **Yield:** 6 servings.

PUMPKIN BURGERS
(Pictured below)

Linda Shuttleworth, Circleville, Ohio

In our town, we have a pumpkin festival in late October and use pumpkins many different ways. This is a popular recipe for "sandwich night" at our house.

1-1/2 pounds ground beef
  1 medium onion, chopped

Main Dishes

1 bottle (12 ounces) chili sauce
1 can (10-3/4 ounces) condensed tomato
    soup, undiluted
1/2 cup canned pumpkin
1 teaspoon salt
1/2 to 1 teaspoon pumpkin pie spice
1/4 teaspoon pepper
6 to 8 hamburger buns, split

In a large skillet, cook beef and onion over medium heat until meat is no longer pink; drain. Add the chili sauce, soup, pumpkin, salt, pumpkin pie spice and pepper. Bring to a boil. Reduce heat; cover and simmer for 1 hour. Serve on buns. **Yield:** 6-8 servings.

TASTY TUNA MELTS

Shannon Phipps, Houston, Texas

Thanks to a dash of mustard, salsa and hot sauce, these warm tuna sandwiches are full of zip! Sometimes I stir chopped pickle and hard-cooked eggs into the tuna mix for additional flavor.

2 cans (6 ounces *each*) tuna, drained
3 tablespoons mayonnaise
1 tablespoon prepared mustard
1 tablespoon salsa
2 to 3 drops hot pepper sauce
1/8 teaspoon grated Parmesan cheese
6 process American cheese slices
6 thin tomato slices
6 bread slices
2 to 4 tablespoons butter

In a bowl, combine the first six ingredients; mix well. Place one cheese slice, two tomato slices and 1/3 cup tuna mixture on three slices of bread; top with the remaining cheese slices and bread slices.

In a large skillet or griddle, melt 2 tablespoons butter. Toast sandwiches until lightly browned on both sides, adding butter if necessary. **Yield:** 3 servings.

BEEFY MUSHROOM MEATBALLS
(Pictured above right)

Lavina Schelter, Oakfield, Wisconsin

Among my memories of a reunion held on my farm are these savory meatballs a family member made. That's where I got this recipe that I now make for potlucks and get-togethers. It's so handy to transport and keep warm in a slow cooker, and it makes a great appetizer, too.

2 slices bread, torn
2 tablespoons milk
1 egg, beaten
3 tablespoons finely chopped onion
1/2 teaspoon salt
1/4 teaspoon pepper
1-1/2 pounds ground beef
1 tablespoon butter
2 tablespoons all-purpose flour
1 can (10-1/2 ounces) beef consomme
2 cans (4 ounces *each*) mushroom stems
    and pieces, drained
1 tablespoon dried parsley flakes
1 teaspoon Worcestershire sauce
1 teaspoon beef bouillon granules
1/2 cup sour cream
Hot cooked noodles, optional
Minced fresh parsley

In a bowl, combine bread and milk. Add the egg, onion, salt and pepper; mix well. Crumble beef over mixture and mix well. Shape into 1-in. balls. In a large skillet, brown meatballs in small batches over medium heat until no longer pink. Drain on paper towels.

In a large saucepan, melt butter. Stir in flour until smooth. Gradually add consomme; bring to a boil. Reduce heat; add the mushrooms, parsley, Worcestershire sauce and bouillon. Add meatballs; simmer, uncovered, for 30 minutes, stirring occasionally. Remove from the heat; stir in sour cream. Serve over noodles if desired. Garnish with parsley. **Yield:** 6-8 servings.

'Cake' Is Fit for April Fools'

NO FOOLING—you can pull the wool over everyone's eyes April 1 with an imaginative "dessert" from Julie Foltz of Newport News, Virginia.

"It's really a pizza," she explains with a grin. "I just bake it in a fluted tube cake pan. Topped with melted mozzarella 'frosting', it looks a lot like a cake."

To round out her April Fools' Day meal, Julie serves "mashed potatoes" and "gravy" (scoops of ice cream with caramel sauce) and "fish nuggets" (toasted coconut-covered candies). "Our kids hoot and holler over the whole dinner," she says.

APRIL FOOLS' CAKE

1 jar (14 ounces) pizza sauce
1/2 pound bulk Italian sausage, cooked and crumbled
1 package (8 ounces) sliced pepperoni
3 cups biscuit/baking mix
3/4 cup milk
2 eggs
2 tablespoons butter, melted
1 teaspoon garlic salt
5 to 6 slices mozzarella cheese

In a bowl, combine pizza sauce, sausage and pepperoni; set aside. In another bowl, combine biscuit mix, milk, eggs, butter and garlic salt. Spread half of batter on bottom and up sides of a greased 10-in. fluted tube pan. Spoon meat mixture over batter; cover with remaining batter.

Bake at 375° for 35-40 minutes or until browned and a toothpick inserted in the crust comes out clean. Invert onto a baking sheet. Arrange cheese over cake. Return to the oven for 5 minutes or until cheese is melted. Using two large metal spatulas, transfer cake to a serving platter; serve immediately. **Yield:** 8 servings.

SPINACH EGG CROISSANTS

Karen Oviatt, Washougal, Washington

This special breakfast entree is a real treat on weekends when I have time to enjoy a relaxing meal.

1 cup sliced fresh mushrooms
1 package (10 ounces) fresh spinach, chopped
1 small onion, chopped
2 to 3 tablespoons vegetable oil
10 eggs, beaten
1 cup (4 ounces) shredded Monterey Jack cheese
8 croissants, split
2 cups prepared hollandaise sauce

In a large skillet, saute mushrooms, spinach and onion in oil until tender. Add eggs; cook and stir over medium heat until eggs are completely set. Stir in cheese. Toast croissant halves under broiler. Top with egg mixture and hollandaise sauce. **Yield:** 8 servings.

MEATY MACARONI BAKE

Connie Helsing, Ashland, Nebraska

We go to lots of rodeos. This is an ideal casserole to make in the morning and bake when we get home.

1-1/2 pounds ground beef
1 medium onion, chopped
1 garlic clove, minced
1 jar (14 ounces) spaghetti sauce
1 cup water
1 can (8 ounces) tomato sauce
1 can (6 ounces) tomato paste
1/2 teaspoon salt
1/8 teaspoon pepper
2 eggs, beaten
1/4 cup vegetable oil
1 package (7 ounces) elbow macaroni, cooked and drained
2 cans (4 ounces *each*) mushroom stems and pieces, drained
1 cup (4 ounces) shredded mozzarella cheese
1/4 cup grated Parmesan cheese
1 cup soft bread crumbs

In a large skillet, cook the beef, onion and garlic over medium heat until meat is no longer pink; drain. Add the spaghetti sauce, water, tomato sauce, tomato paste, salt and pepper. Bring to a boil. Reduce heat; simmer, uncovered, for 10 minutes.

In a bowl, combine the eggs, oil, macaroni, mushrooms, cheeses and bread crumbs. Spoon into a 3-qt. baking dish. Top with meat mixture. Bake, uncovered, at 350° for 30 minutes. Sprinkle with additional mozzarella cheese if desired. Let stand for 10 minutes before serving. **Yield:** 6-8 servings.

BEEF 'N' POTATO PIE

Thelma Musselman, Forest, Ohio

I began entering fairs in the 1970s. This savory pie brought home a Grand Champion ribbon.

    2 cups all-purpose flour
    1 teaspoon salt
  1/2 teaspoon onion powder
  3/4 cup butter-flavored shortening
  1/4 cup cold water
FILLING:
  1/4 cup chopped green pepper
  1/4 cup chopped sweet red pepper
    1 small onion, chopped
    4 teaspoons vegetable oil, *divided*
    3 cups cubed cooked beef roast
    1 can (10-3/4 ounces) condensed beefy
      mushroom soup, undiluted
    1 can (4 ounces) mushroom stems and
      pieces, drained
    1 teaspoon Worcestershire sauce
  1/4 teaspoon garlic powder
Dash pepper
    1 tablespoon cornstarch
    1 tablespoon water
    2 cups sliced cooked peeled potatoes
    1 egg, lightly beaten

In a bowl, combine flour, salt and onion powder; cut in the shortening until crumbly. Gradually add water, tossing with a fork until dough forms a ball. Divide dough in half. Roll out one piece to fit a 9-in. pie plate. Line pie plate with bottom pastry; trim even with edge.

In a large skillet, saute the peppers and onion in 1 tablespoon oil. Add the beef, soup, mushrooms, Worcestershire sauce, garlic powder and pepper. Bring to a boil. Combine cornstarch and water until smooth; stir into skillet. Bring to a boil; cook and stir for 2 minutes or until thickened. Cool. Spoon into crust. Top with potatoes. Brush remaining oil over potatoes.

Roll out remaining pastry to fit top of pie; place over filling. Trim, seal and flute edges. Cut slits in pastry. Brush with egg. Bake at 375° for 45 minutes. Cover edges loosely with foil. Bake 10 minutes longer or until golden brown. **Yield:** 6-8 servings.

PIZZA RICE CASSEROLE

(Pictured at right)

Christine Reimer, Niverville, Manitoba

Anyone who enjoys pizza and lasagna will like this Italian-style recipe that combines those two flavors.

Usually, I make a few casseroles at once and freeze some for future enjoyment.

  3/4 pound ground beef
    1 medium onion, chopped
    2 cans (8 ounces *each*) tomato sauce
    1 teaspoon sugar
    1 teaspoon salt
    1 teaspoon dried parsley flakes
  1/4 teaspoon garlic powder
  1/4 teaspoon oregano
Dash pepper
    2 cups cooked rice
  1/2 cup small-curd cottage cheese
  1/2 cup shredded mozzarella cheese

In a large skillet, cook beef and onion over medium heat until meat is no longer pink; drain. Add the tomato sauce, sugar, salt, parsley, garlic powder, oregano and pepper. Bring to a boil. Reduce heat; cover and simmer for 15 minutes.

Combine the rice and cottage cheese; spoon half into a greased 11-in. x 7-in. x 2-in. baking dish. Top with half of the meat mixture. Repeat layers. Sprinkle with mozzarella cheese. Bake, uncovered, at 325° for 30-35 minutes or until heated through and bubbly. **Yield:** 4 servings.

Speedy Steaks and Chops

IS YOUR GANG craving hearty fare fast? We've rounded up a bunch of quick recipes featuring steaks and chops that will get you cookin' in no time. Each dish calls for no more than 10 ingredients—most you likely have on hand—and many can be finished in less than 30 minutes. Enjoy!

CHOPS WITH CORN SALSA

(Pictured below)

Diane Halferty, Corpus Christi, Texas

This easy recipe is popular with my family and friends. I like to serve it throughout the year.

4-1/2 teaspoons chili powder
   6 boneless pork loin chops (3/4 inch thick)
   2 teaspoons vegetable oil
   1 can (15-1/4 ounces) corn with red and green peppers, drained
   1 can (14-1/2 ounces) diced tomatoes with garlic and onion, undrained

   1 can (2-1/4 ounces) sliced ripe olives, drained
   2 tablespoons minced fresh cilantro

Rub chili powder over both sides of pork chops. Cover and refrigerate for 20 minutes. In a large skillet over medium-high heat, brown chops on both sides in oil; drain.

Add the corn, tomatoes and olives. Reduce heat; cover and simmer for 12-16 minutes or until meat is tender and juices run clear. Remove chops and keep warm. Stir cilantro into corn mixture; serve over chops. **Yield:** 6 servings.

ORANGE SAUCED PORK CHOPS

Cory Cadotte, Winnipeg, Manitoba

It's simple to dress up plain pork chops with a citrus-flavored sauce.

   4 bone-in pork loin chops (1 inch thick)
   1 tablespoon vegetable oil

1/2 cup orange juice
2 tablespoons brown sugar
2 tablespoons orange marmalade
1 tablespoon cider vinegar
3 to 4 teaspoons cornstarch
2 tablespoons cold water
Salt and pepper

In a skillet over medium-high heat, brown pork chops on both sides in oil; drain. Combine the orange juice, brown sugar, marmalade and vinegar; pour over chops. Bring to a boil. Reduce heat; cover and simmer for 14-18 minutes or until meat juices run clear.

Remove chops and keep warm. Combine cornstarch and water until smooth; stir into pan juices. Bring to a boil; cook and stir for 2 minutes or until thickened. Season with salt and pepper. Serve with chops. **Yield:** 4 servings.

PARMESAN PORK SANDWICHES

Mary Kirkland, Las Vegas, Nevada

These saucy sandwiches are a nice change of pace from the traditional chicken variety. Plus, they're quick to fix.

1 garlic clove, minced
4 tablespoons vegetable oil, *divided*
1 can (15 ounces) tomato puree
1 egg, lightly beaten
2 tablespoons water
1/4 cup seasoned bread crumbs
4 boneless pork loin chops (1/4 inch thick)
1/2 cup shredded mozzarella cheese
1/4 cup grated Parmesan cheese
4 sandwich rolls, split

In a saucepan, saute garlic in 2 tablespoons oil. Add the tomato puree. Bring to a boil. Reduce heat; simmer, uncovered, for 5 minutes.

Meanwhile, combine the egg and water in a shallow bowl. Place the bread crumbs in another shallow bowl. Dip pork chops in egg mixture, then coat with crumbs. In a large skillet over medium-high heat, brown chops on both sides in remaining oil.

Spread half of the tomato mixture in a greased 11-in. x 7-in. x 2-in. baking dish. Top with pork chops; drizzle with remaining tomato mixture. Sprinkle with cheeses. Bake, uncovered, at 425° for 8-10 minutes or until meat juices run clear. Serve on rolls. **Yield:** 4 servings.

PEPPER STEAK

Nicky Hurt, APO, England

This speedy steak recipe comes from my mom's files. It's always been a favorite.

1 pound boneless beef sirloin steak, cut into thin strips
1 tablespoon vegetable oil
2 garlic cloves, minced
2 cans (14-1/2 ounces *each*) beef broth
1 small sweet red pepper, sliced
1 small green pepper, sliced
4-1/2 teaspoons cornstarch
1/4 cup water
4 cups hot cooked rice

In a skillet over medium-high heat, brown steak in oil; drain. Add garlic; saute for 3 minutes. Add broth; bring to a boil. Reduce heat; simmer, uncovered, for 12-16 minutes or until broth is reduced by half.

Add peppers. Combine cornstarch and water until smooth; stir into broth. Bring to a boil; cook and stir for 2 minutes or until thickened. Serve over rice. **Yield:** 4 servings.

MAPLE HAM STEAK

Jean Tayntor, Eaton, New York

The family dairy farm has also been a producer of maple syrup. This is a very simple, but delicious, ham steak idea.

1 bone-in fully cooked ham steak (about 2 pounds and 3/4 inch thick)
1/2 cup maple syrup, *divided*

Grill ham, uncovered, over medium-hot heat for 5-7 minutes on each side, basting frequently with 1/4 cup syrup. Warm remaining syrup to serve with ham. **Yield:** 6 servings.

TOSSING together a tasty salad or soup is easy, especially when you feature a refreshing mix of fresh fruits and veggies.

LUNCH DU JOUR. From top: Peanut Chicken Salad and Clam Chowder (both recipes on p. 49).

Soups & Salads

Soups & Salads

CLAM CHOWDER

(Pictured at left)

Melba Horne, Macon, Georgia

Here's a quick chowder that's been in my family for over 30 years. I make a big pot to take to an annual party at work. It's always a hit. Served with crusty bread and a salad, it's the perfect meal for a chilly evening.

6 bacon strips, diced
1/2 cup finely chopped onion
2 cans (10-3/4 ounces *each*) condensed cream of potato soup, undiluted
1-1/2 cups milk
3 cans (6-1/2 ounces *each*) minced clams, undrained
1 tablespoon lemon juice
1/4 teaspoon dried thyme
1/4 teaspoon pepper
Minced fresh parsley

In a large saucepan, cook bacon over medium heat until crisp; remove to paper towels. Drain, reserving 1 tablespoon drippings. In the drippings, saute onion until tender. Stir in soup and milk. Add the clams, lemon juice, thyme, pepper and bacon; heat through. Garnish with parsley. **Yield:** 5 servings.

PEANUT CHICKEN SALAD

(Pictured at left)

Della Byers, Rosamond, California

Our former neighbor, a native of Indonesia, made this peanut chicken salad, which she called "sate". My family liked it so much that after she moved away, I had to learn to make it.

1/3 cup soy sauce
3 tablespoons minced garlic
3 tablespoons peanut butter
1/4 cup minced fresh cilantro
1/2 teaspoon hot pepper sauce
4 boneless skinless chicken breast halves
4 cups torn mixed salad greens
4 small tomatoes, seeded and chopped
4 green onions, chopped

1 cup shredded cabbage
1 medium cucumber, sliced
1 cup honey-roasted peanuts
1 cup ranch salad dressing
2 to 4 drops hot pepper sauce

In a saucepan, combine the soy sauce, garlic, peanut butter, cilantro and hot pepper sauce; cook and stir until heated through and blended. Cool to room temperature. Place the chicken in a large resealable plastic bag; add soy sauce mixture. Seal the bag and turn to coat; refrigerate for 1 hour.

Drain and discard marinade. Grill chicken, uncovered, over medium heat for 3 minutes on each side. Grill 6-8 minutes longer or until juices run clear. Place the salad greens, tomatoes, onions, cabbage, cucumber and peanuts on a serving platter. Slice chicken; arrange over salad. In a small bowl, combine the salad dressing and hot pepper sauce. Serve with salad. **Yield:** 6 servings.

STRAWBERRY SPINACH SALAD

Donna Moorman, Stirling, Ontario

Years ago, my husband and I went to a dinner catered by a high school cooking class, and they served this colorful salad. I begged for the recipe and have been making it ever since.

8 cups torn fresh spinach
1 pint fresh strawberries, sliced
1 can (11 ounces) mandarin oranges, drained
1/4 cup julienned red onion
1/2 cup vegetable oil
1/3 cup sugar
1/4 cup cider vinegar
1 tablespoon poppy seeds
1-1/2 teaspoons finely chopped onion
1/2 teaspoon Worcestershire sauce
1/4 teaspoon paprika

On salad plates, arrange the spinach, strawberries, oranges and onion. In a jar with a tight-fitting lid, combine the remaining ingredients; shake well. Drizzle over salads; serve immediately. **Yield:** 6-8 servings.

starch, celery seed, cinnamon and cloves. Stir in the cranberry juice, vinegar and reserved raspberry puree. Bring to a boil over medium heat; cook and stir for 1 minute or until thickened. Remove from the heat; cool. Cover and refrigerate.

In a large salad bowl, combine the spinach, oranges, cranberries, onions, sunflower kernels, pecans and almonds. Drizzle with dressing; gently toss to coat. Refrigerate any leftover dressing. **Yield:** 12 servings.

SPICED RHUBARB SOUP

(Pictured below)

Renee Parker, Chester, South Carolina

This very pretty soup is perfect for spring. My whole family loves the fresh flavor of rhubarb, so they all really enjoy this chilled soup.

> ✓ **Uses less fat, sugar or salt. Includes Nutritional Analysis and Diabetic Exchanges.**

      8 cups diced fresh *or* frozen rhubarb, thawed
3-1/2 cups water, *divided*
      1 cup sugar
      4 cinnamon sticks (3 inches)
  1/4 teaspoon salt
      3 tablespoons plus 1-1/2 teaspoons cornstarch
      1 lemon slice
      4 tablespoons reduced-fat sour cream

SALAD WITH CRAN-RASPBERRY DRESSING

(Pictured above)

Tannis Williams, Gowanstown, Ontario

I was given this recipe at a bridal shower our rural farming community held for me. It's become my all-time favorite salad. The color and tang the berries add to the lovely mix make it perfect for company or just my husband and me.

      1 package (10 ounces) frozen sweetened raspberries, thawed and drained
  1/4 cup sugar
      2 teaspoons cornstarch
  1/4 teaspoon celery seed
  1/4 teaspoon ground cinnamon
  1/8 teaspoon ground cloves
  1/2 cup cranberry juice
  1/4 cup red wine vinegar
SALAD:
      1 package (6 ounces) fresh baby spinach
      1 can (11 ounces) mandarin oranges, drained
  1/3 cup dried cranberries
      3 green onions, sliced
  1/4 cup sunflower kernels
  1/4 cup chopped pecans
  1/4 cup slivered almonds

Place raspberries in a blender; cover and process until pureed. Strain and discard seeds; set puree aside. In a saucepan, combine the sugar, corn-

In a large saucepan, bring rhubarb, 3-1/4 cups water, sugar, cinnamon sticks and salt to a boil. Reduce heat; simmer, uncovered, for 20 minutes or until rhubarb is tender. Discard cinnamon sticks. Strain rhubarb mixture; discard pulp. Return liquid to the pan; bring to a boil.

Combine cornstarch and remaining water until smooth; stir into saucepan. Cook and stir for 2 minutes or until thickened. Remove from the heat; add lemon slice. Cover and refrigerate until chilled. Discard lemon slice. Ladle soup into bowls. Garnish each serving with 1 tablespoon sour cream. **Yield:** 4 servings.

Nutritional Analysis: One serving (3/4 cup) equals 267 calories, 2 g fat (1 g saturated fat), 5 mg cholesterol, 163 mg sodium, 65 g carbohydrate, 3 g fiber, 2 g protein.

▰▰▰▰▰▰▰▰▰▰▰
TURKEY CHILI

Celesta Zanger, Bloomfield Hills, Michigan

I've taken my mother's milder recipe for chili and made it thicker and more robust. It's a favorite, especially in fall and winter.

> ✓ Uses less fat, sugar or salt. Includes Nutritional Analysis and Diabetic Exchanges.

- 1 pound lean ground turkey
- 3/4 cup chopped onion
- 3/4 cup chopped celery
- 3/4 cup chopped green pepper
- 1 can (28 ounces) diced tomatoes, undrained
- 1 jar (26 ounces) meatless spaghetti sauce
- 1 can (15-1/2 ounces) hot chili beans
- 1-1/2 cups water
- 1/2 cup frozen corn
- 2 tablespoons chili powder
- 1 teaspoon ground cumin
- 1/4 teaspoon pepper
- 1/8 to 1/4 teaspoon cayenne pepper
- 1 can (16 ounces) kidney beans, rinsed and drained
- 1 can (15 ounces) pinto beans, rinsed and drained

In a large nonstick skillet, cook the turkey, onion, celery and green pepper over medium heat until meat is no longer pink and vegetables are tender. Drain; transfer to a slow cooker. Add tomatoes, spaghetti sauce, chili beans, water, corn and seasonings. Cover and cook on high for 1 hour.

Reduce heat to low; cook for 5-6 hours. Add kidney and pinto beans; cook 30 minutes longer. **Yield:** 13 servings.

Nutritional Analysis: One serving (1 cup) equals 190 calories, 4 g fat (1 g saturated fat), 28 mg cholesterol, 739 mg sodium, 27 g carbohydrate, 7 g fiber, 13 g protein. **Diabetic Exchanges:** 2 very lean meat, 2 vegetable, 1 starch.

▰▰▰▰▰▰▰▰▰▰▰
FRUITY TORTELLINI SALAD
(Pictured above)

Vicky McClain, St. Albans, Vermont

Being from Vermont, the nation's leading maple syrup-producing state, I use pure maple syrup for a special sweet taste. By adding chicken, this salad can be a light main course.

- 1 package (9 ounces) refrigerated cheese tortellini
- 1 can (11 ounces) mandarin oranges, drained
- 1 medium grapefruit, peeled and sectioned
- 1 medium lemon, peeled and sectioned
- 2 kiwifruit, peeled and sliced
- 1 cup halved seedless red grapes
- 2 cups cubed cooked chicken, optional
- 1/2 cup maple syrup
- 1/2 cup orange juice
- 1/2 cup cashews

Cook tortellini according to package directions. Drain and rinse with cold water. In a large bowl, combine the tortellini, fruit and chicken if desired. In a small bowl, whisk the syrup and orange juice; pour over salad and toss to coat. Cover and refrigerate for at least 1 hour. Sprinkle with cashews just before serving. **Yield:** 6-8 servings.

CURRIED CHICKEN BARLEY SALAD

(Pictured below)

Patricia Force, Winsted, Connecticut

A trip through the potluck line at a 4-H supper introduced me to this luscious cold summer salad. The ingredients sound a bit unusual, but they blend beautifully together.

5-1/3 cups water
   1 cup uncooked medium pearl barley
   2 cups frozen peas and carrots
   2 cups cubed cooked chicken
3/4 cup salted dry roasted peanuts
   1 celery rib with leaves, finely chopped
   1 green onion, thinly sliced
DRESSING:
1/2 cup mayonnaise *or* salad dressing
1/2 cup plain yogurt
7-1/2 teaspoons orange marmalade
1-1/2 teaspoons spicy brown *or* Dijon
       mustard
1-1/2 teaspoons curry powder

In a large saucepan, bring water and barley to a boil. Reduce heat; cover and simmer for 45-50 minutes or until tender. Remove from the heat; let stand for 5 minutes. Drain and cool. Place 1 in. of water in another saucepan; add peas and carrots. Bring to a boil. Reduce heat; cover and simmer for 5-7 minutes or until tender. Drain and cool.

In a large bowl, combine the barley, peas and carrots, chicken, peanuts, celery and green onion;

mix well. In a small bowl, whisk together the dressing ingredients; pour over barley mixture and toss to coat. Cover and refrigerate for 2-3 hours. **Yield:** 5-7 servings.

PASTA BEAN SOUP

Beverly Ballaro, Lynnfield, Massachusetts

My family loves this soup during our cold New England winters. It's very thick and hearty.

✓ Uses less fat, sugar or salt. Includes Nutritional Analysis and Diabetic Exchanges.

   1 large onion, chopped
   1 large carrot, chopped
   1 celery rib, chopped
   2 tablespoons olive oil
   3 garlic cloves, minced
   4 cups vegetable *or* chicken broth
3/4 cup uncooked small pasta shells
   2 teaspoons sugar
1-1/2 teaspoons Italian seasoning
1/4 teaspoon crushed red pepper flakes
   2 cans (15 ounces *each*) white kidney *or*
       cannellini beans, rinsed and drained
   1 can (28 ounces) crushed tomatoes
   3 tablespoons grated Parmesan cheese

In a Dutch oven, saute the onion, carrot and celery in oil until crisp-tender. Add garlic; saute 1 minute longer. Add the broth, pasta, sugar, Italian seasoning and pepper flakes. Bring to a boil. Reduce heat; simmer, uncovered, for 15 minutes or until pasta is tender. Add the beans and tomatoes; simmer, uncovered, for 5 minutes. Sprinkle each serving with 1-1/2 teaspoons Parmesan cheese. **Yield:** 6 servings.

Nutritional Analysis: One serving (1-1/3 cups) equals 295 calories, 7 g fat (1 g saturated fat), 2 mg cholesterol, 1,208 mg sodium, 48 g carbohydrate, 9 g fiber, 13 g protein. **Diabetic Exchanges:** 3 vegetable, 2 starch, 1 very lean meat, 1 fat.

PENNE PASTA SALAD

(Pictured above right and on front cover)

Melissa Harryman, Lenorah, Texas

I came up with this recipe one day while experimenting in my kitchen. This salad makes a great side dish with just about any kind of meat.

   1 package (16 ounces) penne *or* medium
       tube pasta
   1 cup quartered cherry tomatoes

1/2 cup chopped green pepper
1/4 cup chopped green onions
 1 can (2-1/4 ounces) sliced ripe olives,
    drained
 1 bottle (8 ounces) Italian salad dressing
1/2 teaspoon coarsely ground pepper
1/4 teaspoon *each* dill weed, garlic salt and
    lemon-pepper seasoning

Cook pasta according to package directions. Meanwhile, in a large serving bowl, combine the tomatoes, green pepper, onions and olives. Drain pasta and rinse in cold water; add to vegetables. Combine the salad dressing and seasonings; pour over the salad and toss to coat. Cover and refrigerate salad for at least 2 hours before serving. **Yield:** 8-10 servings.

COWPOKE CORN BREAD SALAD

Shelly Donnelly, Gold Canyon, Arizona

My crew and I lead horseback camping vacations into the untamed areas of Arizona. Our cooks serve trail lunches and cowboy-sized suppers out of our chuck wagon kitchen. This hearty salad is usually on the menu.

10 cups crumbled corn bread
 8 bacon strips, cooked and crumbled
 2 medium tomatoes, chopped
 1 medium green pepper, chopped
1/2 cup chopped onion
 1 to 1-1/3 cups mayonnaise

In a large bowl, combine first five ingredients. Add mayonnaise; toss to coat. Serve immediately. **Yield:** 8-10 servings.

WINTER SQUASH SOUP
(Pictured below)

Angela Liette, Sidney, Ohio

I enjoy trying new recipes and adding different seasonings to enhance the flavor. This is a tasty way to serve squash.

 2 celery ribs, chopped
 1 medium onion, chopped
 1 garlic clove, minced
 3 tablespoons butter
 3 tablespoons all-purpose flour
 3 cups chicken broth
 2 cups mashed cooked butternut, acorn *or*
    Hubbard squash
 2 tablespoons minced fresh parsley
1/2 teaspoon salt
1/8 to 1/4 teaspoon ground nutmeg
1/4 teaspoon dried savory
1/4 teaspoon dried rosemary, crushed
1/8 teaspoon pepper
 1 cup half-and-half cream

In a large saucepan, saute celery, onion and garlic in butter until tender. Stir in flour until blended. Gradually add the broth. Bring to a boil; cook and stir for 2 minutes or until thickened. Reduce heat; stir in the squash, parsley, salt, nutmeg, savory, rosemary and pepper. Simmer, uncovered, for 10 minutes or until heated through. Cool slightly.

In a blender, process soup in batches until smooth. Return to the pan and heat through. Gradually stir in cream. Cook 5 minutes longer, stirring occasionally. **Yield:** 6 servings.

1 package (5 ounces) salad greens
2/3 cup dried cranberries
1 medium ripe pear, peeled and cubed
3/4 cup seasoned croutons
2 tablespoons sunflower kernels
1/4 cup Italian salad dressing

In a bowl, combine the salad greens, cranberries, pear, croutons and sunflower kernels. Just before serving, add the dressing and toss to coat. **Yield:** 6 servings.

KIELBASA CABBAGE SOUP

(Pictured below)

Patricia Bosse, Darien Center, New York

Cabbage is plentiful in upstate New York. During winter, I like to keep this hearty soup simmering on the stovetop all day.

1 small cabbage, coarsely chopped
1 medium onion, chopped
4 to 6 garlic cloves, minced
2 tablespoons olive oil
4 cups water
3 tablespoons cider vinegar
1 to 2 tablespoons brown sugar
1 pound fully cooked kielbasa *or* Polish sausage, cut into 1/2-inch pieces, halved
4 medium potatoes, peeled and cubed
3 large carrots, chopped
1 teaspoon caraway seeds
1/2 teaspoon pepper

TROPICAL FRUIT SLUSH

(Pictured above)

Teresa Weikle, Morehead, Kentucky

This recipe has been in my family for a long time. I have fond childhood memories of cooling off on many hot afternoons with this cold fruit treat.

3 cups water
1-1/2 cups sugar
6 medium ripe bananas, diced
2 cans (11 ounces *each*) mandarin oranges
1 can (20 ounces) crushed pineapple, undrained
1 can (12 ounces) frozen orange juice concentrate, thawed
1 jar (10 ounces) maraschino cherries, drained and halved
1/3 cup lemon juice

In a saucepan, bring water and sugar to a boil; cook and stir for 5 minutes. Remove from the heat; cool completely. In a 4-qt. freezer container, combine the remaining ingredients. Pour sugar water over the fruit. Cover and freeze for at least 8 hours, stirring once or twice. Remove from the freezer 20 minutes before serving. **Yield:** 12-14 servings.

CRANBERRY TOSSED SALAD

Janelle Halbert, Calgary, Alberta

I enjoy making this salad when the usual lettuce salad gets boring. The vegetables and fruit make a nice combination.

In a Dutch oven or soup kettle, sauté the cabbage, onion and garlic in oil for 5 minutes or until tender. Combine water, vinegar and brown sugar; add to cabbage mixture. Stir in remaining ingredients. Bring to a boil. Reduce heat; cover and simmer for 60-70 minutes or until vegetables are tender. **Yield:** 8-10 servings.

CURRIED RICE SALAD

Lula Young, Newport, Arkansas

Rice is truly one of the world's most versatile foods. Arkansas is the top rice-producing state in the country, so this recipe represents our region well.

   1 can (20 ounces) pineapple tidbits
   2 cups cooked rice, cooled
   2 cups cubed cooked chicken
1/2 cup chopped celery
1/3 cup slivered almonds, toasted
1/3 cup raisins
1/4 cup chopped green onions
2/3 cup mayonnaise
   1 tablespoon Dijon mustard
3/4 teaspoon curry powder
1/4 teaspoon salt
Lettuce leaves, optional

Drain pineapple, reserving juice; set aside 1 cup pineapple and 3 tablespoons juice (refrigerate remaining pineapple and juice for another use). In a large bowl, combine the rice, chicken, celery, almonds, raisins, green onions and reserved pineapple. In a small bowl, combine the mayonnaise, mustard, curry powder, salt and reserved juice. Gently stir into rice mixture. Cover and refrigerate for at least 1 hour. Serve in a lettuce-lined bowl if desired. **Yield:** 8 servings.

OLIVE CORN SALAD

Mrs. Raymond Mumaugh, Hawthorne, California

This recipe has been a favorite of mine for years. My grandmother would always ask me to make it for our family picnic.

   1 package (16 ounces) frozen corn,
     thawed
   3 hard-cooked eggs, diced
1/3 cup sliced stuffed olives
1/2 cup mayonnaise
   2 tablespoons snipped chives
1/2 teaspoon chili powder
1/4 teaspoon ground cumin
1/8 teaspoon salt

In a bowl, combine the corn, eggs and olives. In a small bowl, combine the mayonnaise and seasonings. Stir into corn mixture and mix well. Cover and refrigerate for 2 hours or until chilled. **Yield:** 6 servings.

GREENS 'N' FRUIT SALAD

(Pictured above)

Jean Martin, Raleigh, North Carolina

I concocted this recipe in my kitchen, and I've received a lot of compliments on it. I make it often for my husband and me, and I've also served it to guests at brunches and dinner parties.

   6 cups torn salad greens
   2 medium navel oranges, peeled and
     sectioned
   1 cup halved red seedless grapes
1/2 cup golden raisins
1/4 cup chopped red onion
1/4 cup sliced almonds
   4 bacon strips, cooked and crumbled
DRESSING:
1/2 cup mayonnaise
1/2 cup honey
1/4 cup orange juice
   2 tablespoons grated orange peel

In a large salad bowl, combine the first seven ingredients. In a bowl, whisk together the mayonnaise, honey, orange juice and peel. Serve with salad. Refrigerate leftover dressing. **Yield:** 6 servings (1 cup dressing).

TURKEY BEAN CHILI

LaRita Lang, Lincoln, Nebraska

This is a fast, easy recipe that tastes great. It won a ribbon at the Nebraska State Fair.

- 2 cups cubed cooked turkey breast
- 2 cans (14-1/2 ounces *each*) diced tomatoes, undrained
- 1 can (15 ounces) black beans, rinsed and drained
- 1 can (15 ounces) great northern beans, rinsed and drained
- 1 cup barbecue sauce
- 1 medium onion, chopped
- 1 teaspoon chili powder
- 1 teaspoon ground cumin

In a large saucepan, combine all ingredients. Bring to a boil. Reduce heat; simmer, uncovered, for 10 minutes. **Yield:** 6 servings.

PEANUT APPLE SALAD

(Pictured below)

Dorothy Smith, El Dorado, Arkansas

Folks have commented on this interesting mix of crunchy nuts, apples and veggies and the tangy honey-yogurt dressing.

- 1 cup (8 ounces) plain *or* orange yogurt
- 2 tablespoons honey

- 1 teaspoon salt
- 1/8 teaspoon pepper
- 2 large red apples, chopped
- 1 can (11 ounces) mandarin oranges, drained
- 2 celery ribs, finely chopped
- 2 medium carrots, shredded
- 1 cup dry roasted peanuts
Lettuce leaves, optional

In a bowl, combine the yogurt, honey, salt and pepper. Add fruit, vegetables and nuts; gently stir to coat. Cover and refrigerate until serving. Serve in a lettuce-lined bowl if desired. **Yield:** 8 servings.

CRUNCHY CABBAGE SALAD

Linda Miller, Sanford, North Carolina

This salad hits the spot on warm days. It's always popular at potluck dinners.

- 1 package (3 ounces) chicken ramen noodles
- 1/2 cup vegetable oil
- 3 tablespoons cider vinegar
- 2 tablespoons sugar
- 1/2 teaspoon dried oregano
- 1/2 teaspoon salt
- 1/2 teaspoon pepper
- 5 cups shredded green cabbage
- 3/4 cup chopped green pepper
- 3/4 cup chopped sweet red pepper
- 1/2 cup shredded red cabbage
- 1/2 cup shredded carrot
- 1/2 cup chopped green onions
- 1/2 cup slivered almonds, toasted
- 2 tablespoons sesame seeds, toasted

Break noodles; set aside. In a jar with a tight-fitting lid, combine oil, vinegar, sugar, oregano, salt, pepper and half of the contents from the noodle seasoning packet; shake well. (Discard remaining seasoning or save for another use.) In a large bowl, combine the remaining ingredients. Add noodles and dressing; toss to coat. Serve immediately. **Yield:** 10-12 servings.

MEXICAN BEAN BARLEY SOUP

(Pictured above right)

Elizabeth Cole, Mauckport, Indiana

Wonderfully warming, this soup is always on the menu for the retreats we host on our woodland farm. Everyone enjoys spooning up its yummy vegetable broth and hearty mix of beans and barley.

2 medium onions, chopped
3 garlic cloves, minced
2 tablespoons vegetable oil
1 medium turnip, peeled and diced
1 medium carrot, diced
2 tablespoons finely chopped jalapeno
    pepper*
1-1/2 teaspoons ground cumin
1/2 teaspoon ground coriander
3 cans (14-1/2 ounces *each*) vegetable
    broth
2 cups cooked medium pearl barley
1 can (15 ounces) pinto beans, rinsed and
    drained
2 teaspoons lemon juice

In a large saucepan, saute onions and garlic in oil until tender. Add the turnip, carrot and jalapeno; cook and stir until tender. Add cumin and coriander; cook and stir for 2 minutes. Add broth. Bring to a boil. Reduce heat; cover and simmer for 20 minutes. Add the barley, beans and lemon juice. Simmer, uncovered, 10-15 minutes longer or until soup thickens slightly. **Yield:** 7 servings.

*Editor's Note: When cutting or seeding hot peppers, use rubber or plastic gloves to protect your hands. Avoid touching your face.

FOUR-FRUIT SALAD

Debbie Fite, Fort Myers, Florida

Almost any type of fruit will work in this recipe. The first time I made it, I just used the fruits I had on hand in my refrigerator.

2 cups fresh strawberries, sliced
2 cups green grapes, halved
1 small cantaloupe, cut into chunks
1 to 2 medium firm bananas, sliced
1/3 cup orange juice

In a large bowl, combine the fruit. Pour juice over fruit and toss to coat. Cover and refrigerate for 4 hours. Stir just before serving. **Yield:** 10 servings.

CURRIED SHRIMP SALAD

(Pictured below)

Charlotte Smith, Farmington, Connecticut

This recipe is easy to prepare and tastes great as a main dish. The water chestnuts and celery give it just enough crunch.

1 pound cooked large shrimp, peeled and
    deveined
1 can (8 ounces) sliced water chestnuts,
    drained
1 celery rib, thinly sliced
2 green onions, thinly sliced
3/4 cup mayonnaise *or* salad dressing
2 tablespoons soy sauce
1/2 teaspoon curry powder
Leaf lettuce
1/4 cup slivered almonds, toasted

In a bowl, combine the shrimp, water chestnuts, celery and onions. In a small bowl, combine the mayonnaise, soy sauce and curry powder. Stir into shrimp mixture. Cover and refrigerate for at least 2 hours. Serve in a lettuce-lined bowl. Sprinkle with almonds. **Yield:** 4 servings.

▪▪▪▪▪▪▪▪▪▪▪▪▪
SPICY CHICKEN RICE SOUP
(Pictured above)

Mary Shaver, Jonesboro, Arkansas

Arkansas is the top rice-producing state in the country, so this recipe definitely represents our region.

    2 cans (14-1/2 ounces *each*) chicken
       broth
    3 cups cooked rice
    2 cups diced cooked chicken
    1 can (15-1/4 ounces) whole kernel corn,
       undrained
    1 can (11-1/2 ounces) V8 juice
    1 cup salsa
    1 can (4 ounces) chopped green chilies,
       drained
  1/2 cup chopped green onions
    2 tablespoons minced fresh cilantro
  1/2 cup shredded Monterey Jack cheese,
       optional

In a large saucepan, combine the first nine ingredients. Bring to a boil. Reduce heat; cover and simmer for 15 minutes or until heated through. Garnish with cheese if desired. **Yield:** 8 servings.

▪▪▪▪▪▪▪▪▪▪▪▪▪
TOMATO BARLEY SALAD

Sandi Lange, Sherwood Park, Alberta

I like to serve this fuss-free salad alongside barbecued chicken for a hot summer evening dinner on the deck.

    4 cups cold cooked medium pearl barley
  1/3 cup grated Parmesan cheese
  1/4 cup vegetable oil

1-1/2 teaspoons minced fresh basil
       or 1/2 teaspoon dried basil
    1 garlic clove, minced
  1/2 teaspoon salt
  1/4 to 1/2 teaspoon pepper
    4 cups halved cherry tomatoes
    2 cups frozen corn, thawed

Place barley in a large bowl. In a small bowl, combine the cheese, oil, basil, garlic, salt and pepper; mix well. Pour over barley and toss to coat. Add tomatoes and corn; toss to combine. Cover and refrigerate for 2 hours. **Yield:** 12 servings.

▪▪▪▪▪▪▪▪▪▪▪▪▪
SOUTHWESTERN VEGGIE SALAD
(Pictured below)

Rita Addicks, Weimar, Texas

This speedy salad can be stirred up in no time. I enjoy making it because it takes so little effort.

    2 cups whole kernel corn
    1 small zucchini, sliced 1/4 inch thick
    1 ripe avocado, peeled and chopped
  1/4 cup thinly sliced radishes
Boston *or* leaf lettuce, optional
    2 to 3 medium tomatoes, sliced
DRESSING:
    3 tablespoons ketchup
    2 tablespoons cider vinegar
    1 tablespoon vegetable oil
    1 tablespoon minced fresh cilantro
  1/2 teaspoon garlic powder
  1/4 teaspoon salt
  1/4 teaspoon chili powder

In a large bowl, combine the corn, zucchini, avocado and radishes. On a serving plate, arrange lettuce if desired and tomatoes. In a small bowl, whisk the dressing ingredients. Pour over corn mixture; gently toss to coat. Spoon over tomatoes. Serve immediately. **Yield:** 5 servings.

SWEET 'N' SOUR TOSSED SALAD

Dolores Brignac, Braithwaite, Louisiana

My family was skeptical the first time I served this unusual salad—but one taste convinced them it was a winner. Now when I bring it out, everyone digs in and cleans their plates.

- 1 package (3 ounces) ramen noodles
- 1 cup chopped walnuts
- 1/4 cup butter
- 6 cups torn romaine
- 4 cups broccoli florets
- 1 pint cherry tomatoes, halved
- 4 green onions, sliced

DRESSING:
- 1/2 cup vegetable oil
- 1/4 cup sugar
- 3 tablespoons red wine vinegar
- 4-1/2 teaspoons soy sauce

Salt and pepper to taste

Break noodles into small pieces (save seasoning envelope for another use). In a skillet over medium heat, saute noodles and walnuts in butter for 5-6 minutes or until lightly browned. Cool.

In a large salad bowl, combine the romaine, broccoli, tomatoes and onions. Place dressing ingredients in a blender or food processor; cover and process until sugar is dissolved. Add dressing and noodle mixture to salad; toss to coat. Serve with a slotted spoon. **Yield:** 14-16 servings.

THREE-BEAN BARLEY SALAD

Pat Miller, North Fork, California

Kidney beans, black beans and garbanzo beans deliciously combine in this hearty salad.

- 2 cups water
- 1 tablespoon chicken bouillon granules
- 1 cup quick-cooking barley
- 1 can (16 ounces) kidney beans, rinsed and drained
- 1 can (15 ounces) black beans, rinsed and drained
- 1 can (15 ounces) garbanzo beans *or* chickpeas, rinsed and drained

- 4 green onions, thinly sliced
- 1 cup honey Dijon salad dressing

In a saucepan, bring water and bouillon to a boil. Stir in barley. Reduce heat; cover and simmer for 11-13 minutes or until barley is tender and liquid is absorbed. Cool for 10 minutes; transfer to a bowl. Add beans and onions; stir in the dressing. Refrigerate until serving. **Yield:** 12 servings.

BLACK BEAN SOUP

(Pictured above)

Mary Buhl, Duluth, Georgia

Salsa and cumin add just the right zip to this thick, hearty soup. I like to serve it with corn bread.

✓ Uses less fat, sugar or salt. Includes Nutritional Analysis and Diabetic Exchanges.

- 3/4 cup chopped celery
- 1 medium onion, chopped
- 3 garlic cloves, minced
- 1 tablespoon canola oil
- 3 cans (14-1/2 ounces *each*) chicken broth
- 2 cans (15 ounces *each*) black beans, rinsed and drained
- 1 jar (16 ounces) salsa
- 1 cup cubed cooked chicken breast
- 1 cup cooked long grain rice
- 1 tablespoon lime juice
- 1 teaspoon ground cumin

In a large saucepan, saute celery, onion and garlic in oil until tender. Stir in remaining ingredients; heat through. **Yield:** 10 servings (2-1/2 quarts).

Nutritional Analysis: One serving (1 cup) equals 155 calories, 3 g fat (trace saturated fat), 12 mg cholesterol, 965 mg sodium, 20 g carbohydrate, 6 g fiber, 11 g protein. **Diabetic Exchanges:** 1-1/2 meat, 1 starch.

LENTIL CHICKEN SALAD

Margaret Pache, Mesa, Arizona

A great way to use lentils is in this satisfying salad. Besides the combination of textures, the tasty ingredients blend well with the creamy dressing. It merited a blue ribbon and praise from all the tasters at our church fair.

      2 cups shredded iceberg lettuce
      1 cup cooked lentils
      1 cup diced cooked chicken
      1 cup diced celery
  1/2 cup shredded carrot
  1/2 cup chopped pecans
      1 cup mayonnaise
  1/4 cup chunky salsa
      4 green onions, chopped
      1 tablespoon lemon juice

In a large bowl, combine the first six ingredients. In a small bowl, combine the mayonnaise, salsa, onions and lemon juice. Pour over salad and stir gently to coat. Serve immediately. **Yield:** 4-6 servings.

BLUE CHEESE PEAR SALAD

(Pictured below)

Rebecca Baird, Salt Lake City, Utah

The combination of greens, pears, raspberries, nuts and blue cheese in this refreshing salad, topped with a zesty mustard dressing, is just delightful!

      8 cups mixed salad greens
      1 cup unpeeled fresh pear slices
      1 cup fresh raspberries, optional
  1/2 cup (2 ounces) crumbled blue cheese
  1/4 cup chopped walnuts, toasted
  1/3 cup olive oil
  1/4 cup cider vinegar
  1-1/2 teaspoons Dijon mustard
      1 teaspoon sugar
Pepper to taste

In a large salad bowl, combine the greens, pears, raspberries if desired, blue cheese and nuts. In a jar with a tight-fitting lid, combine the remaining ingredients; shake well. Pour over salad and toss to coat. Serve immediately. **Yield:** 10-12 servings.

MANDARIN CHICKEN SALAD

Belinda Gail Brown, Wedowee, Alabama

Living in Alabama, where lots of peanuts are grown, I've learned to fix many different dishes using this locally raised crop. This is one of my family's favorites.

  1/4 cup sugar
  1/4 cup cider vinegar
  1-1/2 teaspoons vegetable oil
  1/2 teaspoon salt
Dash pepper
      4 cups shredded lettuce
      2 cups cubed cooked chicken
      1 can (15 ounces) mandarin oranges,
          drained
      1 celery rib, thinly sliced
      1 green onion, thinly sliced
      1 cup chow mein noodles
  1/2 cup salted peanuts, toasted

In a jar with a tight-fitting lid, combine the first five ingredients; shake well. In a serving bowl, combine the lettuce, chicken, oranges, celery and onion; stir in chow mein noodles and peanuts. Pour dressing over salad and toss to coat. Serve immediately. **Yield:** 2-4 servings.

FRUITY GREEK SALAD

Sue Donnan, Belleville, Ontario

Peaches and oranges add a tasty twist to this Greek salad. The ingredients really complement each other.

☑ **Uses less fat, sugar or salt. Includes Nutritional Analysis and Diabetic Exchanges.**

    12 cups torn romaine
      1 can (11 ounces) mandarin oranges,
          drained

1/2 teaspoon poultry seasoning
1/4 teaspoon pepper
2 cups uncooked instant rice
1 tablespoon minced fresh parsley

In a large saucepan, combine the first six ingredients; bring to a boil over medium heat. Reduce heat; cover and simmer for 5 minutes. Stir in rice and parsley. Remove from heat; cover and let stand for 5 minutes. **Yield:** 6 servings.

TROPICAL COLESLAW
(Pictured below)

Tiffany Anderson-Taylor, St. Petersburg, Florida

A friend sent this recipe to me, and I've been indebted to her ever since. This is one coleslaw kids really like.

1 medium firm banana, sliced
2 tablespoons lemon juice
3 cups shredded cabbage
1 can (20 ounces) pineapple tidbits, drained
1 celery rib, chopped
1 can (11 ounces) mandarin oranges, drained
1/2 cup golden raisins
1 carton (8 ounces) lemon yogurt
1/2 cup coarsely chopped walnuts
1/2 teaspoon salt

In a small bowl, toss banana slices and lemon juice. In a large serving bowl, combine the cabbage, pineapple, celery, oranges and raisins. Drain bananas; discard juice. Add bananas, yogurt, walnuts and salt to cabbage mixture; toss to coat. Serve immediately. **Yield:** 8-10 servings.

2 celery ribs, sliced
1 cup sliced carrots
1 small red onion, thinly sliced
1/2 cup canned unsweetened peach slices, cut into thirds
10 pitted whole ripe olives
3 ounces crumbled feta cheese
1/4 cup olive oil
1/4 cup red wine vinegar
1/2 teaspoon sugar
1/4 teaspoon dried basil
1/4 teaspoon dried oregano
1/4 teaspoon salt

In a large salad bowl, combine the first eight ingredients. In a jar with a tight-fitting lid, combine the oil, vinegar, sugar and seasonings; shake well. Pour over the salad and toss to coat. **Yield:** 12 servings.

Nutritional Analysis: One serving (1-1/4 cups) equals 94 calories, 7 g fat (2 g saturated fat), 6 mg cholesterol, 178 mg sodium, 8 g carbohydrate, 2 g fiber, 2 g protein. **Diabetic Exchanges:** 1-1/2 fat, 1 vegetable.

CHUNKY CHICKEN RICE SOUP
(Pictured above)

Jacquie Olson, West Linn, Oregon

This is a simple and satisfying soup that my family has always enjoyed. It goes great with a grilled sandwich.

2 cans (14-1/2 ounces *each*) chicken broth
1 cup water
1 package (16 ounces) frozen mixed vegetables, thawed
1 package (6 ounces) grilled chicken strips, cut into 1/2-inch cubes

ADDING *a vegetable or relish to your meal can really perk things up. Go ahead and sauce up your next side dish!*

SIDE BY SIDE. From top: Rich and Creamy Potato Bake, Colorful Vegetable Medley and Teapot Cranberry Relish (all recipes on p. 63).

Side Dishes & Condiments

RICH AND CREAMY POTATO BAKE
(Pictured at left)

Joy Simpkins, Cambridge City, Indiana

This delicious side dish goes well with any meat entree. It's a wonderful recipe to make for potluck dinners.

    3 cups half-and-half cream
    1/2 cup butter
    1-1/2 teaspoons salt
    1 package (32 ounces) frozen Southern-
      style hash brown potatoes, thawed
    1/2 cup grated Parmesan cheese
Minced fresh parsley, optional

In a large saucepan, combine cream, butter and salt. Cook and stir over medium heat until butter is melted. Place potatoes in a greased 13-in. x 9-in. x 2-in. baking dish; pour cream mixture over potatoes. Sprinkle with Parmesan cheese.

Bake, uncovered, at 350° for 45-55 minutes or until potatoes are tender and top is golden brown. Sprinkle with parsley if desired. **Yield:** 12 servings.

COLORFUL VEGETABLE MEDLEY
(Pictured at left)

Martha Hiebert, New Bothwell, Manitoba

Our small community is the cheese capital of Manitoba. This is a favorite recipe from my husband's aunt, who works at the local cheese factory.

    2 tablespoons butter
    2 tablespoons vegetable oil
    3 medium carrots, thinly sliced
    3 celery ribs, thinly sliced
    2 cups cauliflowerets
    1 cup broccoli florets
    3/4 cup cubed fully cooked ham
    1 small onion, chopped
    1/2 cup cooked white rice
    1/2 cup shredded cheddar cheese

In a large skillet, melt the butter over medium heat. Add the oil, carrots, celery, cauliflower, broccoli, ham and onion. Cover and cook for 15-20 minutes or until vegetables are crisp-tender, stirring occasionally. Stir in the rice; cook until heated through. Sprinkle with cheese. Remove from the heat; cover for 2 minutes or until cheese is melted. **Yield:** 4 servings.

TEAPOT CRANBERRY RELISH

(Pictured at left)

Carolyn Huston, Jamesport, Missouri

A Christmas party at the tearoom we operate inspired my friend and me to create this relish. An instant hit, it turned everyone who tried it into a cranberry lover.

    1 package (12 ounces) fresh or frozen
      cranberries
    2 cups sugar
    1/2 cup orange juice
    1/2 cup cranberry juice
    2 cups dried cherries or golden raisins
    1 teaspoon grated orange peel

In a large saucepan, cook the cranberries, sugar and juices over medium heat until the berries pop, about 15 minutes. Add the cherries and orange peel. Simmer, uncovered, for 10 minutes. Cool slightly. Transfer to a bowl; cover and refrigerate until serving. **Yield:** 4 cups.

FRIED GREEN TOMATOES

Melanie Chism, Coker, Alabama

My grandmother came up with her own version of fried green tomatoes. It's a traditional taste of the South that anyone anywhere can enjoy!

    4 medium green tomatoes
    1 teaspoon salt
    1/4 teaspoon lemon-pepper seasoning
    3/4 cup cornmeal
    1/2 cup vegetable oil

Slice tomatoes 1/4 in. thick. Sprinkle both sides with salt and lemon-pepper. Let stand for 20-25 minutes. Coat with cornmeal. In a large skillet, heat oil over medium heat. Fry tomatoes for 3-4 minutes on each side or until tender and golden brown. Drain on paper towels. Serve immediately. **Yield:** 6-8 servings.

SOUTHWESTERN RICE BAKE
(Pictured below)

Sheila Johnson, Red Feather Lakes, Colorado

Whenever I have a hard time planning dinner, my husband requests his favorite bake. Often, I use it as an entree, served with warm tortillas. Other times, I eliminate the meat and present it as a spicy side dish.

> 3 cups cooked brown *or* white rice
> 1/2 pound ground beef, cooked and drained
> 1-1/4 cups sour cream
> 1 cup (4 ounces) shredded Monterey Jack cheese, *divided*
> 1 cup (4 ounces) shredded cheddar cheese, *divided*
> 1 can (4 ounces) chopped green chilies
> 1/2 teaspoon salt
> 1/4 teaspoon pepper

Sliced ripe olives and chopped tomatoes and green onions, optional

In a large bowl, combine the rice, beef, sour cream, 3/4 cup of Monterey Jack cheese, 3/4 cup of cheddar cheese, chilies, salt and pepper. Spoon into a greased 1-1/2-qt. baking dish. Sprinkle with remaining cheeses.

Bake, uncovered, at 350° for 20-25 minutes or until heated through. Garnish with olives, tomatoes and onions if desired. **Yield:** 4 servings.

GRILLED VEGGIE MIX
(Pictured above)

Janet Boulger, Botwood, Newfoundland

Living on this beautiful Canadian island, we often grill out, so we can eat while enjoying the scenery. This tempting veggie dish is the perfect accompaniment to any barbecue fare. To make the recipe even more satisfying, I often use my homegrown vegetables and herbs in the mix.

> 2 medium zucchini, cut into 1/2-inch slices
> 1 large green pepper, cut into 1/2-inch squares
> 1 large sweet red pepper, cut into 1/2-inch squares
> 1 pound fresh mushrooms, halved
> 1 large onion, cubed
> 6 medium carrots, cut into 1/4-inch slices
> 2 cups small broccoli florets
> 2 cups small cauliflowerets

DRESSING:
> 1/4 cup olive oil
> 1/4 cup butter, melted
> 1/4 cup minced fresh parsley
> 2 garlic cloves, minced
> 1 teaspoon dried basil
> 1/2 teaspoon dried oregano
> 1/2 teaspoon salt
> 1/4 teaspoon pepper

Place vegetables in the center of two pieces of double-layered heavy-duty foil (about 18 in. square). Combine dressing ingredients; drizzle over vegetables. Fold foil around mixture and seal

TRICOLOR PEPPER PASTA

Roxanne Lynnes, Grand Forks, North Dakota

I am a big fan of pasta, and this dish is one of my favorites. It's very colorful and flavorful.

> ✓ **Uses less fat, sugar or salt. Includes Nutritional Analysis and Diabetic Exchanges.**

    8 ounces uncooked penne *or* medium
      tube pasta
    1 *each* large sweet red, yellow and green
      pepper, cut into 1/2-inch strips
    1 large onion, cut into 1/2-inch strips
  1/2 pound fresh mushrooms, sliced
    3 tablespoons olive oil
    3 tablespoons red wine vinegar
    1 tablespoon sugar
1-1/2 teaspoons salt
  3/4 teaspoon dried basil
  1/2 teaspoon pepper

Cook pasta according to package directions. Meanwhile, in a large nonstick skillet, saute the peppers, onion and mushrooms in oil until tender. Stir in the vinegar, sugar, salt, basil and pepper. Drain pasta; add to vegetables and toss to coat. **Yield:** 6 servings.

Nutritional Analysis: One serving (1 cup) equals 253 calories, 8 g fat (1 g saturated fat), 0 cholesterol, 594 mg sodium, 41 g carbohydrate, 3 g fiber, 7 g protein. **Diabetic Exchanges:** 2 starch, 2 vegetable, 1 fat.

CRAN-RASPBERRY RELISH

Arloa Dahl, Sloan, Iowa

I developed this recipe when my husband was diagnosed with diabetes. It's great during the holidays and throughout the year.

> ✓ **Uses less fat, sugar or salt. Includes Nutritional Analysis and Diabetic Exchanges.**

    1 package (12 ounces) fresh *or* frozen
      cranberries, thawed
    2 medium apples, peeled, cored and cut
      into eighths
    1 can (20 ounces) unsweetened crushed
      pineapple, undrained
    2 teaspoons sugar-free raspberry soft
      drink mix*

In a food processor or blender, combine cranberries and apples; cover and process until coarsely chopped. Transfer to a bowl. Stir in pineapple and drink mix; mix well. Cover and refrigerate until serving. **Yield:** 5 cups.

Nutritional Analysis: One serving (1/4 cup) equals 34 calories, trace fat (0 saturated fat), 0 cholesterol, trace sodium, 9 g carbohydrate, 1 g fiber, trace protein. **Diabetic Exchange:** 1/2 fruit.

*Editor's Note: This recipe was tested with Crystal Light raspberry ice-flavor low-calorie soft drink mix.

CRANBERRY RICE WITH CARAMELIZED ONIONS

(Pictured above)

Tommi Roylance, Charlo, Montana

Rice provides so many options to a creative cook— the stir-in ideas are endless. In this recipe, dried cranberries star. Their sweet-tart flavor accents my rice combination and gives a festive feel to everyday meals.

2-1/2 cups chicken broth
  1/2 cup uncooked wild rice
  1/2 cup uncooked brown rice
    3 medium onions, cut into wedges
    2 teaspoons brown sugar
    3 tablespoons butter
    1 cup dried cranberries
  1/2 teaspoon grated orange peel

In a large saucepan, bring broth to a boil. Add the wild rice. Reduce heat; cover and simmer for 10 minutes. Add the brown rice; cover and simmer for 45-50 minutes or until rice is tender and liquid is absorbed.

In a large skillet over medium heat, cook the onions and brown sugar in butter until golden brown, stirring frequently. Add the cranberries, peel and rice; heat through. **Yield:** 4 servings.

RHUBARB CHUTNEY
(Pictured below)

Jan Paterson, Anchorage, Alaska

It's always fun to serve a meat or poultry dish with a twist. This tangy-sweet chutney is a wonderfully different garnish. With fine chunks of rhubarb and raisins, it has a nice consistency. It's among our favorite condiments.

3/4 cup sugar
1/3 cup cider vinegar
1 tablespoon minced garlic
1 teaspoon ground cumin
1 tablespoon minced fresh gingerroot
1/2 teaspoon ground cinnamon
1/4 to 1/2 teaspoon ground cloves
1/4 teaspoon crushed red pepper flakes
4 cups coarsely chopped fresh *or* frozen rhubarb, thawed
1/2 cup chopped red onion
1/3 cup golden raisins
1 teaspoon red food coloring, optional

In a large saucepan, combine the first eight ingredients. Bring to a boil. Reduce heat; simmer, uncovered, for 2 minutes or until sugar is dissolved. Add the rhubarb, onion and raisins.

Cook and stir over medium heat for 5-10 minutes or until rhubarb is tender and mixture is slightly thickened. Stir in food coloring if desired. Cool completely. Store in the refrigerator. **Yield:** about 3 cups.

PEPPERY HUSH PUPPIES
(Pictured above)

Ruby Ross, Kennett, Missouri

These spicy hush puppies make a wonderful side dish to fish. They taste best when served warm.

2 cups cornmeal
1/2 cup pancake mix
2-1/2 teaspoons sugar
1 teaspoon baking powder
1 teaspoon salt
1 egg
1 cup buttermilk
2 tablespoons vegetable oil
3 jalapeno peppers, seeded and finely chopped*
1/2 cup finely chopped onion
1/8 to 1/4 teaspoon hot pepper sauce
Oil for deep-fat frying

In a bowl, combine the cornmeal, pancake mix, sugar, baking powder and salt. In another bowl, beat the egg, buttermilk, oil, jalapenos, onion and hot pepper sauce. Stir into dry ingredients just until combined.

In an electric skillet or deep-fat fryer, heat oil to 375°. Drop batter by rounded tablespoonfuls into oil. Fry for 3-4 minutes or until golden brown. Drain on paper towels. Serve warm. **Yield:** 4 dozen.

*Editor's Note: When cutting or seeding hot peppers, use rubber or plastic gloves to protect your hands. Avoid touching your face.

Side Dishes & Condiments

CREAMY POTATO CASSEROLE

Patricia Staudt, Marble Rock, Iowa

This comforting casserole has plenty of down-home appeal, and it's sized right to serve a large gathering. The crushed cornflakes you sprinkle on top give it a beautiful golden color when it is baked.

- 4 pounds potatoes, peeled, cooked and cooled
- 1 large onion, chopped
- 7 tablespoons butter, *divided*
- 2 cups (16 ounces) sour cream
- 1 can (10-3/4 ounces) condensed cream of celery soup, undiluted
- 1-1/2 cups (6 ounces) shredded cheddar cheese
- 1/2 to 1 teaspoon salt
- 1/2 cup crushed cornflakes

Shred potatoes; place in a large bowl and set aside. In a skillet, saute onion in 4 tablespoons butter until tender. Remove from the heat; stir in sour cream and soup. Add to potatoes. Stir in cheese and salt. Transfer to a greased 13-in. x 9-in. x 2-in. baking dish.

Melt the remaining butter; toss with cornflakes. Sprinkle over casserole. Bake, uncovered, at 350° for 40-50 minutes or until heated through. **Yield:** 12 servings.

FRENCH PEAS

Pat Walter, Pine Island, Minnesota

Bright green and festive, this side dish has a slightly sweet flavor everyone will favor. Water chestnuts add a nice crunch. A friend shared this tasty recipe that offers a different way to present peas.

- 2 cans (8 ounces *each*) sliced water chestnuts, drained
- 2 tablespoons chopped onion
- 1/4 cup butter
- 2 teaspoons all-purpose flour
- 1/2 teaspoon sugar
- 1/2 teaspoon salt
- 1/2 cup milk
- 8 cups frozen peas, thawed
- 2 cups shredded lettuce

In a large saucepan, saute water chestnuts and onion in butter until onion is tender. Stir in the flour, sugar and salt until blended. Gradually add milk; stir in peas.

Bring to a boil. Reduce heat; cover and cook for 3-5 minutes or until peas are tender and sauce is slightly thickened. Add lettuce; cook until lettuce is wilted. **Yield:** 12-14 servings.

ASPARAGUS CHEESE BUNDLES

(Pictured below)

Pat Habiger, Spearville, Kansas

Here's an interesting side dish that'll have folks asking for seconds.

- 1 cup water
- 1/2 pound fresh asparagus, trimmed and cut into 2-inch pieces
- 2 medium carrots, julienned
- 1 package (8 ounces) cream cheese, softened
- 1 egg
- 2 tablespoons minced fresh basil *or* 2 teaspoons dried basil
- 1/2 cup crumbled feta cheese *or* shredded mozzarella cheese
- 8 flour tortillas (8 inches)
- 2 tablespoons milk
- 2 teaspoons sesame seeds

In a large saucepan, bring water to a boil. Add asparagus and carrots. Cook, uncovered, for 5 minutes; drain. In a small mixing bowl, beat cream cheese, egg and basil; stir in feta cheese.

Place a mound of vegetables in the center of each tortilla. Top with 2 rounded tablespoonfuls of cheese mixture. Fold ends and sides over filling and roll up. Place seam side down on an ungreased baking sheet. Brush with milk; sprinkle with sesame seeds. Bake at 425° for 10-14 minutes until heated through and golden brown. **Yield:** 8 servings.

VEGETABLE RICE SKILLET

Ruth Rigoni, Hurley, Wisconsin

A bag of frozen mixed vegetables conveniently dresses up plain rice in this quick and easy recipe.

- 1 can (14-1/2 ounces) vegetable broth
- 2 tablespoons butter
- 1 package (16 ounces) frozen California-blend vegetables
- 1 package (6.2 ounces) fast-cooking long grain and wild rice mix
- 3/4 cup shredded cheddar cheese

In a large skillet, bring broth and butter to a boil. Stir in the vegetables and rice with seasoning packet. Return to a boil. Reduce heat; cover and simmer for 4-8 minutes or until vegetables and rice are tender. Sprinkle with cheese. **Yield:** 4-6 servings.

MASHED CARROTS AND TURNIPS

(Pictured below)

Rose Pfeiffer, Tinton Falls, New Jersey

This recipe has been in my family for years. It's an inexpensive and easy dish to prepare.

- 2 pounds carrots, peeled and sliced
- 2 medium turnips, peeled and diced
- 1/2 cup butter, cubed
- 1/4 teaspoon salt
- 1/8 teaspoon pepper
Minced fresh parsley, optional

Place carrots and turnips in a large saucepan and cover with water. Cover and bring to a boil; cook

SWEET POTATO PEAR BAKE

(Pictured above)

Ray Taylor, Memphis, Tennessee

A friend made this sweet potato recipe when I had dinner at her house. I liked it so much, I asked her to share the recipe with me.

- 1 can (15-1/4 ounces) pear halves
- 3 cups cold mashed sweet potatoes
- 4 tablespoons butter, melted, *divided*
- 3 tablespoons brown sugar
- 1/4 teaspoon salt
- 1/4 teaspoon ground nutmeg
- 2 tablespoons honey
- 1 tablespoon grated orange peel
- 6 tablespoons whole-berry cranberry sauce

Drain pears, reserving 2 tablespoons juice (discard remaining juice or save for another use). In a mixing bowl, combine the sweet potatoes, 3 tablespoons butter, brown sugar, salt, nutmeg and reserved pear juice. Beat until combined. Spoon into a greased shallow 1-1/2-qt. baking dish. Arrange pear halves on top, cut side up.

In a small saucepan, combine the honey, orange peel and remaining butter. Cook until heated through. Drizzle half over the pears. Bake, uncovered, at 350° for 30 minutes. Drizzle with the remaining honey mixture. Bake 15 minutes longer. Fill pear halves with cranberry sauce. **Yield:** 6 servings.

for 20 minutes or until tender. Drain and mash. Add butter, salt and pepper. Sprinkle with parsley if desired. **Yield:** 8 servings.

MIXED VEGETABLE CASSEROLE

Marilou Robinson, Portland, Oregon

I found a recipe for a layered veggie casserole, then modified it to use produce I had on hand. I sometimes sprinkle bread crumbs or grated cheese on top for a tasty variation.

  2 medium tomatoes, cut into wedges
  1 cup sliced celery
  1 cup sliced carrots
  1 cup cut green beans (2-inch pieces)
  1 medium onion, sliced
  1 small sweet red pepper, julienned
  1/2 cup canned sliced water chestnuts, drained
1-1/2 teaspoons sugar
1-1/2 teaspoons all-purpose flour
  1 teaspoon dried oregano
  1/4 teaspoon salt
  1/4 teaspoon pepper
  2 tablespoons butter

In a large bowl, combine the vegetables. Place half in a greased 1-1/2-qt. baking dish. In a small bowl, combine the sugar, flour, oregano, salt and pepper. Sprinkle half over vegetables in the baking dish. Top with remaining vegetables and seasoning mixture. Dot with butter. Cover and bake at 350° for 55-60 minutes or until vegetables are tender. **Yield:** 4 servings.

EASY TEX-MEX RICE

Margaret Blair, Lorimor, Iowa

My daughter shared this satisfying rice recipe with me. It's appealing to the eye as well as the taste buds.

  2 cups cooked brown rice
1-1/2 cups salsa
  1 can (15 ounces) black beans, rinsed and drained
  1 cup frozen corn, thawed
  2 tablespoons chopped ripe olives
  1 teaspoon chili powder
  1 cup (4 ounces) shredded cheddar cheese

In a bowl, combine the first six ingredients. Transfer to a greased microwave-safe 8-in. square dish. Cover and microwave on high for 5 minutes, rotating once. Stir; microwave 2-3 minutes longer or until heated through. Sprinkle with cheese. Microwave, uncovered, for 30-60 seconds or un-

til cheese is melted. Let stand for 5 minutes. **Yield:** 4-5 servings.

  Editor's Note: This recipe was tested in an 850-watt microwave.

WINTER FRUIT CHUTNEY
(Pictured above)

Helen Littrell, Klamath Falls, Oregon

Pairing sweet and tart fruits makes this chutney a wonderful accompaniment for pork. Not only is it a consistent blue-ribbon winner at fairs, it's a natural way to capture the best of autumn's harvest in a jar.

  2 cups cider vinegar
  1 medium onion, finely chopped
  1/2 cup water
  1 tablespoon ground ginger
  1 tablespoon grated orange peel
1-1/2 teaspoons salt
  2 garlic cloves, minced
  1/2 teaspoon ground cinnamon
  1/4 teaspoon crushed red pepper flakes
  3 cups packed brown sugar
  2 medium ripe unpeeled pears, finely chopped
  2 cups fresh *or* frozen cranberries
  1 large tart unpeeled apple, finely chopped
  1/2 cup dried currants

In a Dutch oven, combine the first nine ingredients. Bring to a boil over medium heat, stirring occasionally. Reduce heat; cover and simmer for 15 minutes. Stir in the brown sugar, pears, cranberries, apple and currants. Return to a boil. Reduce heat; simmer, uncovered, for 1 hour or until fruit is tender and mixture has thickened.

  Pour hot mixture into hot jars, leaving 1/4-in. headspace. Adjust caps. Process for 15 minutes in a boiling-water bath. **Yield:** 4 half-pints.

CHEESY ZUCCHINI RICE CASSEROLE

(Pictured below)

Judy Hudson, Santa Rosa, California

Cheese is one of the major agricultural products in our area of northern California. A colleague gave me this recipe a number of years ago, and it's always a hit at potluck dinners.

   1 cup uncooked long grain rice
   3 medium zucchini, cut into 1/8-inch slices
   1 can (4 ounces) chopped green chilies
   4 cups (16 ounces) shredded Monterey Jack cheese, *divided*
   2 cups (16 ounces) sour cream
   2 tablespoons chopped green pepper
   2 tablespoons chopped onion
   1 tablespoon minced fresh parsley
   1 teaspoon salt
   1 teaspoon dried oregano
   1 large tomato, sliced

Cook rice according to package directions. In a saucepan, cook zucchini in 1 in. of water until crisp-tender; drain and set aside. Place rice in a greased shallow 3-qt. baking dish. Layer with chilies and 1-1/2 cups cheese.

In a bowl, combine the sour cream, green pepper, onion, parsley, salt and oregano. Spread over cheese. Layer with zucchini and tomato. Sprinkle with remaining cheese.

Cover and bake at 350° for 30 minutes. Uncover; bake 5-10 minutes longer or until heated through and cheese is melted. **Yield:** 12 servings.

HARVEST CARROTS

(Pictured above)

Marty Rummel, Trout Lake, Washington

I make this hearty side dish quite often. Once in a while, I add leftover turkey or chicken breasts and turn it into a main dish.

   4 cups sliced carrots
   2 cups water
   1 medium onion, chopped
   1/2 cup butter, *divided*
   1 can (10-3/4 ounces) condensed cream of celery soup, undiluted
   1/2 cup shredded cheddar cheese
   1/8 teaspoon pepper
   3 cups seasoned stuffing croutons

In a large saucepan, bring carrots and water to a boil. Reduce heat; cover and simmer for 10 minutes or until tender. Drain. In a skillet, saute onion in 3 tablespoons butter until tender.

In a bowl, combine the carrots, onion, soup, cheese and pepper. Melt remaining butter; toss with stuffing. Fold into carrot mixture. Transfer to a greased 2-qt. baking dish. Cover and bake at 350° for 20 minutes. Uncover; bake 10 minutes longer or until lightly browned. **Yield:** 6-8 servings.

CHERRY PEAR CONSERVE

Ruth Bolduc, Conway, New Hampshire

I use pears harvested from my own trees to make this conserve. I love it combined with cream cheese and spread between two waffles that are topped with pure maple syrup.

- 2 medium lemons
- 2 medium limes
- 8 cups chopped peeled ripe pears
- 2 cans (16 ounces *each*) pitted tart cherries, drained
- 2 cans (20 ounces *each*) crushed pineapple, undrained
- 2 cups raisins
- 10 cups sugar
- 1-1/3 cups coarsely chopped walnuts

Grate peel from lemons and limes; set peel aside. Remove pith from lemons and limes; section the fruit and place in a large bowl. Add lemon and lime peel, pears, cherries, pineapple, raisins and sugar. Cover and refrigerate overnight.

Transfer to a large kettle or Dutch oven. Cook over medium heat for 50-60 minutes or until thickened. Stir in nuts; bring to a boil. Remove from the heat. Immediately ladle into hot sterilized jars, leaving 1/4-in. headspace. Adjust caps. Process for 15 minutes in a boiling-water bath. **Yield:** 10 pints.

GARLIC-HERBED MASHED POTATOES

(Pictured at right)

Suzi Bonnett, Bellevue, Nebraska

Our family loves these creamy and comforting potatoes. Garlic and other herbs make them so mouth-watering. For an extra-buttery taste, use Yukon Gold potatoes.

- 6 medium potatoes
- 1 garlic clove, minced
- 6 tablespoons butter, *divided*
- 1 cup heavy whipping cream
- 1 teaspoon dried parsley flakes
- 1 teaspoon dried tarragon
- 3/4 teaspoon salt
- 1/2 teaspoon pepper

Peel potatoes if desired and cut into cubes. Place in a large saucepan; cover with water. Bring to a boil. Reduce heat; cover and simmer for 20-25 minutes or until tender.

Meanwhile, in a small skillet, saute garlic in 2 tablespoons butter for 1 minute or until tender. Add the remaining butter; heat until melted.

Drain potatoes and place in a large mixing bowl. Add garlic mixture, cream, parsley, tarragon, salt and pepper; mash until smooth. **Yield:** 6-8 servings.

WALNUT SWEET POTATO BAKE

Pat Habiger, Spearville, Kansas

Cream cheese adds a flavorful twist to this sweet potato dish, and the nuts provide a delightful crunch.

- 1 package (8 ounces) cream cheese, softened
- 1/2 cup butter, softened
- 1/4 cup packed brown sugar
- 2 eggs
- 4 cups mashed cooked sweet potatoes
- 2 tablespoons chicken broth
- 1/2 teaspoon salt
- 1/2 teaspoon ground nutmeg
- 3/4 cup chopped walnuts

In a large mixing bowl, beat the cream cheese, butter and brown sugar until smooth. Add eggs, one at a time, beating well after each addition. Add the sweet potatoes, broth, salt and nutmeg; mix well. Stir in nuts.

Transfer to a greased shallow 1-1/2-qt. baking dish. Bake, uncovered, at 350° for 40-45 minutes or until a thermometer reads 160°. **Yield:** 8 servings.

▚▚▚▚▚▚▚▚▚▚▚▚

CHEESY VEGETABLE MEDLEY

(Pictured above)

Mary Ulrick, Baconton, Georgia

Can't decide whether to cook vegetables or pasta for a side dish? Try combining them in this medley.

  3 cups broccoli florets
  3 cups cauliflowerets
  2 cups julienned carrots
  1 small onion, diced
1/2 teaspoon garlic powder
1/2 teaspoon Italian seasoning
1/8 teaspoon salt
1/8 teaspoon pepper
  8 ounces elbow macaroni, cooked and drained
  2 cups (8 ounces) shredded mozzarella cheese
  2 cups (8 ounces) shredded cheddar cheese
  8 ounces process cheese (Velveeta), sliced
3/4 cup half-and-half cream
3/4 cup seasoned bread crumbs
1/4 cup butter
1/2 cup grated Parmesan cheese

Place broccoli and cauliflower in a steamer basket. Place in a saucepan over 1 in. of water; bring to a boil. Cover and steam for 5-8 minutes or until crisp-tender. Rinse in cold water; drain and set aside. Repeat with carrots and onion, steaming for 4-5 minutes or until tender.

Place vegetables in a large bowl; add garlic powder, Italian seasoning, salt and pepper. Stir in macaroni. Spoon half into a greased 3-qt. baking

dish. Sprinkle with half of the mozzarella, cheddar and process cheese. Repeat layers.

Pour cream over the top. Sprinkle with bread crumbs; dot with butter. Top with Parmesan cheese. Bake, uncovered, at 350° for 30-40 minutes or until bubbly. **Yield:** 12-14 servings.

▚▚▚▚▚▚▚▚▚▚▚▚

GARBANZO BEANS 'N' RICE

(Pictured below)

Michele Ridenour, Oswego, Illinois

I love to use fresh vegetables from my garden in this delicious dish. My whole family loves the recipe.

✓ **Uses less fat, sugar or salt. Includes Nutritional Analysis and Diabetic Exchanges.**

  1 medium onion, chopped
  2 garlic cloves, minced
  1 tablespoon canola oil
  2 medium tomatoes, chopped
  1 medium zucchini, chopped
1/2 teaspoon dried oregano
  1 can (15 ounces) garbanzo beans *or* chickpeas, rinsed and drained
1/2 teaspoon salt
1/4 teaspoon pepper
  3 cups cooked rice
  1 cup (4 ounces) shredded reduced-fat cheddar cheese

In a nonstick skillet, saute onion and garlic in oil until tender. Stir in the tomatoes, zucchini and oregano. Cover and cook for 4-6 minutes or until zucchini is crisp-tender, stirring occasionally.

Add the beans, salt and pepper; cook and stir until heated through. Serve over rice. Sprinkle with cheese. **Yield:** 6 servings.

Side Dishes & Condiments

Nutritional Analysis: One serving (1/2 cup bean mixture with 1/2 cup rice) equals 286 calories, 7 g fat (2 g saturated fat), 10 mg cholesterol, 445 mg sodium, 46 g carbohydrate, 5 g fiber, 12 g protein. **Diabetic Exchanges:** 2 starch, 2 vegetable, 1-1/2 lean meat.

CRANBERRY SYRUP

Teresa Gaetzke, North Freedom, Wisconsin

This flavorful syrup is so appealing over pancakes, your family will think they're in a fancy restaurant.

1 cup sugar
1 cup packed brown sugar
1 cup cranberry juice
1/2 cup light corn syrup

In a saucepan, combine the sugars and cranberry juice; bring to a boil, stirring constantly. Boil for 4 minutes. Add corn syrup; boil and stir 1 minute longer. Serve over pancakes, French toast or waffles. **Yield:** 2 cups.

FOUR-BEAN SUPREME

Jaki Allen, Irons, Michigan

This side dish recipe has long been in my family. It's possible that it came from Ireland with my great-great-grandparents.

1 can (16 ounces) kidney beans, rinsed and drained
1 can (16 ounces) pork and beans, undrained
1 can (15-1/2 ounces) great northern beans, rinsed and drained
1 can (15 ounces) black beans, rinsed and drained
1 medium onion, chopped
1/3 cup packed brown sugar
1 teaspoon sugar
1 teaspoon salt
1 teaspoon lemon juice
1/2 to 1 teaspoon hot pepper sauce
1/4 teaspoon *each* dried basil, dried oregano, ground cumin, garlic powder, onion powder and pepper
3 bacon strips, cut into 2-inch pieces

In a bowl, combine the beans. In another bowl, combine the onion, sugars, salt, lemon juice, hot pepper sauce and seasonings. Stir into beans. Pour into a greased 2-qt. baking dish. Top with bacon pieces. Bake, uncovered, at 350° for 1 hour or until heated through. **Yield:** 8-10 servings.

STUFFED ZUCCHINI

(Pictured above)

Rose LaCore, Elizabeth, Minnesota

When a friend and I grew zucchini, we made everything we could think of to use up our crop. This recipe, with its refreshing flavor, found favor with our families.

4 medium zucchini (about 8 inches)
1/2 cup uncooked long grain rice
1 small onion, chopped
1/2 medium green pepper, chopped
1 garlic clove, minced
1 tablespoon butter
3/4 cup canned bean sprouts, rinsed, drained and chopped
1/2 cup chopped cabbage
1/4 cup chopped fresh mushrooms
1-1/2 teaspoons soy sauce
1/2 teaspoon salt
Dash pepper
1/2 cup shredded cheddar cheese
1/4 cup sliced almonds

Cut zucchini in half lengthwise; scoop out and discard pulp, leaving a 1/4-in. shell. Place zucchini cut side down in a baking dish. Fill dish with hot water to a depth of 1/4 in. Bake, uncovered, at 350° for 15-20 minutes or until tender. Drain; set aside. Cook rice according to package directions.

In a skillet, saute the onion, green pepper and garlic in butter until tender. Stir in the bean sprouts, cabbage, mushrooms, cooked rice, soy sauce, salt and pepper. Reduce heat; simmer, uncovered, for 5 minutes.

Spoon into zucchini shells; sprinkle with cheese and almonds. Place on an ungreased baking sheet. Bake, uncovered, at 350° for 20-25 minutes or until cheese is melted. **Yield:** 8 servings.

RAISING the bar at the next gathering or bake sale is easy with these delicious bread, muffin and coffee cake recipes.

BAKE UP SMILES. From top: Rhubarb Streusel Muffins (p. 75), Strawberry Coffee Cake (p. 77) and Dill Seed Braid (p. 75).

Breads & Rolls

RHUBARB STREUSEL MUFFINS
(Pictured at left)

Sandra Moreside, Regina, Saskatchewan

What a pleasure it is to set out a basket of these rhubarb muffins…although the basket doesn't stay full for very long!

- 1/2 cup butter, softened
- 1 cup packed brown sugar
- 1/2 cup sugar
- 1 egg
- 2 cups all-purpose flour
- 1 teaspoon baking powder
- 1/2 teaspoon baking soda
- 1/8 teaspoon salt
- 1 cup (8 ounces) sour cream
- 3 cups chopped fresh *or* frozen rhubarb, thawed

TOPPING:
- 1/2 cup chopped pecans
- 1/4 cup packed brown sugar
- 1 teaspoon ground cinnamon
- 1 tablespoon cold butter

In a mixing bowl, cream butter and sugars. Add egg; beat well. Combine the flour, baking powder, baking soda and salt; add to creamed mixture alternately with sour cream. Fold in rhubarb. Fill paper-lined or greased muffin cups three-fourths full.

For topping, combine the pecans, brown sugar and cinnamon in a small bowl; cut in butter until crumbly. Sprinkle over batter. Bake at 350° for 22-25 minutes or until a toothpick comes out clean. Cool for 5 minutes before removing from pans to wire racks. **Yield:** about 1-1/2 dozen.

DILL SEED BRAID
(Pictured at left)

Lori Jameson, Chattaroy, Washington

Its pretty braided shape and pleasant dill flavor distinguish this golden-brown loaf from other yeast breads. My family loves it.

- 1 package (1/4 ounce) active dry yeast
- 1/4 cup warm water (110° to 115°)
- 1 cup plain yogurt
- 1 small onion, finely chopped
- 1/4 cup sugar
- 2 tablespoons butter, softened
- 1 egg
- 1 tablespoon dill seed
- 1 teaspoon salt
- 3 to 3-1/2 cups all-purpose flour

In a mixing bowl, dissolve yeast in warm water. Add yogurt, onion, sugar, butter, egg, dill seed, salt and 1 cup flour. Beat until smooth. Stir in enough remaining flour to form a soft dough.

Turn onto a floured surface; knead until smooth and elastic, about 6-8 minutes. Place in a greased bowl, turning once to grease top. Cover and let rise in a warm place until doubled, about 1 hour.

Punch dough down. Turn onto a lightly floured surface; divide into thirds. Shape each portion into a 20-in. rope. Place ropes on a large greased baking sheet and braid; pinch ends to seal and tuck under. Cover and let rise until doubled, about 30 minutes. Bake at 350° for 35-40 minutes or until golden brown. Remove from pan to a wire rack to cool. **Yield:** 1 loaf.

TOP MUFFIN TIPS

Make greasing muffin cups a breeze by using nonstick cooking spray. Or you can use a crumpled piece of paper towel dipped into shortening for greasing muffin cups.

Never grease muffin cups that won't be used—the grease will burn and make a mess of your pan. Put 2-3 tablespoons of water in the unused muffin cups to keep the pan from warping.

For perfectly rounded muffin tops, only grease the bottoms and halfway up the sides of the muffin cup. If you fill muffin cups more than three-quarters full, you're likely to get "flying saucer" tops.

SPICY PUMPKIN BREAD

Andrea Durr, Nicholasville, Kentucky

Cinnamon, nutmeg and cloves give this quick loaf its tasty appeal. The recipe yields three loaves, so we can eat one right away, then freeze the others to enjoy later.

　5　cups all-purpose flour
　3　cups sugar
　1　cup packed brown sugar
　1　tablespoon baking soda
　1　tablespoon ground cinnamon
　2　teaspoons ground nutmeg
1-1/2　teaspoons ground cloves
　1　can (29 ounces) solid-pack pumpkin
　1　cup vegetable oil
　4　eggs, lightly beaten
1/2　teaspoon rum extract
　2　cups coarsely chopped pecans

In a large bowl, combine the flour, sugars, baking soda, cinnamon, nutmeg and cloves. In another bowl, combine the pumpkin, oil, eggs and extract; stir into the dry ingredients just until moistened. Fold in pecans.

　Pour into three greased 8-in. x 4-in. x 2-in. loaf pans. Bake at 325° for 1-1/2 hours or until a toothpick inserted in the center comes out clean. Cool for 10 minutes before removing from pans to wire racks. **Yield:** 3 loaves.

 ## BROWN SUGAR OAT MUFFINS

(Pictured below)

Regina Stock, Topeka, Kansas

With Kansas being one of the top wheat-producing states, it seems only fitting to share a recipe containing whole wheat flour. These are great muffins to have for breakfast or a late night snack with a cup of hot cocoa.

　1　cup old-fashioned oats
　1　cup whole wheat flour
1/2　cup all-purpose flour
　2　teaspoons baking powder
1/2　teaspoon salt
　2　eggs
3/4　cup packed brown sugar
3/4　cup milk
1/4　vegetable oil
　1　teaspoon vanilla extract

In a bowl, combine the first five ingredients. In another bowl, beat eggs, brown sugar, milk, oil and vanilla; mix well. Stir into the dry ingredients just until moistened. Fill greased or paper-lined muffin cups two-thirds full.

　Bake at 400° for 15-17 minutes or until a toothpick comes out clean. Cool for 5 minutes before removing from pan to a wire rack. **Yield:** 1 dozen.

 ## RHUBARB STICKY BUNS

(Pictured above)

Amy Graef, Tacoma, Washington

My husband and two teen sons are crazy about these sticky buns. I discovered the treat in an old recipe file I purchased at a rummage sale.

1/4　cup cold butter
1/2　cup packed brown sugar
　1　cup chopped fresh *or* frozen rhubarb, thawed

BATTER:
- 1/3 cup butter, softened
- 1/3 cup sugar
- 1 egg
- 1-1/2 cups all-purpose flour
- 2 teaspoons baking powder
- 1/2 teaspoon salt
- 1/4 teaspoon ground nutmeg
- 1/2 cup milk

In a bowl, cut butter into brown sugar until crumbly. Stir in rhubarb. Spoon evenly into 12 well-greased muffin cups; set aside.

In a mixing bowl, cream butter and sugar. Beat in egg. Combine the flour, baking powder, salt and nutmeg; add to creamed mixture alternately with milk. Spoon over rhubarb mixture, filling cups three-fourths full. Bake at 350° for 15-20 minutes or until a toothpick comes out clean. Cool for 5 minutes before inverting onto a serving plate. Serve warm. **Yield:** 1 dozen.

STRAWBERRY COFFEE CAKE

(Pictured on page 74)

Mildred Sherrer, Bay City, Texas

I enhance the mild berry flavor of this moist coffee cake with a crunchy cinnamon filling. Baked in a fluted pan, it's pretty for an afternoon party or Sunday brunch.

- 1 cup butter, softened
- 1-1/2 cups sugar
- 3 eggs
- 2 cups all-purpose flour
- 1 teaspoon baking powder
- 1 teaspoon baking soda
- 1 cup (8 ounces) sour cream
- 2 teaspoons vanilla extract
- 2 cups chopped fresh strawberries

FILLING:
- 3/4 cup chopped walnuts
- 1/4 cup sugar
- 1/4 cup packed brown sugar
- 3/4 teaspoon ground cinnamon

In a mixing bowl, cream butter and sugar. Add eggs; mix well. Combine flour, baking powder and baking soda; add to creamed mixture alternately with sour cream. Beat in vanilla. Fold in strawberries. Spoon half into a greased and floured 10-in. fluted tube pan.

Combine the filling ingredients; sprinkle half over batter. Top with remaining batter and filling. Bake at 350° for 50-60 minutes or until a toothpick inserted near the center comes out clean. Cool for 15 minutes before removing from pan to a wire rack to cool completely. **Yield:** 12-16 servings.

APPLE FRUIT BREAD

(Pictured below)

Ginger Wallace, Millville, New Jersey

When it's apple harvesttime, I buy apples by the bushel basket so we have plenty to eat fresh, and some to use in this apple bread recipe.

- 1-1/2 cups all-purpose flour
- 3/4 cup sugar
- 3/4 teaspoon baking soda
- 1/2 teaspoon ground nutmeg
- 1/4 to 1/2 teaspoon ground cinnamon
- 1/4 teaspoon salt
- 1 egg, lightly beaten
- 1/3 cup apple juice
- 1 large tart apple, peeled and coarsely chopped
- 1/4 cup raisins
- 1/4 cup chopped walnuts
- 1/4 cup maraschino cherries, halved

In a bowl, combine the flour, sugar, baking soda, nutmeg, cinnamon and salt. Combine egg and apple juice; stir into dry ingredients. Fold in apple, raisins, walnuts and cherries. Transfer to a greased 8-in. x 4-in. x 2-in. loaf pan.

Bake at 350° for 50-55 minutes or until a toothpick inserted near the center comes out clean. Cool for 10 minutes before removing from pan to a wire rack to cool completely. **Yield:** 1 loaf.

2-1/2 teaspoons baking powder
1/2 teaspoon salt
2 eggs, lightly beaten
1 cup milk
1/3 cup vegetable oil
1/2 cup chopped pecans

In a large bowl, combine the flours, brown sugar, baking powder and salt. In another bowl, combine the eggs, milk and oil; stir into dry ingredients just until moistened. Fold in pecans.

Fill greased or paper-lined muffin cups two-thirds full. Bake at 400° for 13-15 minutes or until a toothpick comes out clean. Cool for 5 minutes before removing from pan to a wire rack. Serve warm. **Yield:** 1 dozen.

TENDER POTATO ROLLS
(Pictured below)

Lisa Owens, Brighton, Tennessee

Filled with wonderful hearty flavor, these rolls are a delicious accompaniment to a meal. If you like, you can shape the dough into loaves. I once baked 52 loaves and sold slices of the bread at a local fund-raiser.

1 medium potato, peeled and diced
2 cups water
1 package (1/4 ounce) active dry yeast
1 egg
1/4 cup honey
1 tablespoon vegetable oil
1-1/2 teaspoons salt
6 to 6-1/2 cups all-purpose flour

WILD RICE PECAN WAFFLES
(Pictured above)

Kris Sackett, Eau Claire, Wisconsin

My mother found this recipe and shared it with me. It has become a favorite of my family's—especially when the waffles are served with my dad's home-made maple syrup.

1 cup all-purpose flour
1 teaspoon baking powder
1/2 teaspoon salt
2 eggs, *separated*
2/3 cup milk
1/4 cup vegetable oil
1-1/2 cups cooked wild rice
1/2 cup chopped pecans

In a bowl, combine the flour, baking powder and salt. In a mixing bowl, beat egg yolks, milk and oil; stir into dry ingredients just until moistened. In another bowl, beat egg whites until stiff peaks form; fold into batter. Fold in the rice and pecans.

Bake in a preheated greased waffle iron according to manufacturer's directions until golden brown. **Yield:** 5-6 waffles (about 6-1/2 inches).

WHOLE WHEAT MUFFINS

Arlene Bontrager, Haven, Kansas

These moist and tender muffins have a nice whole wheat flavor.

1 cup all-purpose flour
1 cup whole wheat flour
1/2 cup packed brown sugar

In a saucepan, cook potato in water until tender. Set cooking liquid aside to cool to 110°-115°. Mash potato (don't add milk or butter); set aside.

In a large mixing bowl, dissolve yeast in cooled cooking liquid. Add the egg, honey, oil, salt, 4 cups flour and mashed potato. Beat until smooth. Stir in enough remaining flour to form a soft dough. Turn onto a floured surface; knead until smooth and elastic, about 7 minutes. Place in a greased bowl, turning once to grease top. Cover and let rise in a warm place until doubled, about 1 hour.

Punch the dough down. Turn onto a lightly floured surface; divide into 36 pieces. Shape each into a ball. Place in a greased 15-in. x 10-in. x 1-in. baking pan. Cover and let rise until doubled, about 30 minutes. Bake at 375° for 20-25 minutes or until golden brown. Serve warm. **Yield:** 3 dozen.

▪▪▪▪▪▪▪▪▪▪▪▪
COBBLE BREAD
(Pictured on page 81)

Bernice Knutson, Soldier, Iowa

To make this tender coffee cake, I dip balls of dough into cinnamon and sugar, then place them in a fluted tube pan. I pour chopped walnuts in the pan first.

    2 packages (1/4 ounce *each*) active dry
      yeast
  1/2 cup warm water (110° to 115°)
    1 cup warm milk (110° to 115°)
  1/2 cup butter, softened, *divided*
1-2/3 cups sugar, *divided*
    1 teaspoon salt
4-1/2 to 5 cups all-purpose flour
  1/2 cup chopped walnuts
    2 teaspoons ground cinnamon
GLAZE:
    1 cup confectioners' sugar
    3 to 5 tablespoons milk

In a large mixing bowl, dissolve yeast in warm water. Add the milk, 1/4 cup butter, 1 cup sugar, salt and 3 cups flour; beat until smooth. Stir in enough remaining flour to form a firm dough.

Turn onto a floured surface; knead until smooth and elastic, about 6-8 minutes. Place in a greased bowl, turning once to grease top. Cover and let rise in a warm place until almost doubled, about 1-1/2 hours.

Melt remaining butter; pour into a greased 10-in. fluted tube pan. Sprinkle walnuts over bottom of pan. Combine cinnamon and remaining sugar; sprinkle 1/4 cup over nuts.

Punch dough down. Divide into six portions; divide each portion into eight pieces. Roll each piece into a ball; dip in remaining cinnamon-sugar. Place in prepared pan. Sprinkle remaining cinnamon-sugar over top. Cover and let rise until almost doubled, about 45 minutes.

Bake at 350° for 40-45 minutes or until golden brown. Cool for 5 minutes before inverting onto a serving plate. Combine glaze ingredients; drizzle over bread. **Yield:** 10-12 servings.

▪▪▪▪▪▪▪▪▪▪▪▪
ORANGE RAISIN MUFFINS
(Pictured above)

Robert Taylor, Mesa, Arizona

Oranges and raisins are grown in our state, so this recipe represents our region well.

    1 medium navel orange
  1/2 cup orange juice
  1/2 cup butter, melted
    1 egg
1-1/2 cups all-purpose flour
  3/4 cup sugar
    1 teaspoon baking powder
    1 teaspoon baking soda
    1 teaspoon salt
  1/2 cup raisins

Peel orange; place peel in a blender or food processor. Separate orange into segments; place in blender. Add orange juice; cover and process until well blended. Add butter and egg. In a bowl, combine the flour, sugar, baking powder, baking soda and salt. Stir in orange mixture just until moistened. Fold in raisins.

Fill greased or paper-lined muffin cups two-thirds full. Bake at 400° for 15-20 minutes or until a toothpick comes out clean. Cool for 5 minutes before removing from pan to a wire rack. **Yield:** 1 dozen.

WARM UP YOUR APPETITES *with these wonderful breads and rolls. They're sure to please your family and friends any day of the week!*

SLICEFULLY SATISFYING. Clockwise from top left: Herb Dinner Rolls (p. 82), Cobble Bread (p. 79), Yuletide Banana Bread (p. 82) and Fruit 'n' Nut Rings (p. 83).

CRANBERRY ORANGE BREAD

Doris Heath, Franklin, North Carolina

Slices of this citrusy bread are scrumptious for breakfast. I've adapted the recipe over the years to fit my needs as a diabetic.

✓ **Uses less fat, sugar or salt. Includes Nutritional Analysis and Diabetic Exchanges.**

    2 cups all-purpose flour
    1 cup quick-cooking oats
  3/4 cup sugar
    2 teaspoons baking powder
  1/2 teaspoon baking soda
  3/4 cup orange juice
  1/2 cup egg substitute
  1/3 cup canola oil
    1 tablespoon grated orange peel
  3/4 cup chopped fresh *or* frozen
        cranberries, thawed

In a large bowl, combine the first five ingredients. In another bowl, combine the orange juice, egg substitute, oil and orange peel; mix well. Stir into dry ingredients just until moistened. Fold in cranberries.

Pour into an 8-in. x 4-in. x 2-in. loaf pan coated with nonstick cooking spray. Bake at 350° for 55-65 minutes or until a toothpick inserted near the center comes out clean. Cool for 10 minutes before removing from pan to a wire rack. **Yield:** 1 loaf (12 slices).

Nutritional Analysis: One slice equals 212 calories, 7 g fat (1 g saturated fat), trace cholesterol, 138 mg sodium, 35 g carbohydrate, 2 g fiber, 4 g protein. **Diabetic Exchanges:** 2 starch, 1 fat.

YULETIDE BANANA BREAD

(Pictured on page 81)

Regina Albright, Southaven, Mississippi

Rich but relatively fuss-free, this is no ordinary banana loaf! I fill my quick bread with macadamia nuts, raisins and coconut to create a memorable treat.

    1 cup whole macadamia nuts, *divided*
  1/2 cup butter, softened
    1 cup sugar
    2 eggs
1-1/2 cups all-purpose flour
    1 teaspoon baking soda
  1/4 teaspoon salt
    1 cup mashed ripe bananas (about 2
        medium)
  1/2 cup raisins
  1/2 cup flaked coconut

In a food processor or blender, process 1/2 cup macadamia nuts until ground; set aside. Chop remaining nuts; set aside.

In a mixing bowl, cream butter and sugar. Add eggs, one at a time, beating well after each addition. Combine the flour, baking soda, salt and ground nuts; stir into creamed mixture just until moistened. Fold in bananas, raisins, coconut and chopped nuts.

Pour into a greased 9-in. x 5-in. x 3-in. loaf pan. Bake at 350° for 65-70 minutes or until a toothpick comes out clean. Cool for 10 minutes; remove from pan to a wire rack. **Yield:** 1 loaf.

HERB DINNER ROLLS

(Pictured on page 80)

Sue Friesen, Thorold, Ontario

When I couldn't find a recipe for dinner rolls, I created my own using a variety of herbs for extra flavor.

    1 package (1/4 ounce) active dry yeast
  1/4 cup warm water (110° to 115°)
    1 cup warm buttermilk* (110° to 115°)
    4 tablespoons butter, melted, *divided*
    2 tablespoons sugar
1-1/2 teaspoons salt
  1/2 teaspoon *each* dried basil, marjoram and
        thyme
  1/4 teaspoon baking soda
    1 egg
2-3/4 to 3-1/4 cups all-purpose flour

In a large mixing bowl, dissolve yeast in warm water. Add the buttermilk, 2 tablespoons butter, sugar, salt, basil, marjoram, thyme, baking soda, egg and 2 cups flour. Beat until smooth. Stir in enough remaining flour to form a soft dough (dough will be sticky). Turn onto a heavily floured surface; knead with floured hands until smooth and elastic, about 6-8 minutes. Place in a greased bowl, turning once to grease top. Cover and let rise in a warm place until doubled, about 75 minutes.

Punch dough down. Turn onto a lightly floured surface; divide into four portions. Divide each portion into six pieces; shape each piece into a ball. Place in a greased 13-in. x 9-in. x 2-in. baking pan. Cover and let rise until doubled, about 50 minutes.

Bake at 375° for 25-30 minutes or until golden brown. Cool for 5 minutes before removing from pan to a wire rack. Brush with remaining butter. **Yield:** 2 dozen.

*Editor's Note: Warmed buttermilk will appear curdled.

FRUIT 'N' NUT RINGS

(Pictured on page 80)

Donna Gordon, Vineland, New Jersey

I based the filling for these yeasty rings on a recipe my grandmother used to make for cookies. She plumped her raisins in water, but I use orange juice to give them a fruitier flavor.

        2 packages (1/4 ounce *each*) active dry
          yeast
1-3/4 cups warm water (110° to 115°)
        1 cup mashed potatoes (prepared without
          milk *or* butter)
      2/3 cup sugar
      1/2 cup shortening
        2 eggs
      1/2 teaspoon salt
        7 to 7-1/2 cups all-purpose flour
FILLING:
        3 cups golden raisins
        1 cup orange juice
      1/2 cup sugar
        1 cup chopped walnuts
GLAZE:
        1 cup confectioners' sugar
        5 teaspoons milk
      1/4 teaspoon vanilla extract

In a large mixing bowl, dissolve yeast in warm water. Add the potatoes, sugar, shortening, eggs, salt and 3 cups flour. Beat until smooth. Stir in enough remaining flour to form a soft dough. Turn onto a lightly floured surface; knead until smooth and elastic, about 6-8 minutes. Place in a greased bowl, turning once to grease top. Cover and let rise in a warm place until doubled, about 45 minutes.

Meanwhile, in a saucepan, bring the raisins, orange juice and sugar to a boil. Reduce heat; simmer, uncovered, for 5 minutes. Cool slightly. Transfer to a food processor or blender; cover and process until coarsely chopped. Pour into a bowl; stir in nuts.

Line two baking sheets with foil and grease well; set aside. Punch dough down. Turn onto a lightly floured surface; divide dough in half. Roll each portion into a 15-in. x 9-in. rectangle. Spread filling over dough to within 1/2 in. of edges. Roll up jelly-roll style, starting with a long side; pinch seams to seal.

Place each roll seam side down on a prepared baking sheet; pinch ends together to form a ring. With scissors, cut from outside edge to two-thirds of the way toward center of the ring at 1-in. intervals. Separate strips slightly; twist to allow filling to show. Cover and let rise until doubled, about 25 minutes.

Bake at 350° for 25-30 minutes or until golden brown. Remove from pans to cool on wire racks. Combine glaze ingredients; drizzle over rings. **Yield:** 2 coffee cakes.

WHOLE WHEAT BREAD

(Pictured below)

Freida Stutman, Fillmore, New York

I'm a teen and make this bread with my mother, who got the recipe from her mother.

        1 package (1/4 ounce) active dry yeast
        3 cups warm water (110° to 115°),
          divided
      3/4 cup vegetable oil
      1/4 cup molasses
      1/4 cup sugar
        1 tablespoon salt
        3 cups whole wheat flour
        5 to 5-1/2 cups all-purpose flour

In a mixing bowl, dissolve yeast in 3/4 cup water. Add the oil, molasses, sugar, salt and remaining water; mix well. Combine flours; add 3 cups to batter. Beat until smooth. Add enough remaining flour to form a firm dough.

Turn onto a floured surface; knead until smooth and elastic, about 6-8 minutes. Place in a greased bowl, turning once to grease top. Cover and let rise in a warm place until doubled, about 1 hour.

Punch dough down. Turn onto a lightly floured surface; divide in half. Shape each portion into a loaf. Place in two greased 9-in. x 5-in. x 3-in. loaf pans. Cover and let rise until doubled, about 30 minutes. Bake at 350° for 40-45 minutes or until golden brown. Remove from pans to cool on wire racks. **Yield:** 2 loaves.

SATISFYING *a sweet tooth? Choose from any one of these old-fashioned cookies, bars and candies for some real treats!*

LAYERED WITH LOVE. From top: Walnut Sandwich Cookies (p. 87), Chocolate Cheese Layered Bars (p. 85) and Cranberry Walnut White Fudge (p. 85).

Cookies, Bars & Candies

Cookies, Bars & Candies

CHOCOLATE CHEESE LAYERED BARS

(Pictured at left)

Sharon Schaa, Murray, Iowa

These rich and chocolaty bars are a hit at church and family gatherings. Folks love the chocolate and cream cheese layers.

- 1/2 cup butter, softened
- 1 cup sugar
- 2 eggs
- 1 square (1 ounce) unsweetened chocolate, melted
- 1 teaspoon vanilla extract
- 1 cup all-purpose flour
- 1 teaspoon baking powder
- 1/2 cup chopped pecans

CHEESE LAYER:
- 6 ounces cream cheese, softened
- 1/4 cup butter, softened
- 1/2 cup sugar
- 1 egg
- 2 tablespoons all-purpose flour
- 1/2 teaspoon vanilla extract
- 1/4 cup chopped pecans
- 1 cup (6 ounces) semisweet chocolate chips
- 3 cups miniature marshmallows

TOPPING:
- 1/4 cup butter
- 2 ounces cream cheese, softened
- 1 square (1 ounce) unsweetened chocolate
- 2 tablespoons milk
- 3 cups confectioners' sugar
- 1 teaspoon vanilla extract

In a mixing bowl, cream butter and sugar. Add eggs, chocolate and vanilla; mix well. Combine flour and baking powder; stir into chocolate mixture. Fold in pecans. Pour into a greased 13-in. x 9-in. x 2-in. baking pan.

In a mixing bowl, combine cream cheese and butter. Beat in the sugar, egg, flour and vanilla; mix well. Fold in pecans. Spread over the chocolate layer; sprinkle with chips.

Bake at 350° for 20-25 minutes or until edges pull away from sides of pan. Sprinkle with marshmallows; bake 2 minutes longer or until puffed. Spread evenly over cream cheese layer. Cool on a wire rack.

In a saucepan, combine first four topping ingredients. Cook and stir over low heat until smooth. Transfer to a mixing bowl. Add the confectioners' sugar and vanilla; beat until smooth. Spread over cooled bars. Store in the refrigerator. **Yield:** 2 dozen.

CRANBERRY WALNUT WHITE FUDGE

(Pictured at left)

Wanda Green, Woodland, California

A visit to several Oregon cranberry farms inspired my unusual fruit-flavored white fudge. I was thrilled when the recipe earned first place at our county fair a number of years ago.

- 1 teaspoon plus 1/2 cup butter, *divided*
- 2 cups sugar
- 3/4 cup sour cream
- 1 package (10 to 12 ounces) vanilla *or* white chips
- 1 jar (7 ounces) marshmallow creme
- 1 teaspoon vanilla extract
- 3 cups coarsely chopped walnuts
- 1 cup dried cranberries, coarsely chopped

Line an 8-in. square pan with foil and grease the foil with 1 teaspoon butter; set aside. In a heavy saucepan, bring sugar, sour cream and remaining butter to a boil over medium heat. Cook and stir until a candy thermometer reads 234° (soft-ball stage), about 15 minutes.

Remove from the heat. Stir in chips, marshmallow creme and vanilla until smooth. Fold in walnuts and cranberries. Pour into prepared pan. Let stand at room temperature. When cool, lift fudge out of pan and remove foil. Cut into squares. Refrigerate in an airtight container. **Yield:** 3 pounds.

Editor's Note: We recommend that you test your candy thermometer before each use by bringing water to a boil; the thermometer should read 212°. Adjust your recipe temperature up or down based on your test.

Remove from the heat; stir in vanilla.

Drop dough by tablespoonfuls 2 in. apart onto ungreased baking sheets. Using the end of a wooden spoon handle, make an indentation in the center of each cookie; fill with a rounded teaspoon of filling. Top with 1/2 teaspoon of dough, allowing some filling to show. Bake at 375° for 8-10 minutes or until lightly browned. **Yield:** about 4-1/2 dozen.

Editor's Note: Any leftover rhubarb filling may be stored, covered, in the refrigerator and used as a spread on toast or a topping for ice cream.

CRANBERRY CHIP COOKIES
(Pictured below)

Betty Albee, Buhl, Idaho

Chock-full of cranberries, chocolate chips and nuts, these cookies are fun to eat. They offer a change of pace from traditional Christmas cookies...but don't wait until December to make them. My family requests them all year-round.

    1 cup butter, softened
    1 cup sugar
    2 eggs
    1 teaspoon vanilla extract
2-1/4 cups all-purpose flour
  1/2 teaspoon baking powder
  1/4 teaspoon salt
1-1/2 cups (9 ounces) semisweet chocolate
      chips
1-1/2 cups dried cranberries
  3/4 cup chopped pecans
  1/2 cup English toffee bits *or* almond
      brickle chips, optional

RHUBARB-FILLED COOKIES
(Pictured above)

Pauline Bondy, Grand Forks, North Dakota

I won a blue ribbon at our local fair for these tender cookies. They're so pretty with the filling peeking through the dough. When not just any cookie will do, try making these and watch the smiles appear.

    1 cup butter, softened
    1 cup sugar
    1 cup packed brown sugar
    4 eggs
4-1/2 cups all-purpose flour
    1 teaspoon baking soda
    1 teaspoon salt
FILLING:
3-1/2 cups chopped fresh *or* frozen rhubarb,
      thawed
1-1/2 cups sugar
    6 tablespoons water, *divided*
  1/4 cup cornstarch
    1 teaspoon vanilla extract

In a mixing bowl, cream butter and sugars. Add eggs, one at a time, beating well after each addition. Combine the flour, baking soda and salt; gradually add to creamed mixture and mix well (dough will be sticky).

For filling, combine the rhubarb, sugar and 2 tablespoons water in a large saucepan. Bring to a boil. Reduce heat; simmer, uncovered, for 10 minutes or until thickened, stirring frequently. Combine cornstarch and remaining water until smooth; stir into rhubarb mixture. Bring to a boil; cook and stir for 2 minutes or until thickened.

In a mixing bowl, cream butter and sugar. Add eggs and vanilla; mix well. Combine the flour, baking powder and salt; gradually add to the creamed mixture and mix well. Stir in chocolate chips, cranberries, pecans and toffee bits if desired (dough will be stiff).

Drop by rounded tablespoonfuls 2 in. apart onto ungreased baking sheets. Flatten slightly. Bake at 350° for 11-14 minutes or until set and edges are lightly browned. Cool for 2 minutes before removing to wire racks. **Yield:** about 6 dozen.

CHOCOLATE MAPLE BARS

(Pictured at right)

Cathy Schumacher, Alto, Michigan

My family runs a maple syrup operation, and I'm always looking for new ways to incorporate maple syrup into my cooking and baking. These bars are delicious!

  1/2 cup shortening
  3/4 cup maple syrup
  1/2 cup sugar
    3 eggs
    3 tablespoons milk
    1 teaspoon vanilla extract
1-1/4 cups all-purpose flour
  1/4 teaspoon baking powder
  1/4 teaspoon salt
1-1/2 squares (1-1/2 ounces) unsweetened
      chocolate, melted
  1/2 cup chopped pecans
  1/2 cup flaked coconut
FROSTING:
  1/4 cup butter, softened
    1 cup confectioners' sugar
  1/2 cup baking cocoa
  1/2 cup maple syrup
    1 cup miniature marshmallows

In a mixing bowl, cream the shortening, syrup and sugar. Beat in the eggs, milk and vanilla. Combine the flour, baking powder and salt; add to creamed mixture and mix well. Remove half of the batter to another bowl.

Combine melted chocolate and pecans; stir into one bowl. Spread into a greased 13-in. x 9-in. x 2-in. baking pan. Add coconut to remaining batter. Spread carefully over chocolate batter. Bake at 350° for 25 minutes or until a toothpick inserted near the center comes out clean. Cool completely on a wire rack.

For frosting, in a small mixing bowl, cream butter. Gradually add confectioners' sugar and cocoa. Slowly add syrup, beating until smooth. Fold in marshmallows. Frost bars. **Yield:** 3 dozen.

WALNUT SANDWICH COOKIES

(Pictured on page 84)

Shirley Barker, Normal, Illinois

These cookies are really easy to prepare. I've made this recipe many times over the years, and the cookies are always a hit.

  3/4 cup butter, softened
    1 cup sugar
1-1/2 cups all-purpose flour
  1/2 teaspoon salt
    1 tablespoon water
  3/4 cup ground walnuts
Additional sugar
FILLING:
    1 package (3 ounces) cream cheese,
      softened
    1 tablespoon butter, softened
1-1/2 cups confectioners' sugar
  1/2 teaspoon grated orange peel

In a mixing bowl, cream butter and sugar. Combine the flour and salt; gradually add to creamed mixture. Add water. Stir in walnuts. Roll into 1-in. balls. Place 1 in. apart on ungreased baking sheets; flatten slightly with a glass dipped in sugar. Bake at 350° for 12-15 minutes or until edges are lightly browned. Cool for 2 minutes. Remove to wire racks; cool completely.

For filling, in a small mixing bowl, beat cream cheese and butter. Add sugar and orange peel; beat until smooth. Spread over the bottom of half of the cookies; top with remaining cookies. Store in the refrigerator. **Yield:** 2 dozen.

Easter Eggs Hatch Smiles

HERE'S a treat you'll want to shell out this Easter! Nest these delicious chocolate peanut butter eggs on the buffet table and watch smiles spring forth on everyone's faces.

Julie Warren of Conyers, Georgia regularly rolls out these eggs at her house when the weather turns warm.

"The recipe is over 35 years old," she explains. "My home economics teacher in high school had us make the eggs as a class project—and the candies have been a big hit ever since.

"Sometimes," Julie adds, "I'll substitute butterscotch pudding for the chocolate pudding the recipe calls for. It combines nicely with the peanut

butter. I've also tried vanilla pudding, and it tastes good, too."

Not only do Julie's confections sweeten meals, they make egg-citing gifts as well. Either way, you'll find yourself gathering compliments by the dozens when you make them for family and friends!

CHOCOLATE EASTER EGGS

   2 packages (3.4 ounces *each*) cook-and-serve chocolate pudding mix
1/2 cup butter, melted
1/2 cup milk
   5 to 6 cups confectioners' sugar
   2 cups peanut butter
   4 cups (24 ounces) semisweet chocolate chips
   2 teaspoons shortening
Assorted decorating icings and cake decorator candy flowers

In a saucepan, combine the pudding mixes, butter and milk. Cook and stir over medium heat until mixture comes to a boil. Cook and stir 1-2 minutes longer or until thickened. Remove from the heat; stir in sugar and peanut butter. Cool slightly. Shape 1/2 cupfuls into egg shapes. Place on a waxed paper-lined baking sheet; refrigerate until set.

In a microwave or heavy saucepan, melt chocolate chips and shortening; stir until smooth. Dip eggs in chocolate; allow excess to drip off. Return eggs to waxed paper to dry. Decorate with icings and candies as desired. **Yield:** 10 eggs.

CRANBERRY PECAN CLUSTERS

Collette Tubman, St. Thomas, Ontario

I have many candy recipes, and this is one of my favorites. The clusters are quick and easy to make.

6 squares (1 ounce *each*) white baking chocolate
1 cup dried cranberries
1/4 to 1/2 cup chopped pecans

Line a baking sheet with foil; set aside. In a microwave-safe bowl, heat the chocolate, uncovered, at 50% power for about 3 minutes or until melted, stirring once. Stir until smooth. Stir in cranberries and pecans. Drop by teaspoonfuls onto prepared pan. Freeze for 5 minutes, then refrigerate until firm. **Yield:** about 20 pieces.

Editor's Note: This recipe was tested in an 850-watt microwave.

TRIPLE-CHOCOLATE BROWNIE SQUARES

Kathy Fannoun, Brooklyn Park, Minnesota

My husband and I have five young children—all chocolate lovers—so these brownies never seem to last long around our house. They have the benefit of being lower in fat than many other brownies.

✓ Uses less fat, sugar or salt. Includes Nutritional Analysis and Diabetic Exchanges.

1 package reduced-fat brownie mix (13-inch x 9-inch pan size)
1-1/2 cups fat-free milk
1 package (1.4 ounces) sugar-free instant chocolate pudding mix
1/4 cup fat-free hot fudge ice cream topping
1/4 cup plus 1 tablespoon miniature semisweet chocolate chips, *divided*
4 cups frozen fat-free whipped topping, thawed, *divided*

Prepare and bake brownies according to package directions, using a 13-in. x 9-in. x 2-in. baking pan coated with nonstick cooking spray. Cool on a wire rack.

In a mixing bowl, whisk milk and pudding mix for 2 minutes or until slightly thickened. Add fudge topping; beat for 1 minute. In a microwave or heavy saucepan, melt 1/4 cup chocolate chips; stir until smooth. Beat into pudding mixture. Fold in 2 cups whipped topping. Spread over cooled brownies. Cover and refrigerate until pudding is set. Spread with remaining whipped topping. Sprinkle with remaining chocolate chips. **Yield:** 15 servings.

Nutritional Analysis: One piece equals 234 calories, 4 g fat (2 g saturated fat), 1 mg cholesterol, 244 mg sodium, 47 g carbohydrate, 2 g fiber, 4 g protein. **Diabetic Exchange:** 3 starch.

NO-FAIL FUDGE
(Pictured below)

Jeannie De Vries, Martinton, Illinois

Our family is very active in our county fair. This fudge was the only fair entry not to melt in the 100°-plus weather we had that year.

1 teaspoon plus 1/2 cup butter, softened, *divided*
3-1/2 cups confectioners' sugar
1/2 cup baking cocoa
1/4 teaspoon salt
1/4 cup milk
1 teaspoon vanilla extract
1 cup M&M miniature baking bits

Line an 8-in. square pan with foil and grease the foil with 1 teaspoon butter; set aside. In a large bowl, combine the confectioners' sugar, cocoa and salt. Melt remaining butter; add milk and vanilla. Stir into sugar mixture until blended; whisk until smooth. Stir in M&M's. Immediately spread into prepared pan. Refrigerate until firm, about 2 hours.

Using foil, lift fudge out of pan. Discard foil; cut fudge into 1-in. squares. Store in an airtight container in the refrigerator. **Yield:** 1-1/2 pounds.

Almond Fudge

Kathryn Maxson, Mountlake Terrace, Washington

This fudge recipe is from my grandfather-in-law, Max. He makes it for holiday gatherings where it's a favorite.

- 1 teaspoon butter
- 2 teaspoons instant coffee granules
- 1 can (14 ounces) sweetened condensed milk
- 3 cups (18 ounces) semisweet chocolate chips
- 1 teaspoon vanilla extract
- 1/2 teaspoon almond extract

Line a 9-in. square pan with foil and grease the foil with butter; set aside. In a heavy saucepan, dissolve coffee in milk over medium heat. Reduce heat to low. Stir in chocolate chips until melted. Remove from the heat; stir in extracts. Spread into prepared pan. Refrigerate until firm.

Using foil, lift fudge out of pan. Discard foil; cut fudge into 1-in. squares. **Yield:** about 2 pounds.

Coconut Chip Nut Bars

(Pictured above)

Judith Strohmeyer, Albrightsville, Pennsylvania

There's something for everyone in these delectable bars, from coconut and chocolate chips to walnuts and toffee. They're popular with kids and adults alike—so make a big batch. You'll be amazed at how fast they vanish!

- 1-3/4 cups all-purpose flour
- 3/4 cup confectioners' sugar
- 1/4 cup baking cocoa
- 1-1/4 cups cold butter
- 1 can (14 ounces) sweetened condensed milk
- 2 cups (12 ounces) semisweet chocolate chips, *divided*
- 1 teaspoon vanilla extract
- 1 cup chopped walnuts
- 1/2 cup flaked coconut
- 1/2 cup English toffee bits *or* almond brickle chips

In a bowl, combine the flour, sugar and cocoa. Cut in butter until mixture resembles coarse crumbs. Press firmly into a greased 13-in. x 9-in. x 2-in. baking pan. Bake at 350° for 10 minutes.

Meanwhile, in a saucepan, combine milk and 1 cup chocolate chips; cook and stir over low heat until smooth and chips are melted. Stir in vanilla. Pour over crust. Sprinkle with walnuts and remaining chocolate chips. Top with coconut and toffee bits. Gently press down into chocolate layer. Bake at 350° for 18-20 minutes or until firm. Cool on a wire rack. Cut into bars. **Yield:** 3 dozen.

Shamrock Cookies

(Pictured below)

Edna Hoffman, Hebron, Indiana

A handy cookie cutter shapes these sensational sweets. With a hint of mint flavor, they're especially yummy.

- 1 cup shortening
- 1 cup confectioners' sugar
- 1 egg
- 1 teaspoon peppermint extract
- 2-1/2 cups all-purpose flour
- 1 teaspoon salt
- Green paste food coloring
- Green colored sugar, optional

In a mixing bowl, cream shortening and confectioners' sugar. Beat in egg and extract. Add flour and salt; mix well. Tint with food coloring; mix well. Cover; chill for 1 hour or until easy to handle.

On a lightly floured surface, roll out dough to 1/4-in. thickness. Cut with a 2-in. shamrock cookie cutter dipped in flour. Place 1 in. apart on ungreased baking sheets. Sprinkle with colored sugar if desired. Bake at 375° for 10-12 minutes or until edges are lightly browned. Cool for 1 minute before removing to wire racks. **Yield:** 3 dozen.

QUICK BROWNIES

Mrs. Ed Fitch, Clifton, Arizona

These moist brownies get a head-start from a convenient chocolate cake mix. Peanut butter chips add fun flavor.

> 1 package (18-1/4 ounces) chocolate cake mix
> 1/2 cup butter, melted
> 1/2 cup vegetable oil
> 2 eggs
> 1 cup peanut butter chips

In a mixing bowl, combine the first four ingredients. Beat on medium speed for 1 minute. Stir in chips. Pour into a greased 11-in. x 7-in. x 2-in. baking pan. Bake at 350° for 35-40 minutes or until a toothpick inserted near the center comes out clean. Cool on a wire rack. **Yield:** 18 servings.

ANN'S CHOCOLATE CHIP COOKIES

Ann Peterson, Camano Island, Washington

My mother used to bake these cookies. I call this recipe my own, though, since I've made a few changes over the years.

> 1 cup shortening
> 1 cup sugar
> 1 cup packed brown sugar
> 2 eggs
> 2 teaspoons vanilla extract
> 2 cups old-fashioned oats
> 2 cups all-purpose flour
> 1 teaspoon baking soda
> 1 teaspoon baking powder
> 3/4 teaspoon salt
> 1/2 teaspoon ground cinnamon
> 2 cups (12 ounces) semisweet chocolate chips
> 1 cup flaked coconut
> 1 cup chopped walnuts, optional

In a large mixing bowl, cream shortening and sugars. Add eggs and vanilla; mix well. Combine the oats, flour, baking soda, baking powder, salt and cinnamon; add to creamed mixture and mix well. Stir in the chips, coconut and walnuts if desired.

Drop by rounded teaspoonfuls 2 in. apart onto greased baking sheets. Bake at 375° for 8-10 minutes or until edges are lightly browned and cookies are set. Cool for 2 minutes before removing from pans to wire racks. **Yield:** about 9 dozen.

COCONUT OATMEAL CRISPIES

(Pictured above)

Mary Schmidt, Eau Claire, Wisconsin

My mother-in-law baked these cookies in the 1930s for her sons, and later for her grandchildren. Now I make them for my grandkids and great-grandkids.

> 1 cup butter-flavored shortening
> 1 cup sugar
> 1 cup packed brown sugar
> 2 eggs
> 1 teaspoon vanilla extract
> 2 cups quick-cooking oats
> 1-1/2 cups all-purpose flour
> 1 cup flaked coconut
> 1 teaspoon baking soda
> 1 teaspoon salt

In a mixing bowl, cream shortening and sugars. Add eggs, one at a time, beating well after each addition. Beat in vanilla. Combine oats, flour, coconut, baking soda and salt; gradually add to creamed mixture. Shape into two 6-in. rolls; wrap each roll in plastic wrap. Refrigerate for 1 hour or until firm.

Unwrap dough and cut into 1/4-in. slices. Place 2 in. apart on ungreased baking sheets. Bake at 350° for 8-10 minutes or until golden brown. Remove to wire racks. **Yield:** 4 dozen.

CHERRY CRUNCH COOKIES
(Pictured below)

Lora Reynolds, Grants Pass, Oregon

These crispy cookies provide a nice change of pace from the traditional chocolate chip, sugar and peanut butter cookies. The cornflakes give them a tasty coating.

    3/4 cup butter, softened
      1 cup sugar
      2 eggs
      2 tablespoons milk
      1 teaspoon vanilla extract
  2-1/4 cups all-purpose flour
      1 teaspoon baking powder
    1/2 teaspoon salt
    1/2 teaspoon baking soda
      1 cup chopped pecans
      1 cup chopped dates
    1/3 cup chopped maraschino cherries
  1-3/4 cups finely crushed cornflakes
     30 to 35 maraschino cherries, halved

In a mixing bowl, cream butter and sugar. Add eggs, one at a time, beating well after each addition. Add milk and vanilla; mix well. Combine the flour, baking powder, salt and baking soda; add to creamed mixture. Stir in the pecans, dates and chopped cherries. Cover and refrigerate for 30 minutes.

Shape dough into 1-in. balls; roll in cornflakes. Place 2 in. apart on ungreased baking sheets; press a cherry half into center of each. Bake at 350° for 14-15 minutes or until golden brown. Remove to wire racks to cool. **Yield:** 5-1/2 dozen.

PECAN PIE BARS
(Pictured above)

Karlen Dentinger, Louisville, Kentucky

If you like pecan pie, you're sure to love these bars. They don't last long at my house.

    1/2 cup butter, softened
      3 tablespoons confectioners' sugar
      1 cup all-purpose flour
      3 eggs
    3/4 cup packed brown sugar
    3/4 cup corn syrup
Dash salt
    3/4 cup chopped pecans

In a mixing bowl, cream butter and confectioners' sugar. Gradually add flour until blended. Pat into an ungreased 9-in. square baking pan. Bake at 350° for 20-22 minutes until golden.

In another mixing bowl, beat the eggs, brown sugar, corn syrup and salt until smooth. Pour over crust; sprinkle with pecans. Bake 40-45 minutes longer or until set. Cool on a wire rack. Cut into bars. **Yield:** 20 servings.

BUS TRIP COOKIES

Dorothy Jacobson, Puyallup, Washington

My friend and I are in charge of bus trips for our senior citizen center and make these treats for the ride.

    1/2 cup butter, softened
      2 cups sugar
      3 eggs, lightly beaten
      1 tablespoon coconut *or* almond extract
      3 cups biscuit/baking mix
      3 cups mashed potato flakes

In a mixing bowl, cream butter and sugar. Add eggs and extract; mix well. Add biscuit mix and potato flakes; mix well. Drop by rounded teaspoonfuls 2 in. apart onto greased baking sheets.

Bake at 350° for 9-12 minutes or until edges are lightly browned. Cool for 2 minutes before removing to wire racks. **Yield:** about 6 dozen.

DOUBLE CHIP CHEESECAKE BARS

Beth Allard, Belmont, New Hampshire

I love to cook and sometimes create my own recipes. I got creative one afternoon, and this dessert is the result.

    2 cups all-purpose flour
  1/2 cup confectioners' sugar
    1 cup cold butter
FILLING:
    2 packages (8 ounces *each*) cream cheese, softened
  1/2 cup packed brown sugar
    2 eggs
    1 teaspoon almond extract
    1 cup (6 ounces) semisweet chocolate chips, *divided*
  1/2 cup butterscotch chips
  1/2 cup chopped walnuts

In a bowl, combine flour and confectioners' sugar. Cut in butter until mixture resembles coarse crumbs. Press into an ungreased 13-in. x 9-in. x 2-in. baking pan. Bake at 350° for 18-22 minutes or until lightly browned.

Meanwhile, in a mixing bowl, beat cream cheese and brown sugar until smooth. Add eggs and extract; beat on low speed just until combined. Stir in 1/2 cup chocolate chips, butterscotch chips and walnuts. Spread over crust. Sprinkle with the remaining chocolate chips.

Bake at 350° for 20-25 minutes or until center is almost set. Cool completely on a wire rack before cutting. Refrigerate leftovers. **Yield:** 3 dozen.

BUTTERSCOTCH FUDGE

Virginia Hipwell, Fenwick, Ontario

I have entered this fudge at our county fair for several years, and it always wins me a ribbon.

    1 teaspoon plus 2 tablespoons butter, *divided*
1-2/3 cups sugar
  2/3 cup evaporated milk
  1/2 teaspoon salt
    2 cups miniature marshmallows
    1 package (10 to 11 ounces) butterscotch chips
  1/2 cup chopped walnuts
    1 teaspoon maple flavoring

Line an 8-in. square pan with foil and grease the foil with 1 teaspoon butter; set aside. In a saucepan, combine the sugar, milk, salt and remaining butter; cook and stir over medium heat until mixture comes to a boil. Boil for 5 minutes, stirring constantly. Remove from the heat; add marshmallows, chips, nuts and maple flavoring. Stir until marshmallows and chips are melted. Spoon into prepared pan. Let stand until set.

Using foil, lift fudge out of pan. Discard foil; cut fudge into 1-in. squares. Store in an airtight container at room temperature. **Yield:** about 1-1/2 pounds.

FILBERTINES

(Pictured below)

Hollis Mattson, Brush Prairie, Washington

Hazelnuts, or filberts, are by far the most important nut crop grown commercially in the Pacific Northwest.

  1/2 cup butter, softened
  1/2 cup sugar
    1 egg
1-1/3 cups all-purpose flour
  1/2 teaspoon baking soda
  1/8 teaspoon ground cardamom
  1/2 cup finely chopped hazelnuts

In a small mixing bowl, cream butter and sugar. Beat in egg. Combine the flour, baking soda and cardamom; add to creamed mixture. Cover and refrigerate for 1 hour.

Shape into 1-in. balls; roll in chopped nuts. Place 2 in. apart on greased baking sheets. Bake at 350° for 15-18 minutes or until lightly browned. Remove to wire racks. **Yield:** 3 dozen.

SAVE ROOM FOR TREATS because, with this selection of cakes, pies and desserts, you'll want to whip up something new every week!

CHOCOLATY DELIGHTS: From top: Rich Chocolate Cake (p. 95), Chocolate-Caramel Supreme Pie (p. 95) and Favorite Chocolate Sheet Cake (p. 97).

Cakes, Pies & Desserts

CHOCOLATE-CARAMEL SUPREME PIE

(Pictured at left)

Diana Stewart, Oelwein, Iowa

At a church fund-raiser, I purchased a pie-a-month package furnished by a local family. From among all the varieties they made, this one was the best with its chocolate crust, creamy caramel filling and fluffy topping.

  30 caramels*
   3 tablespoons butter
   2 tablespoons water
   1 chocolate crumb crust (9 inches)
 1/2 cup chopped pecans, toasted
   1 package (3 ounces) cream cheese, softened
 1/3 cup confectioners' sugar
 3/4 cup milk chocolate chips
   3 tablespoons hot water
   1 carton (8 ounces) frozen whipped topping, thawed
Chocolate hearts *or* curls, optional

In a saucepan, combine the caramels, butter and water. Cook and stir over medium heat until caramels are melted. Spread over crust; sprinkle with pecans. Refrigerate for 1 hour. In a mixing bowl, beat cream cheese and sugar; spread over caramel layer. Refrigerate.

In a saucepan, melt chocolate chips with hot water over low heat; stir until smooth. Cool slightly. Fold in whipped topping. Spread over cream cheese layer. Garnish with chocolate hearts or curls if desired. Chill until serving. Refrigerate leftovers. **Yield:** 8 servings.

*Editor's Note: This recipe was tested with Hershey caramels.

RICH CHOCOLATE CAKE

(Pictured at left)

Connie Scheffer, Salina, Kansas

For Valentine's Day and other special occasions, I treat my sweeties to this fudgy cake. Even a small slice satisfies the biggest chocolate craving.

2-2/3 cups semisweet chocolate chips
   1 cup butter, softened
   1 cup half-and-half cream
   1 cup sugar
   8 eggs
   2 tablespoons vanilla extract
GLAZE:
   1 cup semisweet chocolate chips
   3 tablespoons half-and-half cream
   2 tablespoons butter, softened
   2 tablespoons corn syrup
Fresh raspberries and variegated mint leaves, optional

Grease a 10-in. springform pan and wrap bottom of pan with heavy-duty foil; set aside. In a saucepan, heat the chocolate chips, butter, cream and sugar over low heat until chocolate is melted; stir until smooth. Pour into a large mixing bowl and cool.

In another mixing bowl, beat eggs on high for 3 minutes or until light and fluffy. Beat into chocolate mixture, a third at a time, until well blended. Stir in vanilla. Pour into prepared pan; place on a baking sheet. Bake at 350° for 45-50 minutes or until a toothpick inserted near the center comes out with moist crumbs (top will crack). Cool on a wire rack (cake will settle). Cover and chill for 1 hour. Run a knife around edge of pan before removing sides.

In a saucepan, heat the first four glaze ingredients over low heat until chocolate is melted; stir until smooth. Spread enough of the glaze over top and sides of cake to cover. Chill 10 minutes. Repeat with remaining glaze. Chill overnight. Garnish with raspberries and mint if desired. Refrigerate leftovers. **Yield:** 12-16 servings.

Editor's Note: This cake contains no flour.

CAKE PAN TIPS

Be generous when greasing cake pans (about 1 tablespoon per layer-cake pan) and your cakes won't stick. When a chocolate cake recipe calls for greasing and flouring the pan, grease it, then dust with unsweetened cocoa powder instead for an even more chocolaty flavor!

SAUCY SPICED APPLE PIE

(Pictured above)

Lisa Jedrzejczak, Capac, Michigan

My mom's sweet and saucy apple pie earns a lip-smacking salute from everyone who tastes it. I like to serve slices warm with a scoop of French vanilla ice cream on top.

Pastry for double-crust pie (9 inches)
- 1/4 cup butter, softened
- 2 cups sugar
- 1 egg
- 1 egg, *separated*
- 1/3 cup unsweetened pineapple juice
- 1-1/2 teaspoons vanilla extract
- 1/3 cup all-purpose flour
- 1/2 teaspoon ground cinnamon
- 1/4 teaspoon ground ginger
- 1/4 teaspoon ground nutmeg
- 6 cups sliced peeled tart apples

Additional sugar

Line a 9-in. pie plate with bottom pastry; trim even with edge. In a mixing bowl, cream butter and sugar. Add the egg, egg yolk, pineapple juice and vanilla; mix well (mixture will appear curdled). Combine the flour, cinnamon, ginger and nutmeg; add to creamed mixture. Fill crust with apple slices. Top with the creamed mixture.

Roll out remaining pastry to fit top of pie; place over filling. Trim, seal and flute edges. Cut

slits in top. Beat egg white; brush over pastry. Sprinkle with additional sugar. Bake at 350° for 55-60 minutes or until crust is golden brown and filling is bubbly. Cool on a wire rack. Refrigerate leftovers. **Yield:** 6-8 servings.

CHOCOLATE CARAMEL PEARS

(Pictured below)

Lisa Roberts, Grafton, Wisconsin

Bring out a tray of these fancy fruit treats and watch everybody's eyes widen. The pears wear a nut-dusted caramel coating and elegant drizzle of chocolate.

- 1 package (14 ounces) caramels*
- 2 tablespoons water
- 6 large firm pears with stems
- 1 cup chopped cashews, hazelnuts *or* almonds
- 1/3 cup semisweet chocolate chips
- 1-1/2 teaspoons shortening, *divided*
- 1/3 cup vanilla *or* white chips

In a heavy saucepan, heat caramels and water over low heat just until caramels are melted. Remove from the heat; cool slightly. Cut a thin slice from the bottom of each pear so it sits flat. Dip pears halfway in caramel; turn to coat and allow excess to drip off. Dip in nuts and place on a greased baking sheet; refrigerate for 30 minutes or until coating is firm.

In a heavy saucepan or microwave, melt chocolate chips with 1 teaspoon shortening; stir until smooth. In another saucepan, melt vanilla chips with remaining shortening; stir until

smooth. Drizzle melted chips over pears and stems. Let stand until set. **Yield:** 6 servings.

Editor's Note: This recipe was tested with Hershey caramels.

FAVORITE CHOCOLATE SHEET CAKE

(Pictured on page 94)

Mary Lewis, Escondido, California

My mother adapted this family pleaser from a recipe for vanilla cake that was in a church cookbook. The cake is so flavorful, it wouldn't need frosting—but I always feel you can never have enough chocolate!

  1 cup butter, softened
  2 cups sugar
  4 eggs
  2 teaspoons vanilla extract
2-1/4 cups cake flour
  1 teaspoon baking soda
  1 teaspoon salt
  1 cup buttermilk
  3 squares (1 ounce *each*) bittersweet
    chocolate, melted
FROSTING:
  1/4 cup baking cocoa
  1/3 cup milk
  1/2 cup butter
  1 teaspoon vanilla extract
3-1/2 cups confectioners' sugar

In a mixing bowl, cream butter and sugar. Add eggs, one at a time, beating well after each addition. Beat in vanilla. Combine the flour, baking soda and salt; add to creamed mixture alternately with buttermilk. Beat in chocolate until combined. Pour into a greased 15-in. x 10-in. x 1-in. baking pan. Bake at 350° for 23-27 minutes or until a toothpick inserted near the center comes out clean. Cool on a wire rack.

For frosting, in a saucepan, bring cocoa and milk to a boil over medium heat, stirring constantly. Remove from the heat; stir in butter and vanilla until butter is melted. Whisk in confectioners' sugar until smooth. Drizzle over cake and spread quickly. Let stand until set. **Yield:** 24 servings.

PUMPKIN CAKE ROLL

(Pictured above right)

Mary Gecha, Center Rutland, Vermont

This is one of my family's favorite dessert recipes, especially for holiday gatherings.

  3 eggs
  1 cup sugar
2/3 cup canned pumpkin
  1 teaspoon lemon juice
3/4 cup all-purpose flour
  2 teaspoons ground cinnamon
  1 teaspoon baking powder
  1 teaspoon ground ginger
1/2 teaspoon salt
1/2 teaspoon ground nutmeg
  1 cup finely chopped walnuts
Confectioners' sugar
FILLING:
  2 packages (3 ounces *each*) cream cheese,
    softened
  1 cup confectioners' sugar
1/4 cup butter, softened
1/2 teaspoon vanilla extract

Line a greased 15-in. x 10-in. x 1-in. baking pan with waxed paper. Grease the paper; set aside. In a mixing bowl, beat eggs for 3 minutes. Gradually add sugar; beat for 2 minutes or until mixture becomes thick and lemon-colored. Stir in pumpkin and lemon juice. Combine dry ingredients; fold into pumpkin mixture. Spread batter evenly in prepared pan. Sprinkle with walnuts.

Bake at 375° for 12-14 minutes or until cake springs back when lightly touched in center. Cool for 5 minutes. Turn cake out of pan onto a kitchen towel dusted with confectioners' sugar. Gently peel off waxed paper. Roll up cake in towel jelly-roll style, starting with a long side. Cool completely on a wire rack.

In a mixing bowl, combine filling ingredients; beat until smooth. Unroll cake; spread evenly with filling to within 1/2 in. of edges. Roll up again. Cover and refrigerate for 1 hour before cutting. Refrigerate leftovers. **Yield:** 10-12 servings.

RHUBARB JELLY-ROLL CAKE
(Pictured below)

Donna Stratton, Carson City, Nevada

This jelly-roll recipe came from my mom's cookbook, circa 1940. It continues to be a family classic and is popular at church potlucks. I also introduced this rhubarb cake to kids in my 4-H cooking class.

> 6 cups chopped fresh *or* frozen rhubarb, thawed
> 2-3/4 cups sugar, *divided*
> 2 teaspoons ground cinnamon
> 1/4 teaspoon ground allspice
> 1/8 teaspoon ground cloves
> 4 eggs
> 1 teaspoon lemon extract
> 3/4 cup all-purpose flour
> 1 teaspoon baking powder
> 1/2 teaspoon salt
> Confectioners' sugar

In a saucepan, combine the rhubarb, 2 cups sugar, cinnamon, allspice and cloves. Bring to a boil. Reduce heat; cook, uncovered, over medium heat until thickened. Cool completely.

In a mixing bowl, beat eggs on high speed until thick and lemon-colored. Gradually add remaining sugar, beating until thick and light-colored. Beat in extract. Combine the flour, baking powder and salt; gradually add to egg mixture.

Grease a 15-in. x 10-in. x 1-in. baking pan and line with waxed paper; grease and flour the paper.

Spread batter into pan. Bake at 375° for 15 minutes or until cake springs back when lightly touched. Cool for 5 minutes. Turn onto a kitchen towel dusted with confectioners' sugar. Peel off waxed paper. Roll up cake in towel jelly-roll style, starting with a short side. Cool.

Carefully unroll cake. Spread filling over cake to within 1 in. of edges. Roll up again. Store in the refrigerator. Dust with confectioners' sugar just before serving. **Yield:** 10-12 servings.

CARAMEL RICE DESSERT
(Pictured above)

LaRee Barlow, Bluffdale, Utah

This recipe has been in our family for four generations. It can be prepared well ahead of time, if necessary.

> 1-1/2 cups uncooked long grain rice
> 2 cups heavy whipping cream
> 1/4 cup sugar
> 1-1/2 teaspoons vanilla extract
> **CARAMEL SAUCE:**
> 3 cups sugar
> 1/4 teaspoon salt
> 2 cups heavy whipping cream
> 1 cup light corn syrup
> 1/4 cup butter
> 2 teaspoons vanilla extract

Cook rice according to package directions. Rinse in cold water; drain. Cover and refrigerate. In a mixing bowl, beat cream until soft peaks form. Gradually add sugar and vanilla, beating until stiff peaks form. Fold into the rice. Cover and refrigerate.

In a large saucepan, combine sugar, salt, cream and corn syrup. Cook over medium heat until thermometer reads 238° (soft-ball stage), stirring frequently. Remove from heat; carefully stir in butter and vanilla. Cool slightly. Serve warm over rice. **Yield:** 10-12 servings (4 cups sauce).

Editor's Note: We recommend that you test your candy thermometer before each use by bringing water to a boil; the thermometer should read 212°. Adjust your recipe temperature up or down based on your test.

PEACHES 'N' CREAM PIE

Dana Tittle, Forrest City, Arkansas

Many customers drop by every season to the peach orchard my husband and I own. It's fun to swap recipes with them, and this is one of my favorites.

    3/4 cup all-purpose flour
      1 package (3 ounces) cook-and-serve
        vanilla pudding mix
    1/2 cup milk
      1 egg
      1 teaspoon baking powder
    1/4 teaspoon salt
      4 large fresh peaches, peeled and sliced
      1 package (8 ounces) cream cheese,
        softened
    1/2 cup sugar
TOPPING:
      2 teaspoons sugar
    1/8 to 1/4 teaspoon ground cinnamon

In a mixing bowl, combine the first six ingredients; beat for 2 minutes. Spread into a greased 9-in. pie plate. Arrange peaches over batter to within 1/2 in. of edge. In a small mixing bowl, beat the cream cheese and sugar; spoon over peaches. Combine sugar and cinnamon; sprinkle over top.

Bake at 350° for 35 minutes or until golden brown around the edges and a toothpick inserted comes out clean. Serve warm. Refrigerate leftovers. **Yield:** 8 servings.

FROZEN CHOCOLATE MINT PIE

(Pictured at right)

Jenny Falk, Sauk Rapids, Minnesota

This refreshing pie was featured at a small resort my family visited regularly as I was growing up. When I make it now, I relish compliments from tasters, along with fond memories of sunny days at the beach.

      3 egg whites
    1/4 teaspoon cream of tartar
      1 cup sugar
CHOCOLATE SAUCE:
    1/4 cup butter
      1 square (1 ounce) unsweetened
        chocolate
      1 cup sugar
    3/4 cup evaporated milk
    1/2 teaspoon vanilla extract
    1/8 teaspoon peppermint extract
Dash salt
      2 cups vanilla ice cream, softened
1-1/3 cups heavy whipping cream, whipped

In a mixing bowl, beat egg whites until foamy. Add cream of tartar; beat until soft peaks form. Gradually add sugar, 1 tablespoon at a time, beating until stiff glossy peaks form. Spread onto the bottom and up the sides of a greased and floured 9-in. deep-dish pie plate. Bake at 275° for 1 hour. Turn off oven and do not open door; let meringue cool completely inside the oven.

For chocolate sauce, in heavy saucepan, melt butter and chocolate; stir until smooth. Stir in sugar and evaporated milk. Cook over low heat for 45-60 minutes or until thickened, stirring occasionally. Remove from the heat; stir in extracts and salt. Cool to room temperature.

Spread ice cream into meringue crust. Fold whipped cream into cooled chocolate sauce. Spread over ice cream layer; freeze until firm. **Yield:** 8 servings.

Time-Saving Rhubarb Treats

WHEN YOUR FAMILY craves rhubarb, these five sweet-tart filled recipes cook up fast. Each has nine ingredients or less, so they can be ready in about an hour!

MICROWAVE RHUBARB SAUCE
(Pictured below)

Carol Gode, Lamberton, Minnesota

This sweet sauce is scrumptious served over ice cream. My sister shared the quick and easy recipe with me.

>   3 **cups diced fresh** *or* **frozen rhubarb, thawed**
>   1 **cup water**
> 1/2 **cup sugar**
>   1 **package (3 ounces) cook-and-serve vanilla pudding mix**
> **Vanilla ice cream, optional**

In a microwave-safe bowl, combine the rhubarb, water and sugar. Microwave, uncovered, on high for 8-10 minutes or until rhubarb is tender, stirring occasionally.

Stir in pudding mix until blended; cook for 1-2 minutes or until thickened, stirring occasionally. Serve over ice cream if desired. **Yield:** 6-9 servings.

Editor's Note: This recipe was tested in an 850-watt microwave.

RHUBARB CLOUD

Anna Daley, Montague, Prince Edward Island

The pickings from my rhubarb patch go to good use with this simple dessert. It's a nice light finish to a heavier meal.

>   3 **cups sliced fresh** *or* **frozen rhubarb, thawed**
> 1/2 **cup sugar**
>   1 **tablespoon lemon juice**
>   1 **teaspoon grated orange peel**
>   1 **cup heavy whipping cream**

In a large saucepan, bring the rhubarb, sugar, lemon juice and orange peel to a boil. Reduce heat; cook, uncovered, over medium heat until mixture is reduced to about 1 cup, about 15 minutes. Remove from the heat and cool completely.

In a mixing bowl, beat cream until soft peaks form. Fold in rhubarb mixture. Serve immediately. **Yield:** 4 servings.

STRAWBERRY RHUBARB DUMPLINGS

Beverly Draves, Beloit, Wisconsin

My family is fond of rhubarb and dumplings, so I combined the two in this tasty dessert. It's full of old-fashioned flavor.

4 cups sliced fresh *or* frozen rhubarb,
thawed
1-1/2 cups water
1 cup sugar
1/8 teaspoon salt
1-1/2 cups mashed strawberries
1 cup biscuit/baking mix
1/3 cup milk
Whipped cream

In a large saucepan, bring rhubarb, water, sugar
and salt to a boil. Reduce heat; simmer, uncovered,
for 6-8 minutes or until rhubarb is tender. Stir in
strawberries; return to a boil.

Meanwhile, in a bowl, combine biscuit mix
and milk just until moistened. Drop batter in four
mounds onto rhubarb mixture. Cook, uncovered, for 10 minutes. Cover and cook 5-8 minutes
longer or until a toothpick inserted in a dumpling
comes out clean. Serve warm with whipped
cream. **Yield:** 4 servings.

RHUBARB APPLE PIE

Sandra Lee Marr, Oakhurst, California

*I put apple pie filling in with rhubarb when I was out
of the fresh stalks one day. This delicious pie was the
satisfying result.*

2 cups sliced fresh *or* frozen rhubarb,
thawed
1 can (21 ounces) apple pie filling
1/4 cup sugar
1/4 teaspoon ground cinnamon
1/4 teaspoon ground nutmeg
Pastry for double-crust pie (9 inches)
1/4 cup butter
TOPPING:
1 tablespoon sugar
1/4 teaspoon ground cinnamon

In a bowl, combine the first five ingredients. Line
a 9-in. pie plate with bottom pastry; trim to 1 in.
beyond edge of plate. Add filling; dot with butter.
Place remaining pastry over filling. Cut slits in
top. Trim, seal and flute edges.

Combine sugar and cinnamon. Brush crust
with water; sprinkle with cinnamon-sugar. Cover edges loosely with foil.

Bake at 400° for 20 minutes. Remove foil. Reduce heat to 350°; bake 15 minutes longer or until crust is golden brown. Cool on a wire rack.
Store in the refrigerator. **Yield:** 6-8 servings.

PINEAPPLE-RHUBARB STREUSEL DESSERT

Bobbi Miles, Waupaca, Wisconsin

*Convenient canned pineapple and fresh rhubarb deli-
ciously combine in this dessert. It's quick, easy and,
best of all, yummy!*

5 cups sliced fresh *or* frozen rhubarb,
thawed (1-inch pieces)
2 cans (8 ounces *each*) crushed pineapple,
undrained
1 cup sugar
1/4 teaspoon ground nutmeg
1 package (18-1/2 ounces) golden cake
mix (butter recipe)
2 cups finely chopped pecans
1/2 cup cold butter

In a large bowl, combine the first four ingredients; mix well. Pour into a greased 13-in. x 9-in.
x 2-in. baking dish.

In another bowl, combine dry cake mix and
pecans. Cut in butter until mixture resembles
coarse crumbs; spread evenly over rhubarb mixture. Bake at 350° for 35-40 minutes or until lightly browned. **Yield:** 12 servings.

TIME'S RIPE FOR RHUBARB

Two kinds of rhubarb are on the market.
Hothouse has pink to pale red stalks and yel-
low-green leaves. *Field-grown* is found with
cherry red stalks, bright green leaves and a
more pronounced flavor.

Choose rhubarb that has crisp, brightly
hued stalks. The leaves should look fresh and
be free of blemishes.

APPLE BUNDT CAKE

(Pictured above)

Virginia Horst, Mesa, Washington

I love this recipe because the cake has a thin, crunchy crust and a soft, delicious inside. With the butter cream sauce, it's almost like eating candy.

2 eggs
2 cups sugar
1-1/2 cups vegetable oil
3 cups all-purpose flour
1 teaspoon baking soda
1 teaspoon ground cinnamon
1/2 teaspoon salt
3 cups diced peeled apples
1 cup chopped pecans

BUTTER CREAM SAUCE:
1/2 cup butter
1 cup sugar
1/2 cup heavy whipping cream
1 teaspoon vanilla extract

In a large mixing bowl, beat the eggs, sugar and oil. Combine the flour, baking soda, cinnamon and salt; gradually add to batter (batter will be very stiff). Fold in apples and pecans. Pour into a greased 10-in. fluted tube pan. Bake at 325° for 1-1/4 to 1-1/2 hours or until a toothpick inserted near the center comes out clean. Cool for 10 minutes before removing from pan to a wire rack.

For sauce, melt butter in a small saucepan. Add the sugar, cream and vanilla. Cook and stir over low heat until sugar is dissolved and sauce is heated through. Slice cake; serve with warm sauce. Refrigerate leftover sauce. **Yield:** 12-16 servings.

CRAN-APPLE COBBLER

(Pictured below)

Jo Ann Sheehan, Ruther Glen, Virginia

My cranberry-packed cobbler is the crowning glory of many of our late fall and winter meals. My family isn't big on pies, so this favorite is preferred at our Thanksgiving and Christmas celebrations. The aroma of cinnamon and fruit is so inviting!

2-1/2 cups sliced peeled apples
2-1/2 cups sliced peeled firm pears
1 to 1-1/4 cups sugar
1 cup fresh *or* frozen cranberries, thawed
1 cup water
3 tablespoons quick-cooking tapioca
3 tablespoons red-hot candies
1/2 teaspoon ground cinnamon
2 tablespoons butter

TOPPING:
3/4 cup all-purpose flour
2 tablespoons sugar
1 teaspoon baking powder
1/4 teaspoon salt
1/4 cup cold butter
3 tablespoons milk

Vanilla ice cream

In a large saucepan, combine the first eight ingredients; let stand for 5 minutes. Cook and stir over medium heat until mixture comes to a full rolling boil, about 18 minutes. Transfer cran-apple mixture to a greased 2-qt. baking dish; dot with butter.

102

Cakes, Pies & Desserts

Combine the flour, sugar, baking powder and salt in a bowl. Cut in butter until mixture resembles coarse crumbs. Stir in milk until a soft dough forms.

Drop topping by heaping tablespoonfuls onto hot fruit. Bake at 375° for 30-35 minutes or until golden brown. Serve warm with ice cream. **Yield:** 6-8 servings.

COOL 'N' CREAMY CHOCOLATE PIE

Christie Pyle, Owasso, Oklahoma

My mother-in-law fixes this pie often for family get-togethers. It's one of my husband's favorite desserts. My two sons love it as well.

1-1/2 cups milk
1 package (3.9 ounces) instant chocolate pudding mix
1 package (3 ounces) cream cheese, softened
1 cup confectioners' sugar
1 carton (8 ounces) frozen whipped topping, thawed, *divided*
1 chocolate crumb crust (8 *or* 9 inches)
1 milk chocolate candy bar (1.55 ounces), chopped

In a mixing bowl, beat milk and pudding mix on low speed for 2 minutes or until thickened; set aside. In another mixing bowl, beat the cream cheese and confectioners' sugar until blended. Mix in 1 cup whipped topping.

Spread into crust. Top with pudding mixture and remaining whipped topping. Sprinkle with chopped candy bar. Cover and refrigerate overnight. **Yield:** 8 servings.

CHOCOLATE TRUFFLE PIE

(Pictured above right)

Mercelle Jackson, Rochester, New York

Warm days warrant a cool dessert like this frosty and refreshing pie. The raspberry sauce combined with rich chocolate and ice cream make each slice irresistible. All eyes will light up when you pull out this pleaser!

1 cup chocolate wafer crumbs
1/4 cup butter, melted
1 pint chocolate ice cream, softened
1 cup (6 ounces) semisweet chocolate chips
1/3 cup heavy whipping cream
1 pint vanilla ice cream, softened
2 tablespoons slivered almonds, toasted

1 package (10 ounces) frozen sweetened raspberries, thawed
1 tablespoon cornstarch

In a bowl, combine wafer crumbs and butter. Press onto the bottom and up the sides of a 9-in. pie plate coated with nonstick cooking spray. Freeze for 30 minutes. Spread chocolate ice cream over crust; freeze for 1 hour or until firm.

In a microwave or small saucepan, heat chocolate chips and whipping cream until chips are melted; stir until smooth. Cool slightly. Quickly and carefully spread over chocolate ice cream. Freeze for 30 minutes. Top with vanilla ice cream; sprinkle with almonds. Cover and freeze until firm.

For sauce, puree the raspberries in a blender or food processor until smooth. Strain and discard seeds. In a saucepan, combine cornstarch and raspberry juice until smooth. Bring to a boil; cook and stir for 1-2 minutes or until thickened. Cool completely. Remove pie from the freezer 10 minutes before cutting. Serve over raspberry sauce. **Yield:** 8 servings.

APPLE A DAY

Apple yields: 1 pound fresh = 2 large, 3 medium or 4 small; 2 to 2-1/2 cups chopped or sliced. Dried apples: 1 pound = 4-1/3 cups; 8 cups cooked.

STRAWBERRY-LEMON CREAM PUFFS
(Pictured below)

Janice Mitchell, Aurora, Colorado

A tangy lemon filling chock-full of berry slices is tucked inside these tender puffs. My husband is impressed with their great taste and appearance. I like how easy the puffs are to make.

- 1 cup water
- 1/4 cup butter
- 1 cup all-purpose flour
- 4 eggs

FILLING:
- 1/4 cup sugar
- 1-1/2 tablespoons cornstarch
- 1 can (5 ounces) evaporated milk
- 1 cup (8 ounces) vanilla yogurt
- 1-1/2 teaspoons lemon extract
- 1/4 teaspoon butter flavoring
- 1 cup sliced fresh strawberries
- 1/2 teaspoon confectioners' sugar

In a saucepan, bring water and butter to a boil. Add flour all at once, stirring until a smooth ball forms. Remove from the heat; let stand for 5 minutes. Add eggs, one at a time, beating well after each addition. Continue beating until mixture is smooth. Drop by 1/4 cupfuls 3 in. apart onto greased baking sheets.

Bake at 400° for 30 minutes or until golden brown. Remove to wire racks. Immediately split puffs open and remove tops; discard soft dough from inside. Set puffs and tops aside to cool.

For filling, combine sugar and cornstarch in a saucepan. Stir in milk and yogurt until smooth.

Bring to a boil; cook and stir for 2 minutes or until thickened. Remove from the heat. Stir in lemon extract and butter flavoring. Cool. Fold in strawberries. Refrigerate until serving. Fill cream puffs; replace tops. Dust with confectioners' sugar. **Yield:** 10 servings.

BLACK FOREST TRIFLE
(Pictured above)

Peggy Linton, Cobourg, Ontario

When I want a dessert that's fit for a feast, I turn to this trifle. The recipe calls for a brownie mix, so it's simple to make.

- 1 package brownie mix (13-inch x 9-inch pan size)
- 2 packages (2.8 ounces *each*) chocolate mousse mix
- 1 can (21 ounces) cherry pie filling
- 1 carton (16 ounces) frozen whipped topping, thawed
- 4 Skor candy bars, crushed

Prepare and bake brownies according to package directions; cool completely on a wire rack. Prepare mousse according to package directions.

Crumble brownies; sprinkle half into a 4-qt. trifle dish or glass bowl. Top with half of the pie filling, mousse, whipped topping and candy bars. Repeat layers. Cover and refrigerate for 8 hours or overnight. **Yield:** 16 servings.

Cakes, Pies & Desserts

RHUBARB FROZEN YOGURT

Sarah Bradley, Athens, Texas

My frozen yogurt makes a refreshing end to any meal. The rhubarb flavor is fantastic.

✓ Uses less fat, sugar or salt. Includes Nutritional Analysis and Diabetic Exchanges.

  5 cups chopped fresh *or* frozen rhubarb, thawed
1-1/4 cups sugar, *divided*
  2 cups fat-free plain yogurt
  2 tablespoons orange juice
1/8 teaspoon red liquid food coloring

In a large saucepan, combine rhubarb and 3/4 cup sugar; let stand for 15 minutes. Bring to a boil. Reduce heat; simmer, uncovered, for 10 minutes or until thickened, stirring frequently. Remove from the heat; cool completely. Stir in yogurt, orange juice, food coloring and remaining sugar. Cover and refrigerate overnight. Freeze in an ice cream freezer according to manufacturer's instructions. Transfer to a freezer container. Cover and freeze in a refrigerator freezer for 2-4 hours before serving. **Yield:** 8 servings.

Nutritional Analysis: One serving (1/2 cup) equals 177 calories, 1 g fat (1 g saturated fat), 4 mg cholesterol, 46 mg sodium, 39 g carbohydrate, 1 g fiber, 4 g protein. **Diabetic Exchanges:** 1-1/2 starch, 1 vegetable, 1/2 fat-free milk.

FRUIT KUCHEN

Sandra Fischer, Sturgis, South Dakota

This dessert is quicker to make than traditional fruit kuchens because frozen bread dough forms the crust.

  1 cup heavy whipping cream
3/4 cup sugar
2/3 cup soft bread crumbs
  1 loaf (1 pound) frozen bread dough, thawed
  3 tablespoons cherry *or* raspberry pie filling
TOPPING:
  3 tablespoons all-purpose flour
  2 tablespoons butter, melted
  1 tablespoon sugar

In a saucepan, combine the cream, sugar and bread crumbs. Cook over medium heat until mixture begins to thicken. Remove from the heat; cool for 15 minutes. Meanwhile, divide the dough in half; press into the bottom and up the sides of two 9-in. pie plates to form a crust. Pour half of cream mixture into each crust.

Drop spoonfuls of pie filling over cream layer. Combine topping ingredients; sprinkle over filling. Bake at 350° for 25-30 minutes or until edges are golden brown and center is set. **Yield:** 2 kuchens (8-10 servings each).

CHOCOLATE SNACK CAKE
(Pictured below)

Sandra Carroll, Avoca, Iowa

My husband always asks me to make this cake for his birthday. But we enjoy it so much, I make it year-round.

✓ Uses less fat, sugar or salt. Includes Nutritional Analysis and Diabetic Exchanges.

1/2 cup butter, softened
1-1/2 cups sugar
  1 cup cold water
  2 cups cake flour
1/2 cup baking cocoa
  1 teaspoon baking soda
1/4 teaspoon salt
  1 teaspoon vanilla extract
  3 egg whites
  2 teaspoons confectioners' sugar

In a mixing bowl, cream butter and sugar. Beat in water. Combine the flour, cocoa, baking soda and salt; add to creamed mixture and mix well. Add vanilla. In another bowl, beat egg whites on medium speed until soft peaks form. Gently fold into the creamed mixture.

Pour into a 9-in. square baking pan coated with nonstick cooking spray. Bake at 350° for 40-45 minutes or until a toothpick inserted near the center comes out clean. Cool on a wire rack. Dust with confectioners' sugar. **Yield:** 12 servings.

Nutritional Analysis: One piece equals 260 calories, 8 g fat (5 g saturated fat), 21 mg cholesterol, 247 mg sodium, 45 g carbohydrate, 2 g fiber, 4 g protein. **Diabetic Exchanges:** 3 starch, 1-1/2 fat.

or until thickened. Remove from the heat; stir in vanilla. Serve warm sauce over cake. If desired, garnish with mint. **Yield:** 12-15 servings.

RHUBARB BREAD PUDDING
(Pictured below)

Virginia Andersen, Palermo, North Dakota

My mother gave me the recipe for this old-fashioned pudding. It's a great way to use up day-old bread. Nothing enhances this traditional dessert better than garden-grown rhubarb.

        8 slices bread, lightly toasted
    1-1/2 cups milk
      1/4 cup butter
        5 eggs, lightly beaten
        3 cups chopped fresh *or* frozen rhubarb, thawed
    1-1/2 cups sugar
      1/2 teaspoon ground cinnamon
      1/4 teaspoon salt
      1/2 cup packed brown sugar

Remove crusts from bread; cut into 1/2-in. cubes. Place in a greased 1-1/2-qt. baking dish. In a saucepan, heat milk over medium heat until bubbles form around sides of pan; remove from the heat. Stir in butter until melted. Pour over bread; let stand for 15 minutes.

In a bowl, combine the eggs, rhubarb, sugar, cinnamon and salt; stir into bread mixture. Sprinkle with brown sugar. Bake at 350° for 45-50 minutes or until set. Serve warm. Refrigerate leftovers. **Yield:** 8 servings.

CHOCOLATE CAKE WITH FUDGE SAUCE
(Pictured above)

Lydia Briscoe, Scott Depot, West Virginia

My whole family makes sure to leave room for dessert when this wonderful cake is on the menu. We all love chocolate and agree this rich, quick and easy recipe is one of the yummiest ways to enjoy it.

        1 package (3.4 ounces) cook-and-serve chocolate pudding/pie filling mix
        2 cups milk
        1 package (18-1/4 ounces) chocolate cake mix
SAUCE:
      1/2 cup butter
        1 cup (6 ounces) semisweet chocolate chips
        1 can (12 ounces) evaporated milk
        2 cups confectioners' sugar
        1 teaspoon vanilla extract
Variegated mint, optional

In a saucepan or microwave, prepare pudding with milk according to package directions for pudding. Pour into a mixing bowl; add dry cake mix and beat until well blended. Spread into a greased 13-in. x 9-in. x 2-in. baking pan. Bake at 350° for 30-35 minutes or until cake springs back when lightly touched and edges pull away from sides of pan. Cool on a wire rack.

For sauce, in a heavy saucepan, melt butter and chocolate over low heat. Stir in evaporated milk and sugar until smooth. Bring to a boil over medium heat; cook and stir for 8 minutes

Cakes, Pies & Desserts

TROPICAL PINEAPPLE DESSERT

Darlene Markel, Salem, Oregon

We love Hawaii, and when we aren't visiting the beautiful Islands, I keep the Hawaiian spirit at home by serving this delicious dessert.

✓ **Uses less fat, sugar or salt. Includes Nutritional Analysis and Diabetic Exchanges.**

- 1 cup all-purpose flour
- 1 cup sugar
- 1 teaspoon salt
- 1/2 teaspoon baking soda
- 1 egg, lightly beaten
- 1 can (20 ounces) unsweetened crushed pineapple, drained
- 1/2 cup flaked coconut
- 1/2 cup chopped macadamia nuts
- 3 tablespoons brown sugar

In a bowl, combine the flour, sugar, salt and baking soda. Stir in egg and pineapple until well blended. Transfer to a 9-in. pie plate coated with nonstick cooking spray. Combine the coconut, nuts and brown sugar; sprinkle over batter.

Bake at 350° for 40-45 minutes or until a toothpick inserted near the center comes out clean. Serve warm. **Yield:** 8 servings.

Nutritional Analysis: One piece equals 307 calories, 9 g fat (3 g saturated fat), 27 mg cholesterol, 420 mg sodium, 54 g carbohydrate, 3 g fiber, 4 g protein. **Diabetic Exchanges:** 2 starch, 2 fat, 1 fruit.

HEAVENLY CHEESECAKE

Rhonda Drullard, San Joaquin Valley, California

This cheesecake is one of my family's favorites. The chocolaty creation really lives up to its name.

- 1-1/2 cups chocolate wafer crumbs
- 5 tablespoons butter, melted
- 1 envelope unflavored gelatin
- 1 cup milk
- 5 Milky Way candy bars (2.05 ounces *each*), *divided*
- 2 packages (8 ounces *each*) cream cheese, softened
- 2 tablespoons sugar
- 1 teaspoon vanilla extract
- 1 cup heavy whipping cream

In a bowl, combine wafer crumbs and butter. Press onto the bottom and 1 in. up the sides of a greased 9-in. springform pan. Refrigerate. In a saucepan, sprinkle gelatin over milk; let stand for 1 minute. Cook and stir over low heat until

gelatin is dissolved. Cut four candy bars into quarters; add to gelatin mixture. Cook until candy bars are melted and mixture is smooth. Remove from the heat; set aside.

In a mixing bowl, beat cream cheese and sugar; add gelatin mixture and vanilla. Add cream; beat on high speed for 4 minutes. Pour into crust. Refrigerate for at least 4 hours or until firm. Slice or chop remaining candy bar for garnish. **Yield:** 12 servings.

RASPBERRY BREEZE PIE

(Pictured above)

Pamela Baldwin, Columbia, Tennessee

One way to my family's heart is through great-tasting food. Luckily, I've learned to take a few shortcuts to get there. This no-bake pie is a good example. Using canned pie filling and a prepared crust gets me out of the kitchen quickly.

- 1 package (8 ounces) cream cheese, softened
- 1 cup confectioners' sugar
- 1 teaspoon vanilla extract
- 1 cup whipped topping
- 1 graham cracker crust (8 or 9 inches)
- 1-3/4 cups raspberry, cherry *or* strawberry pie filling
- 1/4 teaspoon almond extract
- Sliced almonds

In a mixing bowl, beat the cream cheese, sugar and vanilla until smooth. Fold in the whipped topping. Spoon into crust. Combine the pie filling and extract; spread over the cream cheese layer. Garnish with sliced almonds. **Yield:** 6-8 servings.

MAPLE SUGAR CAKE
(Pictured below)

Elin Lee, Lancaster, Massachusetts

Old-fashioned maple sugar frosting tops this tasty spice cake. Its homemade goodness and simplicity were just what the judges were looking for at the local fair where it won a blue ribbon.

  1/2 cup butter, softened
1-1/4 cups packed brown sugar
    3 eggs
  1/2 cup maple syrup
  1/4 cup milk
  1/4 cup sour cream
    1 teaspoon maple flavoring
2-1/2 cups cake flour
    2 teaspoons baking powder
  1/2 teaspoon baking soda
  1/2 teaspoon salt
  1/2 teaspoon ground cloves
  1/4 teaspoon *each* ground allspice, nutmeg
     and mace
MAPLE SUGAR FROSTING:
    6 tablespoons butter, softened
1-1/2 teaspoons maple flavoring
4-1/2 cups confectioners' sugar
  1/2 to 3/4 cup sour cream
Chopped walnuts, optional

In a mixing bowl, cream butter and brown sugar. Add eggs, one at a time, beating well after each addition. In a bowl, combine the syrup, milk, sour cream and maple flavoring. In another bowl, com-

bine the flour, baking powder, baking soda, salt, cloves, allspice, nutmeg and mace; add to creamed mixture alternately with syrup mixture.

Pour into two greased and floured 9-in. round baking pans. Bake at 350° for 20-25 minutes or until a toothpick inserted near the center comes out clean. Cool for 10 minutes before removing from pans to a wire rack to cool.

For frosting, in a mixing bowl, cream butter and maple flavoring. Gradually beat in the confectioners' sugar. Add enough sour cream to achieve spreading consistency. Spread frosting between layers and over top and sides of cake. Sprinkle with walnuts if desired. Store in the refrigerator. **Yield:** 12-14 servings.

CHOCOLATE MALTED ICE CREAM
(Pictured above)

Rose Hare, Mountain Home, Idaho

As a child, I helped crank out gallons of homemade ice cream. And thanks to this recipe, I'm carrying on the tradition in my family. We're chocolate fans—so you can imagine the reaction when we spoon up this fudgy summer treat.

    5 eggs, beaten
    1 cup sugar
  1/2 cup chocolate malted milk powder
    2 cups milk
    1 tablespoon vanilla extract
    4 cups heavy whipping cream
    1 cup malted milk balls, coarsely crushed

In a heavy saucepan, combine the eggs, sugar and malted milk powder. Gradually add milk.

Cook and stir over low heat until mixture reaches 160° and coats the back of a metal spoon. Remove from the heat.

Cool quickly by placing pan in a bowl of ice water; stir for 2 minutes. Stir in vanilla. Press plastic wrap onto surface of custard. Refrigerate for several hours or overnight.

Stir in cream and malted milk balls. Fill cylinder of ice cream freezer two-thirds full; freeze according to manufacturer's instructions. Refrigerate remaining mixture until ready to freeze. Allow to ripen in ice cream freezer or firm up in your refrigerator freezer 2-4 hours before serving. **Yield:** 2 quarts.

STRAWBERRY TRIFLE

Norma Steiner, Monroe, Wisconsin

I won first prize in a dairy recipe contest with this tasty trifle. You can double the recipe and make two for large groups.

    1 cup cold milk
    1 cup (8 ounces) sour cream
    1 package (3.4 ounces) instant vanilla
        pudding mix
    1 teaspoon grated orange peel
    2 cups heavy whipping cream, whipped
    8 cups cubed angel food cake
    4 cups sliced fresh strawberries

In a mixing bowl, beat the milk, sour cream, pudding mix and orange peel on low speed until thickened. Fold in whipped cream.

Place half of the cake cubes in a 3-qt. glass bowl. Arrange a third of the strawberries around sides of bowl and over cake; top with half of the pudding mixture. Repeat layers once. Top with remaining berries. Refrigerate for 2 hours before serving. **Yield:** 8-10 servings.

LEMON SURPRISE CHEESECAKE
(Pictured at right)

Karen Chesnut, Clarksburg, California

I love lemon pie and cheesecake—and when I whip up this treat, I can have them both for dessert!

1-1/2 cups lemon cream-filled sandwich
        cookie crumbs
    1/4 cup butter, melted
    2 tablespoons sugar
LEMON FILLING:
    2/3 cup plus 2 tablespoons sugar
    5 tablespoons cornstarch

    1 cup water
    2 egg yolks, slightly beaten
    1/3 cup lemon juice
    2 tablespoons butter
    1 teaspoon grated lemon peel
CHEESECAKE LAYER:
    1 envelope unflavored gelatin
    1/2 cup lemon juice
    3 packages (8 ounces *each*) cream cheese,
        softened
    3/4 cup sugar
    1 cup heavy whipping cream, whipped
    2 teaspoons grated lemon peel

Combine the cookie crumbs, butter and sugar; press onto the bottom of a lightly greased 9-in. springform pan. Bake at 350° for 8-10 minutes or until crust just begins to brown. Cool on a wire rack.

In saucepan, combine sugar and cornstarch. Stir in water until smooth. Bring to a boil; cook and stir for 2 minutes or until thickened. Remove from the heat. Stir a small amount of hot filling into egg yolks. Return all to pan, stirring constantly. Bring to a gentle boil; cook and stir for 2 minutes. Remove from the heat; stir in lemon juice, butter and peel. Cool.

In a small saucepan, sprinkle gelatin over lemon juice; let stand for 1 minute. Heat over low heat, stirring until gelatin is dissolved. Remove from heat. In a mixing bowl, beat cream cheese and sugar. Gradually beat in gelatin mixture until combined. Fold in the whipped cream and lemon peel.

Spoon three-fourths of cheesecake mixture into crust; build up edges slightly. Chill for 5 minutes. Spoon lemon filling over cheesecake layer to within 1/2 in. of edges. Top with remaining cheesecake mixture. Cover and refrigerate overnight. Carefully run a knife around edge of pan; remove sides of pan. Refrigerate leftovers. **Yield:** 12 servings.

3/4 cup plus 2 tablespoons sugar
2/3 cup baking cocoa
1/2 cup plus 2 tablespoons all-purpose flour
1/2 teaspoon salt
2-1/2 cups milk
2 cups heavy whipping cream
2 teaspoons vanilla extract

In a 2-1/2-qt. microwave-safe bowl, combine the sugar, cocoa, flour and salt. Gradually whisk in milk and cream until smooth. Cover with waxed paper. Microwave on high for 12 minutes or until thickened, whisking every 4 minutes. Whisk in the vanilla. Pour into dessert dishes. Serve warm, or press a piece of waxed paper or plastic wrap on top of pudding and refrigerate. **Yield:** 6 servings.

Editor's Note: This recipe was tested in an 850-watt microwave.

ALMOND CRANBERRY SAUCE
(Pictured above)

Doris Eastlund, Isanti, Minnesota

This homemade sauce is scrumptious served over pound cake. It's nice for when company's coming because it can be made ahead of time.

    2 cups fresh *or* frozen cranberries
1-1/4 cups sugar
  1/2 cup water
  1/3 cup apricot preserves
    5 teaspoons cornstarch
    2 tablespoons cold water
  1/4 cup slivered almonds
    1 tablespoon lemon juice
    1 loaf (10-3/4 ounces) frozen pound
       cake, thawed and sliced
Whipped topping

In a large saucepan, combine cranberries, sugar, water and preserves. Bring to a boil over medium heat. Reduce heat; simmer, uncovered, until cranberries pop, about 10 minutes, stirring occasionally.

Combine cornstarch and cold water until smooth; stir into cranberry mixture. Bring to a boil; cook and stir for 2 minutes or until thickened. Stir in almonds and lemon juice. Serve over pound cake. Garnish with whipped topping. Refrigerate leftovers. **Yield:** 2-1/4 cups.

HOMEMADE COCOA PUDDING

Lynn Steele, Brookville, Ohio

You can make this pudding into a rocky road version by stirring in mini marshmallows and pecans. It also makes a great pie when poured into a crust.

PLUM KUCHEN
(Pictured below)

Gretchen Berendt, Carroll Valley, Pennsylvania

I remember my mother making plum kuchen. She never followed a recipe, but this recipe tastes like hers.

    2 eggs
  1/3 cup milk
    3 tablespoons butter, melted
    1 cup all-purpose flour
  1/2 cup plus 2 tablespoons sugar, *divided*
    1 teaspoon baking powder

1-1/4 teaspoons ground cinnamon, *divided*
1/4 teaspoon salt
1/4 teaspoon ground nutmeg
6 medium plums, pitted and halved
Whipped cream and additional ground nutmeg,
optional

In a mixing bowl, beat the eggs, milk and butter. Combine the flour, 1/2 cup sugar, baking powder, 3/4 teaspoon cinnamon, salt and nutmeg; add to the egg mixture and beat just until combined. Pour into a greased 9-in. round baking pan. Place plums cut side up over batter. Combine remaining sugar and cinnamon; sprinkle over the top.

Bake at 375° for 20-25 minutes or until a toothpick inserted near the center comes out clean. Cool for 10 minutes before removing from pan to a wire rack to cool completely. Serve with whipped cream and sprinkle with nutmeg if desired. **Yield:** 6 servings.

BROWN SUGAR ANGEL FOOD CAKE

Nina Summan, Connersville, Indiana

For a new twist on angel food cake, give this recipe a try. It's light and tasty!

☑ **Uses less fat, sugar or salt. Includes Nutritional Analysis and Diabetic Exchanges.**

1-1/2 cups egg whites (about 1 dozen)
2 cups packed brown sugar, *divided*
1-1/4 cups cake flour
1-1/2 teaspoons cream of tartar
1 teaspoon salt
2 teaspoons vanilla extract

Place egg whites in a mixing bowl; let stand at room temperature for 30 minutes. Sift 1 cup brown sugar and flour together twice; set aside. Sift remaining sugar; set aside.

Beat egg whites until foamy. Add cream of tartar and salt; beat until soft peaks form. Add vanilla. Gradually add reserved sugar, about 2 tablespoons at a time, beating well after each addition; beat until stiff glossy peaks form. Gradually fold in flour mixture, about 1/2 cup at a time.

Gently spoon into an ungreased 10-in. tube pan. Bake at 350° for 40-45 minutes or until lightly browned and entire top appears dry. Immediately invert pan onto a wire rack and cool completely, about 1 hour. Run a knife around side of cake and remove to a serving plate. **Yield:** 12 servings.

Nutritional Analysis: One piece equals 197 calories, trace fat (trace saturated fat), 0 cholesterol, 265 mg sodium, 45 g carbohydrate, trace fiber, 4 g protein.

CRUSTLESS NEW YORK CHEESECAKE

(Pictured above)

Mrs. George Parsell, Flushing, New York

This rich and flavorful cheesecake uses an abundance of dairy products. Even without a crust, this is a cheesecake I guarantee everyone will love.

1-1/2 cups sugar
3 tablespoons cornstarch
3 cups (24 ounces) ricotta cheese
2 tablespoons lemon juice
2 packages (8 ounces *each*) cream cheese, softened
1/2 cup butter, softened
4 eggs
1 teaspoon vanilla extract
2 cups (16 ounces) sour cream
3 tablespoons all-purpose flour
Assorted fresh fruit

In a large mixing bowl, combine the sugar, cornstarch, ricotta and lemon juice until smooth. Add cream cheese and butter; mix well. Add eggs and vanilla; beat on low speed just until combined. Add sour cream and flour; beat just until combined. Pour into a greased 9-in. springform pan. Place pan on a baking sheet.

Bake at 325° for 70-75 minutes or until edges are lightly brown and top is dry to the touch (center 5 in. of cheesecake will not be set). Cool on a wire rack for 10 minutes. Carefully run a knife around the edge of pan to loosen; cool 1 hour longer. Refrigerate overnight. Remove sides of pan. Garnish with fruit. Refrigerate leftovers. **Yield:** 12-16 servings.

BLUEBERRY ICE CREAM TOPPING

(Pictured at right)

Betty Leibnitz, Hallock, Minnesota

Here's the scoop on a sensational ice cream sauce! It has fresh-fruit flavor and is delicious served with angel food cake, too.

> 2 cups fresh *or* frozen blueberries
> 1 tablespoon water
> 2 tablespoons sugar
> Pinch salt
> 1/2 teaspoon cornstarch
> 1 teaspoon cold water
> 1-1/2 teaspoons lemon juice
> 1/4 teaspoon vanilla extract
> 1/8 teaspoon ground cinnamon
> Ice cream

In a saucepan, combine the blueberries, water, sugar and salt; cook and stir over low heat until sugar is dissolved. Bring to a boil. Reduce heat and simmer, uncovered, for 7 minutes or until the blueberries burst.

Combine cornstarch and cold water until smooth; stir into hot blueberry mixture. Bring to a boil; cook and stir for 1 minute or until thickened. Remove from the heat; stir in the lemon juice, vanilla and cinnamon. Serve over ice cream. **Yield:** 1-1/4 cups.

WATERMELON GELATIN DESSERT

(Pictured below)

For a refreshing change from the usual birthday cake, flavor your party with this "fruitful" favorite from our Test Kitchen staff! Since the treat is so easy to prepare, you'll likely want to serve it for other occasions...or even any day at all!

> 2 packages (3 ounces *each*) lime gelatin
> 6 cups boiling water, **divided**
> 1 package (3 ounces) watermelon gelatin
> 1 package (3 ounces) strawberry gelatin
> 2 envelopes unflavored gelatin
> 1/3 cup cold water
> 1-1/2 cups white grape juice
> 1 carton (12 ounces) frozen whipped topping, thawed

In a bowl, dissolve the lime gelatin in 3 cups boiling water. Pour into an 8-in. square dish coated with nonstick cooking spray. In a bowl, combine the watermelon and strawberry gelatins; stir in the remaining boiling water until gelatin is dissolved. Pour into another 8-in. square dish coated with nonstick cooking spray. Refrigerate both dishes until gelatin is very firm.

Meanwhile, sprinkle the unflavored gelatin over cold water; let stand for 1 minute. In a saucepan, bring grape juice to a boil; stir in softened unflavored gelatin. Stir over low heat until gelatin is dissolved. Pour into a bowl; refrigerate for 45 minutes or until slightly thickened. Gently fold in whipped topping.

Cut green gelatin into 1/2-in. cubes and red gelatin into 1-in. cubes. Place 2 cups whipped topping mixture in a bowl; fold in green gelatin. Spread into a 13-in. x 9-in. x 2-in. dish coated with nonstick cooking spray. Fold red gelatin into remaining whipped topping; spread over green gelatin layer. Refrigerate for 2 hours or until set. Cut into squares. **Yield:** 12-15 servings.

COOL STRAWBERRY CREAM

Joyce Cooper, Mount Forest, Ontario

This fruity, luscious dessert makes a wonderful ending to a special dinner. When fresh strawberries are not available, I substitute two packages of the frozen unsweetened kind, thawed and drained.

2 packages (8 ounces *each*) cream cheese, softened
3/4 cup sugar
1/2 cup sour cream
3 cups fresh strawberries, mashed
1 cup whipped topping

BLUEBERRY SAUCE:

1 package (12 ounces) frozen unsweetened blueberries
1/3 cup sugar
1/4 cup water

Line the bottom and sides of a 9-in. x 5-in. x 3-in. loaf pan with a double layer of heavy-duty foil; set aside.

In a mixing bowl, beat the cream cheese, sugar and sour cream until light. Fold in strawberries and whipped topping. Pour into prepared pan. Cover; freeze for several hours or overnight.

In a saucepan, bring the blueberries, sugar and water to a boil; cook and stir for 3 minutes. Cool slightly. Transfer to a blender; cover and puree until smooth. Cover and refrigerate.

Remove strawberry cream from the freezer 15-20 minutes before serving. Use foil to lift out of pan; remove foil. Cut into slices with a serrated knife. Serve with blueberry sauce. **Yield:** 10-12 servings.

CHOCOLATE STRAWBERRY TORTE

(Pictured at right)

Paula Magnus, Republic, Washington

I made this one year for my father-in-law's birthday, and it was a big hit. I've since made it for Easter and other spring occasions.

5 squares (1 ounce *each*) semisweet chocolate
3/4 cup butter
1-1/2 cups sugar
3 eggs
2 teaspoons vanilla extract
2-1/2 cups all-purpose flour
1 teaspoon baking soda
1/4 teaspoon salt
1-1/2 cups water

STRAWBERRY FILLING:

4 cups sliced fresh strawberries
2 tablespoons sugar
1 teaspoon vanilla extract

GLAZE:

3 squares (1 ounce *each*) semisweet chocolate
1 tablespoon butter
1 cup confectioners' sugar
3 tablespoons water
1/2 teaspoon vanilla extract
1 carton (8 ounces) frozen whipped topping, thawed

In a microwave or heavy saucepan, melt chocolate and butter; stir until smooth. Transfer to a large mixing bowl; add sugar. Add the eggs, one at a time, beating well after each addition. Beat in the vanilla.

Combine the flour, baking soda and salt; add to chocolate mixture alternately with water and beat until smooth.

Pour into two greased and floured 9-in. round baking pans. Bake at 350° for 28-33 minutes or until a toothpick inserted near the center comes out clean. Cool for 10 minutes before removing from pans to wire racks.

In a bowl, combine filling ingredients; set aside. For the glaze, in a microwave or heavy saucepan, melt chocolate and butter. Stir in confectioners' sugar, water and vanilla until smooth. Cool slightly.

To assemble, place one cake layer on a serving plate. Spread with half of whipped topping; drizzle with half of glaze. Top with half of filling. Repeat layers. **Yield:** 10-12 servings.

vanilla. Beat on low speed until well mixed. Spoon half into crust. Cut four pineapple rings in half; arrange in a spoke fashion over filling. Evenly spoon remaining filling over pineapple. Refrigerate for 6 hours or overnight.

Beat marmalade until soft and spreadable; brush 6 tablespoons on top of cheesecake. Cut remaining pineapple rings in half; arrange over marmalade. Place kiwi slices between pineapple rings. Brush with remaining marmalade. Just before serving, run a knife around edge of pan to loosen. Remove sides of pan. Refrigerate leftovers. **Yield:** 12-14 servings.

KIWI PINEAPPLE CHEESECAKE

(Pictured above and on cover)

Kimie Taziri, Fort Collins, Colorado

When I was a teacher, this dessert was the one co-workers and my students requested most often. It's light and refreshing and very easy to make.

1-3/4 cups crushed vanilla wafers (about
    50 wafers)
1/4 cup sugar
1/2 cup butter, melted
FILLING:
  1 can (20 ounces) sliced pineapple
  1 envelope unflavored gelatin
  2 packages (8 ounces *each*) cream cheese,
    softened
  1 carton (15 ounces) ricotta cheese
  1 cup confectioners' sugar
  1 tablespoon grated orange peel
  1 teaspoon vanilla extract
TOPPING:
1/2 cup orange marmalade
  1 kiwifruit, peeled, halved and sliced

In a bowl, combine the wafer crumbs and the sugar; stir in the butter. Press onto the bottom and 2 in. up the sides of a greased 9-in. springform pan. Bake at 350° for 8 minutes. Cool on a wire rack; refrigerate for 30 minutes.

Meanwhile, drain pineapple, reserving 1/2 cup juice (discard remaining juice or save for another use). In a small saucepan, sprinkle gelatin over reserved juice; let stand for 1 minute. Cook over low heat, stirring until gelatin is completely dissolved. Cool to room temperature, about 10 minutes.

In a mixing bowl, beat cream cheese, ricotta cheese and confectioners' sugar until smooth; gradually add gelatin mixture, orange peel and

STRAWBERRY YOGURT CRUNCH

(Pictured below)

Becky Palac, Escondido, California

This is a very light and delicious dessert. It's a wonderful dish to top off a spring meal.

3/4 cup butter, softened
1/3 cup packed brown sugar
1/2 cup all-purpose flour
1/2 teaspoon ground cinnamon
1/4 teaspoon baking soda
  1 cup quick-cooking oats
  1 cup flaked coconut, toasted
1/3 cup chopped nuts

1 carton (8 ounces) frozen whipped
  topping, thawed
2 cartons (6 ounces *each*) strawberry
  custard-style yogurt *or* flavor of your
  choice

In a mixing bowl, cream butter and brown sugar.
Combine the flour, cinnamon and baking soda;
gradually add to creamed mixture. Stir in the
oats, coconut and nuts. Remove 1 cup for topping. Press remaining oat mixture into an ungreased 13-in. x 9-in. x 2-in. baking dish. Bake at
350° for 12-13 minutes or until light brown. Cool
on a wire rack.

In a bowl, fold whipped topping into yogurt.
Spread over crust. Sprinkle with reserved oat
mixture. Cover and refrigerate for 4 hours or
overnight. **Yield:** 12-15 servings.

RASPBERRY RIBBON PIE
(Pictured above right)

Anita Ohlson, Oak Harbor, Washington

*It's fun to go out as a family and pick raspberries.
We always freeze some, so we can make this pie
year-round.*

1 cup vanilla wafer crumbs
1/4 cup butter, melted
1 package (3 ounces) raspberry gelatin
1 cup boiling water
1/4 cup sugar
1 cup fresh raspberries
1 tablespoon lemon juice
1 package (3 ounces) cream cheese,
  softened
1/3 cup confectioners' sugar
1 teaspoon vanilla extract
Pinch salt
1 cup heavy whipping cream
Additional whipped cream and fresh
  raspberries

In a bowl, combine the wafer crumbs and butter;
press onto the bottom and up the sides of an ungreased 9-in. pie plate. Bake at 350° for 10 minutes or until golden brown.

In a bowl, dissolve gelatin in boiling water. Add
the sugar, raspberries and lemon juice. Refrigerate
until partially set, about 1-1/2 hours.

In a mixing bowl, beat cream cheese and confectioners' sugar until smooth. Add vanilla and
salt. In a another mixing bowl, beat whipping
cream until stiff peaks form. Fold into cream
cheese mixture. Spread 3/4 cup over bottom of
crust. Spread 3/4 cup raspberry mixture over the
top; repeat layers. Refrigerate for 8 hours or

overnight before serving. Garnish pie with additional whipped cream and berries. **Yield:** 6-8
servings.

BAKED BARLEY PUDDING

Judy Berarducci, Port St. Lucie, Florida

*This dessert recipe has the same sweet and satisfying
flavor as traditional rice pudding. Smooth and cus-
tardy, it bakes up firm and golden.*

1-1/4 cups water
1/2 cup uncooked medium pearl barley
1/4 teaspoon salt
2 cups milk
1 cup heavy whipping cream
1/2 cup sugar
2 eggs
1 teaspoon vanilla extract
1/2 cup golden raisins
1/4 teaspoon ground cinnamon

In a saucepan, bring water to a boil. Stir in barley and salt. Reduce heat; simmer, uncovered, for
15 minutes, stirring occasionally. Add milk; cook
over medium-low heat for 10 minutes or until barley is almost tender, stirring frequently. In a
bowl, whisk the cream, sugar, eggs and vanilla;
gradually stir into the barley mixture.

Spoon into eight greased 6-oz. custard cups.
Sprinkle with raisins and cinnamon. Place custard
cups in two 9-in. baking pans. Fill both pans
with boiling water to a depth of 1 in. Bake, uncovered, at 350° for 30-35 minutes or until a knife
inserted near the center comes out clean. **Yield:** 8
servings.

Editor's Note: Pudding will appear layered
when baked.

KENTUCKY PEACH COBBLER

Maybellene Griffin, Beattyville, Kentucky

I've made this very easy peach cobbler for years. Not long after my son moved away from home, he called to ask me for the recipe.

> 6 medium ripe peaches, peeled and sliced (about 4 cups)
> 2 tablespoons butter, softened
> 1-1/4 cups sugar, *divided*
> 1 teaspoon vanilla extract
> 1 cup all-purpose flour
> 2 teaspoons baking powder
> Dash salt
> 1/2 cup milk
> 1/2 cup cold water
> Vanilla ice cream

Arrange peaches in a greased 11-in. x 7-in. x 2-in. baking dish. In a mixing bowl, combine butter and 1/2 cup sugar. Beat in vanilla. Combine the flour, baking powder and salt; add to creamed mixture alternately with milk. Pour over peaches; sprinkle with remaining sugar.

Pour cold water over the top. Bake at 350° for 35-40 minutes or until golden brown. Serve warm with ice cream. **Yield:** 6 servings.

PEANUT ICE CREAM PIE

(Pictured below)

Lois Sieck, Goodland, Kansas

Everyone is nuts about this rich, refreshing pie. It comes in handy as a quick and easy no-bake dessert

for church dinners, card parties, showers and drop-in company. Judges at a northwest Kansas fair declared it a grand-prize winner.

> 1-1/2 cups graham cracker crumbs (about 24 squares)
> 1/4 cup sugar
> 1/3 cup butter, softened
> 1 quart vanilla ice cream, softened
> 1/2 cup light corn syrup
> 1/3 cup chunky peanut butter
> 2/3 cup dry roasted peanuts

In a bowl, combine the cracker crumbs, sugar and butter; press onto the bottom and up the sides of an ungreased 9-in. pie plate. Spoon half of the ice cream into crust. In a small bowl, combine the corn syrup and peanut butter; spoon half over ice cream. Sprinkle with half of the peanuts. Repeat layers. Freeze until firm. **Yield:** 6-8 servings.

CHOCOLATE 'N' TOFFEE RICE PUDDING

(Pictured above)

JoAnn Vess Hilliard, East Liverpool, Ohio

I can't think of a more comforting dessert than this pudding. The toffee bits add a crunch to its creamy consistency. My husband, Frank, and I enjoy making treats like this together. It looks especially pretty layered in a parfait glass.

Cakes, Pies & Desserts

3 cups milk
3 cups cooked rice
1/2 cup packed brown sugar
3 tablespoons butter
1/4 teaspoon salt
1 teaspoon vanilla extract
1/4 cup flaked coconut, toasted
1/4 cup English toffee bits *or* almond
   brickle chips
1/4 cup miniature semisweet chocolate
   chips
1/2 cup whipped topping
7 maraschino cherries

In a large saucepan, combine the milk, rice, brown sugar, butter and salt; bring to a boil over medium heat. Cook for 15 minutes or until thick and creamy, stirring occasionally. Remove from the heat; stir in vanilla. Cool.

Spoon half of the pudding into the dessert dishes. Combine the coconut, toffee bits and chocolate chips; sprinkle half over the pudding. Repeat the layers. Refrigerate until serving. Garnish with the whipped topping and cherries.
Yield: 7 servings.

INCREDIBLE CHOCOLATE CAKE

Janice Britz, Lexington, Michigan

My brother-in-law calls this "Snicker Bar Cake" and has me make it for every family occasion. It's always the first dessert to go.

1 package (18-1/4 ounces) chocolate
   cake mix
1 can (14 ounces) sweetened
   condensed milk
1 jar (12-1/4 ounces) caramel ice cream
   topping
1 carton (12 ounces) frozen whipped
   topping, thawed
2 tablespoons baking cocoa
2 Heath candy bars (1.4 ounces *each*),
   crushed

Prepare and bake the cake mix according to the package directions, using a greased 13-in. x 9-in. x 2-in. baking pan. Place on a wire rack for 10 minutes.

Using the end of a wooden spoon handle, poke 20 holes in warm cake. Pour milk over cake; cool for 10 minutes. Pour caramel topping over cake; cool completely.

In a bowl, combine whipped topping and cocoa; spread over cake. Sprinkle with crushed candy bars. Cover and store in the refrigerator.
Yield: 12-15 servings.

TROPICAL CAKE
(Pictured below)

Doris Wendling, Palm Harbor, Florida

The lemon-lime soda and pineapple give this cake a refreshing taste.

1 package (18-1/4 ounces) yellow cake
   mix
1 package (3.4 ounces) instant vanilla
   pudding mix
1/3 cup vegetable oil
3 eggs
1-1/4 cups lemon-lime soda
TOPPING:
1 cup sugar
2 tablespoons all-purpose flour
2 eggs, lightly beaten
1/2 cup butter
1 can (8 ounces) crushed pineapple,
   drained
1 cup flaked coconut

In a large mixing bowl, combine the cake and pudding mixes, oil and eggs; beat on low speed until smooth. Add soda; beat on medium for 2 minutes. Pour into a greased 13-in. x 9-in. x 2-in. baking pan. Bake at 350° for 35-40 minutes or until a toothpick inserted near the center comes out clean. Place on a wire rack.

In a saucepan, combine the sugar, flour, eggs, butter and pineapple. Cook and stir over medium heat until mixture is thickened and a thermometer reads 160°. Remove from the heat; stir in coconut. Spread over warm cake. Cool for 1 hour. Cover and refrigerate. **Yield:** 12-16 servings.

In a mixing bowl, combine the eggs, brown sugar, oil and orange peel; mix well. Combine the flour, baking soda, cinnamon, baking powder, salt and cloves; beat into egg mixture. Stir in carrots and cranberries. Pour into two greased and floured 9-in. round baking pans.

Bake at 350° for 25-30 minutes or until a toothpick inserted near the center comes out clean. Cool for 10 minutes before removing from pans to wire racks to cool completely.

For frosting, in a mixing bowl, beat cream cheese and butter until fluffy. Gradually beat in confectioners' sugar, milk, ginger and orange peel if desired. Split each cake into two horizontal layers. Spread frosting between layers and over top and sides of cake. **Yield:** 12-14 servings.

BUTTERNUT APPLE CRISP
(Pictured below)

Therese Butler, Ijamsville, Maryland

Someone brought this crisp to a parish dinner at my church. I asked for the recipe, and now I take this yummy dessert to every potluck I attend.

  3/4 cup packed brown sugar, *divided*
    1 teaspoon ground cinnamon
  1/2 teaspoon salt
    2 pounds butternut squash, peeled, seeded and thinly sliced (about 4 cups)
    1 can (21 ounces) apple pie filling
    2 tablespoons lemon juice
  1/2 cup all-purpose flour
  1/2 cup quick-cooking oats
    6 tablespoons cold butter

CRANBERRY-CARROT LAYER CAKE
(Pictured above)

Nellie Runne, Rockford, Illinois

This moist cake smothered with rich cream cheese frosting makes any dinner festive. Every autumn, I go to a cranberry festival in Wisconsin and load up on fresh cranberries to freeze for year-round cooking.

    4 eggs
1-1/2 cups packed brown sugar
1-1/4 cups vegetable oil
    1 teaspoon grated orange peel
    2 cups all-purpose flour
    1 teaspoon baking soda
    1 teaspoon ground cinnamon
  3/4 teaspoon baking powder
  1/2 teaspoon salt
  1/4 teaspoon ground cloves
    2 cups shredded carrots
    1 cup dried cranberries
CREAM CHEESE FROSTING:
    2 packages (8 ounces *each*) cream cheese, softened
  3/4 cup butter, softened
    4 cups confectioners' sugar
    1 tablespoon milk
  1/2 teaspoon ground ginger
  1/2 teaspoon grated orange peel, optional

In a bowl, combine 1/2 cup brown sugar, cinnamon and salt. Add squash, pie filling and lemon juice. Pour into a greased 9-in. square baking dish. Cover and bake at 350° for 30 minutes.

In a small bowl, combine the flour, oats and remaining brown sugar. Cut in butter until mixture resembles coarse crumbs. Sprinkle over squash mixture. Bake 45-50 minutes longer or until topping is golden brown and squash is tender. **Yield:** 9 servings.

CITRUS APPLE PIE

Beatrice Jacobs, Portland, Oregon

I found this recipe in my early years of cooking, and it's been a favorite of my five children ever since. It's different, zesty and flavorful. I prefer to serve it warm.

Pastry for double-crust pie (9 inches)
- 1-1/2 cups sugar
- 5 teaspoons all-purpose flour
- 2 teaspoons grated orange peel
- 1 teaspoon grated lemon peel
- 1/4 cup orange juice
- 1 tablespoon lemon juice
- 4 cups shredded peeled tart apples (about 4 large)
- 2 eggs, beaten

Line a 9-in. pie plate with bottom pastry; trim pastry even with edge of plate. In a bowl, combine the sugar, flour, and orange and lemon peels. Stir in juices. Add apples and toss to coat. Stir in eggs. Pour into crust.

Roll out remaining pastry; make a lattice crust. Seal and flute edges. Cover edges loosely with foil. Bake at 450° for 15 minutes. Remove foil; reduce heat to 350°. Bake 30-35 minutes longer or until crust is golden brown and filling is bubbly. Cool on a wire rack. **Yield:** 6-8 servings.

BLUEBERRY BUCKLE

(Pictured above right)

Helen Dodge, Meriden, Connecticut

I used to buy baskets of delicious blueberries from a man who had numerous bushes. One of my co-workers gave me this recipe, and it's become a favorite.

- 1/4 cup shortening
- 3/4 cup sugar
- 1 egg
- 2 cups all-purpose flour
- 2 teaspoons baking powder
- 1/2 teaspoon salt
- 1/2 cup milk
- 2 cups fresh *or* frozen blueberries*

TOPPING:
- 1/2 cup sugar
- 1/3 cup all-purpose flour
- 1/2 teaspoon ground cinnamon
- 1/4 cup cold butter

In a mixing bowl, cream the shortening and sugar. Beat in egg; mix well. Combine the flour, baking powder and salt; add alternately to creamed mixture with milk. Fold in blueberries. Pour into a greased 9-in. square baking dish.

For topping, combine the sugar, flour and cinnamon; cut in butter until mixture resembles coarse crumbs. Sprinkle over batter. Bake at 350° for 40-45 minutes or until a toothpick inserted near the center comes clean. Cool for 10 minutes before cutting. Serve warm or cooled. **Yield:** 9 servings.

Editor's Note: If using frozen blueberries, do not thaw before adding to batter.

BEFORE YOU BEGIN BAKING...

Here are a few tips to keep in mind next time you're ready to bake:

- Always place the oven rack(s) in the desired position before heating the oven.
- Unless a recipe indicates otherwise, always preheat an oven for 10 to 15 minutes before beginning to bake.
- Glass bakeware conducts and retains heat better than metal, so oven temperatures should be reduced by 25° whenever glass containers are used.

Rhubarb Hints

• For a tasty change of pace, use raspberries instead of strawberries in rhubarb pies. I like to serve the pie warm with a dollop of real whipped cream. —*Alicia Spychala*
St. Joseph, Minnesota

• Thaw frozen rhubarb in a colander placed over a bowl to catch the rhubarb juice. The juice can be used in place of water for a flavor boost in many fruit recipes.
—*Donna Lewis*
Antwerp, New York

• Rhubarb will react with aluminum, so it's best to always bake it in a glass dish. —*Pat Rankin*
Parry Sound, Ontario

• When planting new rhubarb, I sow the roots in the spring and let them grow undisturbed until the following spring—when the stalks will be ready for picking.
—*Monica Pink*
Jordan, Minnesota

• Protect rhubarb in the winter by covering plants with mulch.
—*Kathy Bardwell*
Roy, Utah

• As a birthday treat for my grandchildren, I bake them their own "personal" 7-inch rhubarb pie.
—*Florence Fuller*
Houghton, New York

• Tender, young stalks are easiest to use. They need only to be cut before cooking. Rhubarb with tougher stalks can be peeled with a vegetable peeler to remove fibrous strings before they are cut or cooked. —*Marie Mertz*
Racine, Wisconsin

• Instead of making one large rhubard coffee cake, I'll bake the batter as cupcakes and share with friends and co-workers. I find the cupcakes bake in about 15-17 minutes. —*Shirley Perley*
Nesbit, Manitoba

• Treat unexpected guests to rhubarb pies by making two or three at one time. Bake one for your family and freeze the remaining unbaked pies. The frozen pies should take only 20-30 minutes longer to bake. —*Linda Sterenberg*
Nobleford, Alberta

• To harvest rhubarb, just give the stalk a good pull and it will pop right off of the plant.
—*Hilde Tompkins*
Greenville, New York

• To save time when I make rhubarb crunch, I cook the cornstarch, water and flavoring in the microwave oven rather than on the stovetop. —*Lorraine Black*
Barnum, Iowa

• To help prevent the crust from getting soggy on my rhubarb custard pie, I sprinkle sugar on the crust before pouring in the filling. —*Connie Dahmer*
Marion, Illinois

• Rhubarb freezes so easily and is great to have all year-round. I cut the rhubarb into various sizes before freezing—large chunks for fruit pies, thin pieces for breads, etc. Then I package the rhubarb in just the amount needed for each type of recipe. And I label each container with the amount and size of rhubarb inside. —*Michele Trevathan*
Grand Rapids, Michigan

FANTASTIC FLAN PIE

Ireta Schoun, Montgomery, Michigan

I made this pie recently for the first time, and it was delicious! It's creamy and slightly sweet.

Pastry for single-crust pie (9 inches)
    4 eggs
    1 cup milk
    1 can (14 ounces) sweetened condensed milk
  1/2 cup sugar
    1 teaspoon vanilla extract
  1/2 teaspoon salt
Fresh raspberries and blackberries

Line a 9-in. pie plate with pastry. Trim, seal and flute edges. Prick dough several times with a fork. Bake at 450° for 8-9 minutes or until lightly browned. Meanwhile, in a blender or food processor, combine the eggs, milk, condensed milk, sugar, vanilla and salt; cover and process until smooth.

Pour filling into crust. Cover edges with foil. Bake at 400° for 15 minutes. Reduce heat to 350°; bake 20 minutes longer or until a knife inserted near the center comes out clean. Cool on a wire

rack for 1 hour. Cover and refrigerate until chilled. Garnish with fruit. Refrigerate leftovers. **Yield:** 6-8 servings.

WHITE CHOCOLATE LIME MOUSSE CAKE

(Pictured above)

Margery Richmond, Fort Collins, Colorado

The line at the dessert table convinced me this cake was a winner when I served it at a party. The zippy lime and gingersnap flavors really come through.

    2 cups crushed gingersnaps (about 38 cookies)
    2 tablespoons sugar
    1/3 cup butter, melted
FILLING:
    1 envelope unflavored gelatin
    6 tablespoons lime juice
    9 squares (1 ounce *each*) white baking chocolate, chopped
2-1/2 cups heavy whipping cream, *divided*
    3 packages (8 ounces *each*) cream cheese, softened
    1 cup sugar
    1 tablespoon grated lime peel

Combine the gingersnaps, sugar and butter; press onto the bottom and 1 in. up the sides of a greased 9-in. springform pan. Set aside.

In a microwave-safe dish, sprinkle gelatin over lime juice. Let stand for 1 minute. Microwave on high for 10-20 seconds; stir until gelatin is dissolved. Set aside. In a heavy saucepan or microwave, melt chocolate with 1/2 cup cream; stir until smooth. Cool slightly; stir in dissolved gelatin.

In a mixing bowl, beat cream cheese and sugar until smooth. Gradually add chocolate mixture and lime peel; mix well. In another mixing bowl, beat the remaining cream until stiff peaks form. Gently fold into cream cheese mixture. Spoon over the crust. Cover and chill overnight. Refrigerate leftovers. **Yield:** 12-16 servings.

WALNUT APPLE PIE

(Pictured below)

Diane Laverty, Marysville, Pennsylvania

Adding walnuts gives a slight twist to traditional apple pie recipes and adds a unique flavor we really enjoy.

    4 to 5 large tart apples, peeled and sliced
    1 tablespoon lemon juice
    1/2 cup sugar
    1/4 cup packed brown sugar
    1/2 cup chopped walnuts
    2 tablespoons quick-cooking tapioca
    1/2 teaspoon ground cinnamon
    1/4 teaspoon ground nutmeg
Pastry for double-crust pie (9 inches)
    2 tablespoons butter

In a bowl, toss apples with lemon juice. Combine the sugars, nuts, tapioca, cinnamon and nutmeg; add to apples and toss to coat. Let stand for 15 minutes.

Line a 9-in. pie plate with bottom pastry; trim even with edge. Add apple mixture; dot with butter. Roll out remaining pastry to fit top of pie; place over filling. Trim, seal and flute edges. Cut slits in top. Cover edges loosely with foil. Bake at 400° for 40-45 minutes or until crust is brown and filling is bubbly. Cool on a wire rack. **Yield:** 6-8 servings.

Meanwhile, for sauce, combine the sugar, cornstarch and cinnamon in a saucepan. Stir in rhubarb. Bring to a boil over medium heat; cook and stir for 2 minutes or until slightly thickened and rhubarb is tender. Remove from the heat; cool slightly.

For filling, in a mixing bowl, beat cream cheese and 1/4 cup of the rhubarb sauce until smooth and creamy. Place a rounded tablespoonful on each crepe; fold in half and in half again, forming a triangle. Dust with confectioners' sugar. Serve with remaining sauce. **Yield:** 10 crepes.

CREAMY RHUBARB CREPES
(Pictured above)

Stasha Wampler, Gate City, Virginia

Fixing rhubarb this way brings a spring "zing" to the table. I adapted this crepe recipe, which originally featured strawberry jelly, from one I loved as a child. My husband declared it a "winner". He even came up with its name.

    3 eggs
    1 cup milk
    5 tablespoons butter, melted
1/4 cup sugar
1/4 teaspoon salt
    1 cup all-purpose flour
Additional butter
SAUCE/FILLING:
    1 cup sugar
    1 tablespoon cornstarch
1/4 teaspoon ground cinnamon
    2 cups thinly sliced fresh *or* frozen
        rhubarb, thawed
    1 package (8 ounces) cream cheese,
        softened
Confectioners' sugar

In a bowl, whisk eggs, milk, melted butter, sugar and salt. Beat in flour until smooth; let stand for 30 minutes. Melt 1/2 teaspoon butter in an 8-in. nonstick skillet. Pour 1/4 cup batter into the center of skillet; lift and turn pan to cover bottom.

Cook until lightly browned; turn and brown the other side. Remove to a wire rack; cover with paper towel. Repeat with remaining batter, adding butter to skillet as needed.

FRUIT-FILLED WHITE CAKE
(Pictured below)

Sally Beardsworth, Warwick, Rhode Island

Your guests may think this dessert is too pretty to eat. But the flavorful cake, fluffy frosting and fun fruit filling will tempt them into changing their minds.

1/2 cup butter, softened
1-1/2 cups sugar
    4 egg whites
    2 teaspoons vanilla extract
2-1/4 cups cake flour
    3 teaspoons baking powder
1/2 teaspoon salt
    1 cup milk
FILLING/TOPPING:
    2 envelopes whipped topping mix
2/3 cup milk

1 cup vanilla *or* white chips, melted
1/4 cup strawberry jam
1 can (8 ounces) crushed pineapple, well
  drained
1 cup sliced fresh strawberries

In a large mixing bowl, cream butter and sugar. Add egg whites, two at a time, beating well after each addition. Beat in vanilla. Combine the flour, baking powder and salt; add to creamed mixture alternately with milk.

Pour into two greased and floured 9-in. baking pans. Bake at 350° for 18-22 minutes or until a toothpick inserted near the center comes out clean. Cool for 10 minutes before removing from pans to wire racks.

In a mixing bowl, beat topping mix and milk on high speed for 4 minutes or until thickened. Combine melted chips and jam; gradually beat into topping. Set aside 1 cup for filling. Cover and chill remaining mixture for 20 minutes or until it reaches spreading consistency.

Add pineapple and strawberries to reserved filling. Place one cake layer on a serving plate; spread with fruit mixture. Top with remaining cake layer. Frost top and sides of cake with chilled topping. Store in the refrigerator. **Yield:** 10-12 servings.

WHITE CHOCOLATE CONES

Hand out these dipped delights, and they'll disappear lickety-split! Our Test Kitchen staff made the ice cream extra-special by topping it with melted white chocolate.

4-1/2 cups ice cream
  6 sugar cones
1-1/4 pounds white chocolate
1/4 cup vegetable oil

Spoon a small amount of ice cream into each cone; press gently. Place a large scoop on cone; press gently. Place each cone in a glass; freeze for 2 hours.

Cut 3/4 pound of white chocolate into chunks; set the remaining chocolate aside. In a microwave-safe bowl, combine the chocolate chunks and oil. Microwave at 50% power for 3 minutes, stirring every minute or until melted and smooth. Let stand until mixture reaches room temperature, about 45 minutes.

Using a vegetable peeler, shave the remaining chocolate. Dip ice cream into melted chocolate mixture; immediately sprinkle with shaved chocolate. Return cones to glasses; freeze until chocolate is set. **Yield:** 6 servings.

Editor's Note: This recipe was tested in an 850-watt microwave.

CRANBERRY RAISIN PIE

(Pictured above)

Ruth Judson, Oakham, Massachusetts

There are many cranberry bogs in our state, especially on Cape Cod. The delicious combination of cranberries and raisins make this pie memorable.

  1 cup sugar
4-1/2 teaspoons all-purpose flour
1/2 cup water
1-1/2 cups chopped fresh *or* frozen
  cranberries
3/4 cup raisins, finely chopped
  1 tablespoon butter
1-1/2 teaspoons vanilla extract
Pastry for a double-crust pie (9 inches)
Half-and-half cream, optional

In a large saucepan, combine sugar and flour. Stir in water until blended; bring to a boil. Add cranberries and raisins. Reduce heat; cover and simmer for 15 minutes, stirring occasionally. Remove from the heat; stir in butter and vanilla until butter is melted. Cool slightly.

Line a 9-in. pie plate with bottom pastry; trim to 1 in. beyond edge of pie plate. Pour filling into crust. Roll out remaining pastry; cut into lattice strips and place over filling. Seal and flute edges. Brush lattice crust with cream if desired.

Bake at 375° for 30 minutes or until crust is golden brown and filling is bubbly, covering edges with foil during the last 10 minutes. Cool on a wire rack. Refrigerate leftovers. **Yield:** 6-8 servings.

Cooking for Two

Cooking for Two

Want fulfilling meals without the leftovers? These recipes provide perfect portions for two!

APRICOT-GLAZED CHICKEN

(Pictured at left)

Retha Kaye Naylor, Frankton, Indiana

My husband knows what's on the menu when our boys come home from college. This main dish has become our homecoming tradition.

- 2 boneless skinless chicken breast halves
- 1/4 cup mayonnaise
- 1/4 cup apricot preserves
- 2 tablespoons dried minced onion

Place chicken in a greased 9-in. square baking dish. Combine the mayonnaise, preserves and onion; spoon over chicken.

Bake, uncovered, at 350° for 25 minutes or until chicken juices run clear. **Yield:** 2 servings.

WALNUT COOKIE STRIPS

(Pictured at left)

June Grimm, San Rafael, California

This recipe is over 70 years old. It came from the grandmother of a friend of my son's, when he was a Boy Scout. This was his troop's favorite cookie.

- 1/2 cup all-purpose flour
- 1/8 teaspoon salt
- 1/4 cup cold butter
- FILLING:
- 1 egg
- 3/4 cup packed brown sugar
- 2 tablespoons all-purpose flour
- 1/2 teaspoon vanilla extract
- 1/8 teaspoon baking powder
- 1/2 cup chopped walnuts
- 1/4 cup flaked coconut
- FROSTING:
- 3/4 cup confectioners' sugar
- 1 tablespoon butter, softened
- 1 tablespoon orange juice
- 1/2 teaspoon lemon juice
- 1/4 cup chopped walnuts

In a bowl, combine flour and salt; cut in butter until crumbly. Press into a greased 9-in. x 5-in. x 3-in. loaf pan. Bake at 350° for 15 minutes or until lightly browned.

Meanwhile, in a small mixing bowl, beat egg. Add brown sugar, flour, vanilla and baking powder; mix well. Stir in nuts and coconut. Pour over hot crust. Bake 15 minutes longer or until set. Cool completely on a wire rack.

For frosting, combine the confectioners' sugar, butter and juices in a mixing bowl; beat until smooth. Spread over filling; sprinkle with nuts. Chill for 1-2 hours or until frosting is set. Store in the refrigerator. **Yield:** 2 dozen.

CORN RICE MEDLEY

(Pictured at left)

Cheryl Ivers, Orangeburg, South Carolina

Adding colorful vegetables to rice is a simple way to dress it up. This is a versatile side dish for many entrees.

- 1 cup chicken broth
- 1/2 cup uncooked long grain rice
- 1/4 cup chopped sweet red pepper
- 1 green onion, chopped
- 1 tablespoon olive oil
- 1/2 cup frozen corn, thawed
- 1 tablespoon grated Parmesan cheese

In a saucepan, bring broth to a boil; add rice. Reduce heat; cover and simmer for 10 minutes. Meanwhile, in a small skillet, saute the red pepper and green onion in oil until tender. Stir into rice. Add the corn. Cover and cook for 5 minutes or until rice is tender. Sprinkle with Parmesan cheese. **Yield:** 2 servings.

RICE TIPS

To keep rice (especially brown rice) fresh longer, store it in the refrigerator. Never stir rice while it cooks; it will crush the grains, releasing starch, and make the rice gummy.

1-1/2 teaspoons sugar
    1 medium carrot, cut into 1-1/2-inch
        julienne strips
1-1/2 cups frozen cut green beans
    1/4 to 1/2 teaspoon salt
Dash pepper
    2 bacon strips, cooked and crumbled

In a skillet, heat oil. Stir in vinegar and sugar. Add carrot strips; cook and stir for 2 minutes. Add beans; cook and stir 4-5 minutes longer or until vegetables are crisp-tender. Sprinkle with salt, pepper and bacon. **Yield:** 2 servings.

CHEESY BAKED POTATOES
(Pictured below)

Dolores Nemec, Garfield Heights, Ohio

This is a perfect recipe for two, but I also prepare it in larger quantities for special occasions when we have dinner guests. One of these potatoes is practically a meal in itself.

2 large russet potatoes
1 egg, beaten
2 tablespoons milk
2 tablespoons mayonnaise
3/4 cup shredded cheddar cheese, *divided*
1/4 teaspoon salt
Dash pepper
    2 tablespoons sliced green onion
    2 bacon strips, cooked and crumbled

TOMATO SOUP WITH A TWIST
(Pictured above)

Eleanor Stamen, Whitehall, Pennsylvania

In 1932, our junior high school cooking class teacher taught us a simple recipe starting with a can of tomato soup. As I was preparing tomato soup for lunch recently, I remembered those two additional ingredients. I had forgotten what a tasty difference the peanut butter and cheese make.

1 can (10-3/4 ounces) condensed tomato
    soup, undiluted
1 tablespoon creamy peanut butter
1-1/3 cups milk
2 tablespoons shredded cheddar cheese
Additional cheddar cheese

In a saucepan, combine the soup and peanut butter. Gradually stir in milk. Add cheese; cook and stir until peanut butter and cheese are melted and soup is heated through. Garnish with additional cheese. **Yield:** 2 servings.

GREEN BEANS WITH CARROTS

Pat MacIntosh, Delanco, New Jersey

Want to add some zip to a meal? Dish up these colorful veggies. Not only are they eye-catching, the beans and carrots are tasty, too.

1 tablespoon olive oil
1 tablespoon white wine vinegar

Bake potatoes at 375° for 1 hour or until tender. When cool enough to handle, cut a thin slice off the top of each potato; scoop out pulp, leaving a thin shell. In a bowl, mash the pulp, egg, milk, mayonnaise, 1/2 cup of cheese, salt and pepper. Spoon into potato shells. Top with onion, bacon and remaining cheese.

Place in a small ungreased baking pan. Bake, uncovered, at 375° for 25-30 minutes or until heated through. **Yield:** 2 servings.

PEACH COBBLER

Doris Heath, Franklin, North Carolina

Old-fashioned, delicious and easy-to-make describe this peach cobbler. Fresh from the oven and served with a scoop of ice cream, it will earn you rave reviews at the table.

1-1/2 teaspoons cornstarch
    1 tablespoon water
    1 can (8-1/2 ounces) sliced peaches, undrained
1/2 cup biscuit/baking mix
    2 teaspoons sugar
    2 tablespoons milk
    1 tablespoon vegetable oil

In a small saucepan, combine cornstarch and water until smooth. Stir in peaches. Cook and stir over medium heat for 5-8 minutes or until thickened. Pour into a greased 1-qt. baking dish.

In a bowl, combine biscuit mix and sugar. Stir in the milk and oil just until moistened. Drop by spoonfuls over peaches. Bake at 400° for 20-25 minutes or until the top is golden brown. **Yield:** 2 servings.

TANGY CUCUMBER GELATIN

Bernadeane McWilliam, Decatur, Illinois

A friend shared this recipe with me years ago. She had a vegetable garden and always had a good yield of cucumbers. This pleasant salad is the right amount for one or two. The cucumber and green onions give a nice texture contrast and refreshing crunch.

    1 package (3 ounces) lemon gelatin
1/2 cup boiling water
    1 medium cucumber, peeled and diced
    4 green onions, chopped
    1 cup (8 ounces) small-curd cottage cheese
1/2 cup mayonnaise *or* salad dressing

In a bowl, dissolve gelatin in boiling water. Add the cucumber and onions. Stir in cottage cheese and mayonnaise until blended. Pour into two 1-1/2-cup molds coated with nonstick cooking spray. Refrigerate overnight or until set. Unmold just before serving. **Yield:** 2 servings.

SAUCY PORK CHOPS

(Pictured above)

Dorothy Toben, Blackwell, Oklahoma

This entree brightens up the usual routine of chops and rice. I reach for this recipe when the weather is brisk and our appetites are hearty.

    2 bone-in pork loin chops (3/4 inch thick)
    2 tablespoons butter
1/4 cup chopped onion
1/4 cup water
1/4 cup maple syrup
    1 tablespoon cider vinegar
    2 teaspoons Worcestershire sauce
    1 teaspoon chili powder
1/4 teaspoon salt
1/4 teaspoon pepper
1/8 teaspoon garlic powder

In a skillet, brown pork chops on both sides in butter. Transfer to a small greased baking dish; sprinkle with onion.

In a bowl, combine the remaining ingredients. Pour over chops. Cover and bake at 350° for 20 minutes or until a meat thermometer reads 160°. **Yield:** 2 servings.

FRUIT-STUFFED CHICKEN
(Pictured at right)

Claudette Mogle, Federal Way, Washington

I created this recipe to serve at the wedding dinner for the pastor of our church. After experimenting with many different kinds of chicken dishes, I finally hit on a winner. The bride and groom were pleased, and I've made it many times for myself since!

> 2 boneless skinless chicken breast halves
> 3 tablespoons chopped dried apricots
> 3 tablespoons chopped dried cranberries
> 3 tablespoons chopped dried plums
> 1/2 cup apricot preserves
> 1 teaspoon lemon juice

Flatten chicken to 1/4-in. thickness. Combine the apricots, cranberries and plums; place half on each chicken breast. Roll up tightly; secure with toothpicks. Place seam side down in a greased 8-in. square baking dish.

In a saucepan, combine preserves and lemon juice. Cook and stir for 5 minutes over medium heat; pour half over the chicken. Keep the remaining sauce warm. Bake the chicken, uncovered, at 350° for 25 minutes or until juices run clear. Serve with warm sauce. **Yield:** 2 servings.

MERINGUE PUDDING CUPS
(Pictured at right)

Mary McMenamin, Spring City, Pennsylvania

My mother, who didn't own a cookbook, created this recipe. She fussed over ingredients until she was satisfied with the results. With nine children to feed on a limited budget, she came up with many variations of the same dish. This dessert was a special treat that we always enjoyed.

> 1 cup graham cracker crumbs (about 16 squares)
> 2 tablespoons butter, melted
> 1 tablespoon sugar
> 1 tablespoon water
> 1-3/4 cups milk
> 1 package (3 ounces) cook-and-serve vanilla pudding mix
> MERINGUE:
> 2 egg whites
> 1/4 teaspoon cream of tartar
> 2 tablespoons sugar

In a bowl, combine the cracker crumbs, butter, sugar and water; press onto the bottom and up the sides of two 10-oz. custard cups. Bake at 350° for 6 minutes or until crust is lightly browned; set aside.

In a saucepan, combine the milk and pudding mix; prepare according to package directions. Keep warm.

In a small mixing bowl, beat egg whites and cream of tartar on medium speed until soft peaks form. Gradually beat in sugar, 1 tablespoon at a time, until stiff peaks form. Spoon warm pudding into crust; spread with meringue, sealing edges to crust.

Bake at 350° for 15 minutes or until golden brown. Cool on a wire rack for 1 hour; refrigerate for 1-2 hours before serving. **Yield:** 2 servings.

BAKED ZUCCHINI
(Pictured at right)

Betty Castleberry, Livonia, Michigan

I've been preparing zucchini this way for years. It's a great side dish with many entrees.

> 2 medium zucchini, cut into 1/4-inch slices
> 2 tablespoons butter, melted
> 1 tablespoon minced fresh oregano *or* 1 teaspoon dried oregano
> 1/4 cup grated Parmesan cheese
> Salt and pepper to taste

In a bowl, toss the zucchini, butter and oregano. Arrange in a single layer on a greased baking sheet or shallow baking dish; sprinkle with Parmesan cheese. Bake, uncovered, at 350° for 35-40 minutes or until golden brown. Season with salt and pepper. **Yield:** 2-3 servings.

ORANGE MINT COFFEE
(Pictured at right)

Wanda Whitfield, Eastanollee, Georgia

One of my favorite beverages to serve during the holidays is wassail, but to satisfy so many of my friends who love coffee, I found this recipe. Once they sampled it, their taste buds were hooked.

> 2 fresh mint sprigs
> 2 unpeeled fresh orange slices
> 2 cups hot strong brewed coffee
> 1/3 cup heavy whipping cream
> 2 teaspoons sugar

In two coffee cups, place a mint sprig and an orange slice. Pour hot coffee into cups. In a small mixing bowl, beat cream until soft peaks form. Gradually add sugar, beating until stiff peaks form. Serve with the coffee. **Yield:** 2 servings.

PECAN-CRUSTED SALMON
(Pictured below)

Cheryl Bykowski, Punta Gorda, Florida

This nutty coating and cool sauce turn ordinary salmon into something special. My husband was thrilled the first time I served this.

    2 salmon fillets (6 ounces *each*)
    2 tablespoons mayonnaise
  1/2 cup finely chopped pecans
  1/3 cup seasoned bread crumbs
    2 tablespoons grated Parmesan cheese
    1 tablespoon minced fresh parsley
    1 tablespoon butter, melted
CUCUMBER SAUCE:
  1/2 cup chopped seeded peeled cucumber
  1/2 cup vanilla yogurt
  1/2 teaspoon snipped fresh dill *or* 1/4
      teaspoon dill weed
  1/8 teaspoon garlic powder

Place salmon skin side down in a greased 11-in. x 7-in. x 2-in. baking dish. Spread 1 tablespoon mayonnaise over each fillet. Combine the pecans, bread crumbs, Parmesan cheese, parsley and butter; spoon over salmon. Bake at 425° for 10-15 minutes or until fish flakes easily with a fork.

  Meanwhile, in a small bowl, combine the cucumber sauce ingredients. Serve with the salmon. **Yield:** 2 servings.

SPINACH CHEDDAR BAKE
(Pictured above)

Julie Dixon, Hazelwood, Missouri

Spinach is one of my favorite foods, so I make this easy recipe often. You can use frozen or canned spinach.

    1 package (10 ounces) frozen chopped
      spinach, thawed and undrained
  1/3 cup crushed saltines (about 6 crackers)
    1 egg, beaten
  1/2 teaspoon onion powder
Salt to taste
    1 cup (4 ounces) shredded cheddar
      cheese, *divided*

In a bowl, combine the spinach, crackers, egg, onion powder and salt. Stir in 1/2 cup cheese. Transfer to a greased 2-cup baking dish; sprinkle with remaining cheese. Bake, uncovered, at 350° for 30 minutes or until cheese is melted and bubbly. **Yield:** 2 servings.

HAMBURGER MAC SKILLET

Barbara Kemmer, Rohnert Park, California

This recipe makes just the right amount for my husband and me. I like the idea of cooking it all in one pan. A touch of Worcestershire sauce adds a distinctive taste.

  1/2 pound ground beef
  1/4 cup chopped onion
  1/4 cup chopped green pepper
    1 garlic clove, minced
    1 can (11-1/2 ounces) tomato juice

1/2 cup uncooked elbow macaroni
1 teaspoon Worcestershire sauce
3/4 teaspoon salt
1/8 teaspoon pepper

In a skillet, cook the beef, onion, green pepper and garlic over medium heat until meat is no longer pink; drain. Add the tomato juice, macaroni, Worcestershire sauce, salt and pepper; bring to a boil. Reduce heat; cover and simmer for 20 minutes or until macaroni is tender. **Yield:** 2 servings.

CHEESY SPANISH RICE

Ann Wagenecht, Prophetstown, Illinois

This hearty rice can accompany chicken or beef—or stand alone as a tasty meatless entree. It's quick, easy and delicious.

1/2 pound ground beef
1 large green pepper, diced
1/2 cup chopped onion
1 garlic clove, minced
2 cups cooked white rice
1 can (10-3/4 ounces) condensed tomato soup, undiluted
4 ounces process cheese (Velveeta), cubed
1 teaspoon chili powder
1/4 teaspoon salt
1/4 teaspoon pepper

In a skillet, cook the beef, green pepper, onion and garlic over medium heat until meat is no longer pink; drain. Add the rice, soup, cheese, chili powder, salt and pepper. Cook until cheese is melted. Transfer to a 3-cup baking dish. Cover and bake at 350° for 30-35 minutes. **Yield:** 2 servings.

MARINATED TOMATOES

Maryalice Kieffer, Pittsburgh, Pennsylvania

My mom made this salad often, and I have made it for my family. The bread is delicious dipped in the dressing. It's something you can enjoy all summer.

2 medium tomatoes, sliced
1/4 cup olive oil
1/4 teaspoon dried oregano
1/4 teaspoon garlic salt
2 soft breadsticks *or* Italian rolls

Place tomato slices in a bowl. In a small bowl, whisk oil, oregano and garlic salt. Pour over tomatoes; stir gently to coat. Cover and refrigerate for 1-2 hours. Serve with breadsticks or rolls for dipping into marinade. **Yield:** 2 servings.

OLD-FASHIONED CUTOUT COOKIES

(Pictured below)

Elizabeth Turner, Lula, Georgia

These simple cookies are so crisp and buttery, it's hard to eat just one. I make them for special holidays, but they're welcome anytime.

1/4 cup butter, softened
3/4 cup sugar
1 egg
1 teaspoon milk
1/2 teaspoon vanilla extract
1-1/2 cups self-rising flour*
Additional sugar

In a small mixing bowl, cream butter and sugar. Beat in the egg, milk and vanilla. Add flour and mix well. On a lightly floured surface, roll out dough to 1/8-in. thickness. Cut with 3-in. cookie cutters dipped in flour. Sprinkle with additional sugar. Place 1 in. apart on greased baking sheets. Reroll scraps if desired. Bake at 375° for 7-8 minutes or until edges are lightly browned. Remove to wire racks to cool. **Yield:** about 1-1/2 dozen.

Editor's Note: As a substitute for 1-1/2 cups of self-rising flour, place 2-1/4 teaspoons baking powder and 3/4 teaspoon salt in a measuring cup. Add all-purpose flour to measure 1 cup. Then add another 1/2 cup all-purpose flour to the recipe.

132

SHAKE AND SCRAMBLE
(Pictured at left)

Carla Reid, Charlottetown, Prince Edward Island

This is a fast and hearty egg recipe. To make it even easier to prepare, I cut up the turkey and the vegetables, shred the cheese and freeze them in 1/2-cup portions. So when I want to serve this dish, I simply take out the number of bags needed.

    4 eggs, lightly beaten
  1/2 cup milk
  1/2 cup chopped green *and/or* sweet red
       pepper
  1/2 cup diced deli smoked turkey
  1/2 cup shredded cheddar cheese
    2 tablespoons butter
Salt and pepper to taste

In a container with a tight-fitting lid, combine the first five ingredients. Cover and shake until well mixed. In a small skillet, melt butter over medium heat. Add egg mixture; cook and stir until eggs are completely set. Season with salt and pepper. **Yield:** 2 servings.

PRUNE QUICK BREAD
(Pictured at left)

Shirley Kmiotek, Northbridge, Massachusetts

I bake this bread weekly and use a variety of fruits available in the junior baby food lines. The recipe came from a friend, who made it for our Christian Mothers' Club. When I'm asked to bake for lunches, bake sales or other benefits, I usually make this bread.

    2 tablespoons shortening
  1/2 cup sugar
    1 egg
  1/2 cup milk
    2 jars (2-1/2 ounces *each*) prune baby
       food
1-1/2 cups all-purpose flour
    1 teaspoon baking soda
  1/2 teaspoon salt
  1/2 cup chopped pecans

In a small mixing bowl, cream shortening and sugar. Add the egg, milk and prunes; mix well. Combine the flour, baking soda and salt; add to creamed mixture just until moistened. Stir in nuts.

Pour into two greased and floured 5-3/4-in. x 3-in. x 2-in. loaf pans. Bake at 350° for 30-35 minutes or until a toothpick inserted near the center comes out clean. Cool for 5 minutes before removing from pans to a wire rack. **Yield:** 2 mini loaves.

CRANBERRY COOLER
(Pictured at left)

Carolyn Griffin, Macon, Georgia

I am a retired assistant lunchroom manager for an elementary school. In addition to serving lunches, we were often called upon to serve refreshments for school meetings and other occasions. Everyone always enjoyed this cranberry punch.

    1 cup cranberry juice
    1 cup pineapple juice
  1/4 cup sugar
  1/4 teaspoon almond extract
1-1/4 cups ginger ale, chilled

In a pitcher, combine the juices, sugar and extract. Stir until sugar is dissolved. Refrigerate for at least 2 hours. Just before serving, stir in ginger ale. **Yield:** 2 servings.

HONEY-BAKED BANANAS
(Pictured at left)

Claudette Mogle, Federal Way, Washington

I created this recipe one day out of desperation. We had invited guests for dinner, and about a half hour before they were due to arrive, I realized I had forgotten all about preparing a dessert! I discovered I had plenty of bananas on hand, so I "fancied" them up and baked them. It was a big hit!

    2 medium firm bananas, sliced
    1 tablespoon butter, melted
    2 teaspoons honey
  1/2 teaspoon lemon juice
  1/4 cup flaked coconut, toasted
  1/4 cup chopped pecans, toasted
Whipped topping

Place the bananas in a greased 1-qt. baking dish. Combine the butter, honey and lemon juice; drizzle over bananas.

Bake, uncovered, at 350° for 10-12 minutes or until heated through. Sprinkle each serving with coconut and pecans; top with a dollop of whipped topping. **Yield:** 2 servings.

GO BANANAS!

For a cool and refreshing treat, cut bananas into chunks and put them in the freezer. You can enjoy them after a couple of hours. Or try carrying bananas in your lunch or using them as a snack.

SHRIMP CREOLE

(Pictured above)

Edna Boothe, Richmond, Virginia

Years ago, when we visited relatives on the eastern coast of North Carolina, they served this dish. I asked for the recipe and it quickly became one of our favorite meals.

- 1/2 cup chopped green pepper
- 1/4 cup chopped onion
- 1 celery rib, chopped
- 1 garlic clove, minced
- 1-1/2 teaspoons vegetable oil
- 1 can (15 ounces) tomato sauce
- 1 teaspoon dried oregano
- 1 bay leaf
- 1/2 pound cooked medium shrimp, peeled and deveined

Hot cooked rice

In a skillet, saute the green pepper, onion, celery and garlic in oil until tender. Add the tomato sauce, oregano and bay leaf.

Reduce heat; simmer, uncovered, for 20 minutes. Stir in the shrimp and cook for 3 minutes longer. Discard the bay leaf. Serve over rice. **Yield:** 2 servings.

MUSTARD VEGETABLE DIP

Irene Malew, Medinah, Illinois

I like to keep some of this dip in the fridge at all times so my husband and I have something to munch on. It

should keep for about 1 week in a tightly sealed container.

- 1/2 cup mayonnaise
- 1/4 cup sugar
- 1 tablespoon vegetable oil
- 1 tablespoon Dijon *or* other prepared mustard
- 1/2 teaspoon garlic powder

Assorted raw vegetables

In a bowl, combine the mayonnaise, sugar, oil, mustard and garlic powder; stir until smooth. Cover and refrigerate dip until serving. Serve with vegetables. Refrigerate any leftover dip. **Yield:** 3/4 cup.

CREAM CHEESE CORN BAKE

Tamma Foster, Blanchard, Oklahoma

This side dish recipe gives corn a whole new look. Don't be surprised if even your pickiest eater loves it! It's that good.

- 1-3/4 cups frozen corn
- 4 ounces cream cheese, cubed
- 2 tablespoons butter, cubed
- 2 tablespoons canned chopped green chilies
- 1 small garlic clove, minced
- 1/8 teaspoon salt

Dash pepper

In a bowl, combine all the ingredients. Place in a greased 3-cup baking dish.

Bake, uncovered, at 350° for 25-30 minutes or until bubbly around the edges. Stir before serving. **Yield:** 2 servings.

PEANUT BUTTER FRUIT DIP

Cloyd Sensenig, West Lawn, Pennsylvania

My wife was a great cook and I loved to help her. She liked to serve this dip with crackers, pretzels or fresh fruit at our family get-togethers, especially during the holidays.

- 1 cup (8 ounces) vanilla yogurt
- 1/2 cup peanut butter
- 1/8 teaspoon ground cinnamon
- 1/2 cup whipped topping

Assorted fresh fruit

In a bowl, combine the yogurt, peanut butter and cinnamon; mix well. Fold in the whipped topping. Refrigerate until serving. Serve with fruit. **Yield:** 1-2/3 cups.

OVEN BEEF STEW

(Pictured below)

Ruth Ushman, Waterford, Michigan

My husband has always liked this stew and I thought others would, too.

    2 tablespoons all-purpose flour
  3/4 teaspoon salt
  1/8 teaspoon pepper
  3/4 pound boneless beef chuck roast, cut
        into 1-inch cubes
    1 tablespoon vegetable oil
    1 can (10-3/4 ounces) condensed tomato
        soup, undiluted
1-1/4 cups water
  3/4 cup chopped onion
  1/4 teaspoon dried basil
    2 medium potatoes, peeled and diced
    2 medium carrots, cut into 1-inch pieces

In a resealable plastic bag, combine the flour, salt and pepper. Add beef cubes, a few at a time, and shake to coat.

In a Dutch oven, brown meat in oil. Add the soup, water, onion and basil; mix well. Cover and bake at 350° for 1 hour. Add potatoes and carrots. Bake 1 hour longer or until meat and vegetables are tender. **Yield:** 2-3 servings.

TURKEY MEATBALLS IN GARLIC SAUCE

(Pictured above)

Audrey Thibodeau, Mesa, Arizona

This is a pared-down recipe that my husband and I enjoy. Served over hot rice or noodles, it makes a satisfying dinner for two. I like to accompany it with baked acorn squash.

    2 tablespoons milk
  1/2 teaspoon Worcestershire sauce
    2 to 3 drops hot pepper sauce
  1/2 cup finely crushed butter flavored
        crackers (about 10 crackers)
    1 tablespoon minced fresh parsley
  1/4 teaspoon salt
  1/8 teaspoon pepper
  1/2 pound ground turkey breast
    1 cup V8 juice
  1/4 cup chicken broth
    2 garlic cloves, minced
Hot cooked rice

In a large bowl, combine the first seven ingredients. Crumble turkey over mixture and mix well. Shape into six meatballs. Place in a greased 9-in. pie plate. Bake, uncovered, at 400° for 10 minutes.

Meanwhile, in a small bowl, combine the V8 juice, broth and garlic. Turn meatballs; spoon sauce over top. Reduce heat to 350°. Bake 20 minutes longer, basting every 5 minutes. Serve over rice. **Yield:** 2 servings.

FISH FILLETS ITALIANO
(Pictured at right)

Margaret Risinger, Pacifica, California

My husband is an avid fisherman, so we enjoy a lot of fresh ocean fish. I found this recipe in a cookbook but adjusted it to serve two and changed the seasonings. Served with rice and a salad, it makes a delicious low-fat entree.

    1/4 cup chopped onion
      1 garlic clove, minced
      2 teaspoons olive oil
      1 cup diced zucchini
    1/2 cup sliced fresh mushrooms
    1/2 teaspoon dried oregano
    1/4 teaspoon dried basil
      1 can (8 ounces) tomato sauce
      1 tablespoon tomato paste
    3/4 pound cod, perch *or* haddock fillets
      2 tablespoons shredded Parmesan cheese

In a skillet, saute onion and garlic in oil until tender. Add the zucchini, mushrooms, oregano and basil. Cook for 3 minutes or until tender. Stir in the tomato sauce and paste. Cook for 8-10 minutes or until heated through.

Place fillets in an ungreased 11-in. x 7-in. x 2-in. baking dish; top with vegetable mixture. Bake, uncovered, at 350° for 20 minutes or until fish flakes easily with a fork. Sprinkle with Parmesan cheese. **Yield:** 2 servings.

MASHED POTATOES WITH CUCUMBER
(Pictured at right)

Stella Paukovich, Apollo, Pennsylvania

The first time I tasted this combination was more than 50 years ago at my mother-in-law's house. My husband assured me I'd love this side dish, and he was right. I changed the recipe slightly and like to make it with the first crop of Vidalia onions.

      2 medium potatoes, peeled and cubed
      1 tablespoon butter
      4 tablespoons milk, *divided*
    1/2 small cucumber, peeled and diced
      2 tablespoons chopped sweet onion
    1/2 teaspoon salt
    1/4 teaspoon pepper
    1-1/2 teaspoons white vinegar
      1 teaspoon sugar

Place the potatoes in a saucepan and cover with water. Cover and bring to a boil; cook for 20-25 minutes or until very tender. Drain well; mash

with butter and 2 tablespoons of milk. Stir in the cucumber, onion, salt and pepper.

In a small bowl, stir vinegar and sugar into the remaining milk. Stir into potato mixture. Serve immediately. **Yield:** 2 servings.

CHEESY BLT SALAD
(Pictured at right)

Maxine Wheeler, Columbus, Indiana

"Frank's Salad" is what this was called at Palm's Cafe in Columbus, Indiana. When my new husband and I were just out of college with little money for entertainment or dining out, we enjoyed this salad often.

      3 cups torn mixed salad greens
      8 cherry tomatoes, halved
      6 bacon strips, cooked and crumbled
      3 tablespoons chopped sweet pickles
    1/4 cup cubed Monterey Jack cheese
    1/4 cup mayonnaise
    1/2 cup French salad dressing

In a salad bowl, toss the greens, tomatoes, bacon, pickles and cheese. In a small bowl or pitcher, combine mayonnaise and French dressing; serve with the salad. **Yield:** 2 servings.

ORANGE CHOCOLATE MOUSSE
(Pictured at right)

Shirley Glaab, Hattiesburg, Mississippi

This easy-to-make dessert is one of my favorites to serve. It looks so elegant, and the velvety texture, with a subtle hint of orange, is a perfect ending to any meal.

      1 egg, beaten
      1 egg yolk, beaten
      2 tablespoons brown sugar
    1/2 to 1 teaspoon grated orange peel
    1/2 cup heavy whipping cream
    4-1/2 teaspoons orange juice
      3 squares (1 ounce *each*) semisweet
        chocolate, melted
Whipped cream and orange peel strips, optional

In a saucepan, combine the first six ingredients until blended. Cook and stir over medium-low heat for 15 minutes or until the mixture is thickened and reaches at least 160°. Remove from the heat; stir in melted chocolate until smooth.

Pour into dessert dishes. Refrigerate for at least 2 hours or until serving. Garnish with whipped cream and orange peel if desired. **Yield:** 2 servings.

TURKEY MEAT LOAF

(Pictured below)

Judy Prante, Portland, Oregon

I created this recipe when I cooked for a private business. One of the staff members thought it was the best turkey meat loaf she had ever eaten.

4-1/2 teaspoons water
1-1/2 teaspoons teriyaki sauce
    1 cup cubed bread
    1 egg, beaten
    2 tablespoons chopped onion
    1 tablespoon chopped green pepper
    1 tablespoon shredded mozzarella cheese
    1 tablespoon shredded cheddar cheese
Pinch garlic powder
Pinch celery seed
  1/2 pound ground turkey
    1 tablespoon grated Parmesan cheese

In a bowl, combine the water, teriyaki sauce and bread cubes; let stand for 5 minutes. Add the egg, onion, green pepper, mozzarella and cheddar cheeses, garlic powder and celery seed. Crumble turkey over mixture and mix well.

Pat into an ungreased 5-3/4-in. x 3-in. x 2-in. loaf pan. Sprinkle with Parmesan cheese. Bake, uncovered, at 350° for 1 hour or until meat is no longer pink and a meat thermometer reads 165°; drain. **Yield:** 2 servings.

STEWED TOMATOES WITH DUMPLINGS

(Pictured above)

Viola Stutz, Greenwood, Delaware

When I was young and did not feel well, my mother made one of my favorite dishes. Just smelling it cook made me feel better, along with her tender loving care.

    1 can (14-1/2 ounces) diced tomatoes, undrained
    1 tablespoon sugar
  1/4 teaspoon salt
  1/4 teaspoon pepper
    2 tablespoons butter
  1/2 cup biscuit/baking mix
    3 tablespoons milk

In a saucepan, combine the tomatoes, sugar, salt, pepper and butter. Bring to a boil over medium heat, stirring occasionally. In a bowl, combine the biscuit mix and milk. Drop batter in four mounds onto the tomatoes.

Reduce heat; cover and simmer for 10 minutes or until a toothpick inserted in a dumpling comes out clean (do not lift cover while simmering). **Yield:** 2 servings.

MARINATED TURKEY THIGHS

Enid Karp, Carlsbad, California

This recipe was one I originally used for lamb shanks. I decided it just might work for turkey, too—and I was right! The meat turns out tender, juicy and very flavorful every time.

1-1/2 cups buttermilk
    3 tablespoons dried minced onion

      1 teaspoon salt
  1/2 teaspoon pepper
  1/2 teaspoon celery seed
  1/2 teaspoon ground coriander
  1/2 teaspoon ground ginger
      2 turkey thighs (about 3/4 pound *each*)

In a resealable plastic bag, combine the buttermilk, onion, salt, pepper, celery seed, coriander and ginger; add turkey. Seal bag and turn to coat; refrigerate for 8 hours or overnight.

Drain and discard marinade. Place turkey in a shallow greased baking dish. Cover and bake at 325° for 45 minutes. Uncover; bake 30-35 minutes longer or until the turkey juices run clear and a meat thermometer reads 180°. **Yield:** 2 servings.

HERBED BREADSTICKS

Jeanne Collevechio, Ft. Pierce, Florida

Growing up, my children loved Italian food. Now my grandchildren are enjoying these breadsticks as special treats.

  3/4 to 1 cup all-purpose flour
  1/4 cup cornmeal
      1 teaspoon active dry yeast
  1/2 teaspoon garlic salt
  1/4 teaspoon dried basil
  1/4 teaspoon dried oregano
  1/3 cup milk
      2 tablespoons butter
      1 egg
  1/2 cup shredded Monterey Jack cheese
Additional butter, melted, optional

In a mixing bowl, combine 1/2 cup flour, cornmeal, yeast, garlic salt, basil and oregano. In a saucepan, heat milk and butter to 120°-130°. Add to dry ingredients; beat just until moistened. Add egg; beat until smooth. Stir in cheese and enough remaining flour to form a soft dough (do not knead). Cover and let rest for 15 minutes.

Divide dough into six pieces; roll each piece into a 7-in. rope. Place on a greased baking sheet. Cover and let rise in a warm place for 30 minutes. Bake at 375° for 14-16 minutes or until golden brown. Brush with butter if desired. **Yield:** 6 breadsticks.

AUTUMN CHOWDER
(Pictured at right)

Sheena Hoffman
North Vancouver, British Columbia

When the weather gets chilly, we enjoy "comfort foods", like this hearty chowder. It's easy to prepare, and the aroma as it simmers makes my mouth water.

      2 bacon strips, diced
  1/4 cup chopped onion
      1 medium red potato, diced
      1 small carrot, halved lengthwise and thinly sliced
  1/2 cup water
  3/4 teaspoon chicken bouillon granules
      1 cup milk
  2/3 cup frozen corn
  1/8 teaspoon pepper
2-1/2 teaspoons all-purpose flour
      2 tablespoons cold water
  3/4 cup shredded cheddar cheese

In a saucepan, cook bacon over medium heat until crisp; remove to paper towels. Drain, reserving 1 teaspoon drippings. In the drippings, saute onion until tender. Add the potato, carrot, water and bouillon. Bring to a boil. Reduce heat; cover and simmer for 15-20 minutes or until the vegetables are almost tender.

Stir in the milk, corn and pepper. Cook 5 minutes longer. Combine the flour and cold water until smooth; gradually whisk into soup. Bring to a boil; cook and stir for 1-2 minutes or until thickened. Remove from the heat; stir in cheese until melted. Sprinkle with bacon. **Yield:** 2 servings.

CHICKEN PARMESAN

(Pictured at left)

Mary Dennis, Bryan, Ohio

This unique combination of chicken breasts in spaghetti sauce makes a pretty dish, and it's so flavorful.

    2 boneless skinless chicken breast
      halves
    2 teaspoons vegetable oil
1-1/2 cups spaghetti sauce
    1 can (4 ounces) mushrooms stems and
      pieces, drained
  1/2 cup shredded mozzarella cheese
    2 tablespoons grated Parmesan cheese
Hot cooked linguine

In an ovenproof skillet, brown the chicken in oil over medium heat. Add spaghetti sauce and mushrooms.

Bring to a boil. Reduce heat; cover and simmer for 10-15 minutes or until chicken juices run clear. Sprinkle with cheeses.

Broil 4-6 in. from the heat for 3-4 minutes or until cheese is melted. Serve over linguine. **Yield:** 2 servings.

WEST TENNESSEE CORN BREAD

(Pictured at left)

Betty Kaytis, Elizabethton, Tennessee

My husband never liked corn bread until I started making this recipe—then he'd eat half of it. I like to serve this bread piping hot with lots of real butter on the side.

    1 egg
  1/4 cup mayonnaise*
  1/4 cup buttermilk
    1 tablespoon vegetable oil
    1 cup yellow cornmeal
  1/4 cup sugar
1-1/2 teaspoons baking powder
  1/2 teaspoon salt

In a mixing bowl, beat the egg, mayonnaise, buttermilk and oil until smooth. Combine the cornmeal, sugar, baking powder and salt; add to egg mixture and beat just until combined.

Grease an ovenproof 6-in. skillet or round baking dish; dust with the cornmeal. Add the batter. Bake at 425° for 18-20 minutes or until a toothpick inserted near the center comes out clean. **Yield:** 2 servings.

*Editor's Note: Reduced-fat or fat-free mayonnaise may not be substituted for regular mayonnaise in this recipe.

SAVORY SUMMER SQUASH

(Pictured at left)

Nadine Daniels, Curtis, Washington

I'm always looking for good-tasting recipes that are low in fat and quick to fix. This delicious squash dish fits the bill. Because zucchini is so abundant, it's almost an annual game to find new ways to fix it. This makes a perfect side dish for any meal.

    1 small zucchini, julienned
    1 small yellow summer squash,
      julienned
    1 medium tomato, diced
    3 tablespoons finely chopped onion
    1 tablespoon olive oil
  1/4 teaspoon garlic powder
  1/4 teaspoon dried marjoram
  1/4 teaspoon seasoned salt
  1/8 teaspoon pepper

In a skillet, saute the zucchini, yellow squash, tomato and onion in oil for 1 minute. Sprinkle with seasonings.

Cook 5-7 minutes longer or until vegetables are tender. Serve with a slotted spoon. **Yield:** 2 servings.

RASPBERRY TARTS

(Pictured at left)

Patricia York, Phillipsburg, New Jersey

This versatile recipe can be made with either raspberries or strawberries, whatever's in season. Combined with chocolate and marshmallows, it's a tasty and pretty dessert.

    2 tablespoons seedless red raspberry
      preserves
    2 individual graham cracker shells
    3 tablespoons heavy whipping cream
  1/3 cup semisweet chocolate chips
    2 tablespoons marshmallow creme
   16 fresh raspberries

In a saucepan or microwave, heat preserves until melted; stir. Spoon into graham cracker shells. In a small saucepan, bring cream to a boil. Remove from the heat; stir in the chocolate chips until melted and smooth. Spoon into the shells.

Heat marshmallow creme just until softened; drop by teaspoonfuls onto chocolate. Cut through with a knife to swirl the marshmallow creme. Place raspberries around the outer edge of crust. Refrigerate until serving. **Yield:** 2 servings.

1-1/2 cups cauliflowerets
1/4 cup finely chopped walnuts *or* pecans
3 tablespoons dry bread crumbs
3 tablespoons butter
1/4 cup chopped green onions
1-1/2 teaspoons minced fresh parsley
1 teaspoon lemon juice

In a saucepan, place 1 in. of water; add cauliflower. Bring to a boil. Reduce heat; cover and simmer for 4-6 minutes or until crisp-tender.

Meanwhile, in a small skillet, cook nuts and bread crumbs in butter for 1 minute. Add onions and parsley; cook and stir until onions are tender and nuts and crumbs are lightly browned. Stir in lemon juice. Drain cauliflower; top with crumb mixture. **Yield:** 2 servings.

EGGPLANT PARMESAN
(Pictured above)

Donna Wardlow-Keating, Omaha, Nebraska

We really like eggplant and would rather have it baked than fried. This can be served as a main dish or side.

2 tablespoons olive oil
1 garlic clove, minced
1 small eggplant, peeled and cut into 1/4-inch slices
1 tablespoon minced fresh basil *or* 1 teaspoon dried basil
1 tablespoon grated Parmesan cheese
1 medium tomato, thinly sliced
1/2 cup shredded mozzarella cheese

Combine oil and garlic; brush over both sides of eggplant slices. Place on a greased baking sheet. Bake at 425° for 15 minutes; turn. Bake 5 minutes longer or until golden brown. Cool on a wire rack.

Place half of the eggplant in a greased 1-qt. baking dish. Sprinkle with half of the basil and Parmesan cheese. Arrange tomato slices over top; sprinkle with the remaining basil and Parmesan cheese. Layer with half of the mozzarella cheese and the remaining eggplant; top with the remaining mozzarella.

Cover and bake at 350° for 20 minutes. Uncover; bake 5 minutes longer or until the cheese is melted. **Yield:** 2 servings.

CRUMB-TOPPED CAULIFLOWER

Kathy Cochill, Ocqueoc, Michigan

Here's a tasty way to liven up cooked cauliflower! I got the recipe from my mother-in-law. I serve it often because it is so easy to prepare and quite delicious.

ITALIAN TORTE
(Pictured below)

Theresa Stewart, New Oxford, Pennsylvania

This is one of my favorite dessert recipes because it's easily and quickly prepared, yet it's very different and delicious, good for any occasion. It is sure to impress your guests as it has mine.

1 cup ricotta cheese
3 tablespoons sugar
1/4 cup miniature chocolate chips
1 loaf (10-3/4 ounces) frozen pound cake, thawed

In a bowl, combine the ricotta cheese and sugar; mix well. Stir in chocolate chips. Split cake into

three horizontal layers. Place bottom layer on a serving plate; top with half of the cheese mixture. Repeat layers. Top with the remaining cake layer. Cover and refrigerate until serving. **Yield:** 6 servings.

RADISH CUCUMBER SALAD
(Pictured at right)

Mildred Sherrer, Bay City, Texas

I put this salad together with vegetables I had left in my garden. My family liked it so well, I started bringing it to community suppers and was often asked for the recipe. It's a refreshing side dish for any meat entree.

  1/2 medium cucumber, peeled, seeded and cut into 1-inch julienne strips
    2 radishes, julienned
    2 tablespoons chopped red onion
    1 tablespoon olive oil
1-1/2 teaspoons lemon juice
  1/8 to 1/4 teaspoon garlic salt
  1/8 teaspoon lemon-pepper seasoning

In a serving bowl, combine the cucumber, radishes and onion. In another bowl, combine the remaining ingredients. Pour over vegetables and toss to coat. Serve immediately. **Yield:** 2 servings.

CARROT ZUCCHINI SOUP

Joanne Novellino, Bayville, New Jersey

Carrots were never my family's favorite, but with this delicious soup, they hardly know they're eating them.

    2 small onions
    2 cups water
  1/2 pound carrots, cut into 1-inch pieces
  1/8 teaspoon celery salt
  1/8 teaspoon pepper
    2 cups diced zucchini (3 to 4 medium)
1-1/2 teaspoons olive oil
1-1/2 teaspoons butter
  1/2 cup diced seeded peeled tomatoes
  2/3 cup evaporated milk
    2 tablespoons minced fresh parsley

Chop one onion; set aside. Quarter the other onion and place in a 3-qt. saucepan. Add water, carrots, celery salt and pepper; bring to a boil. Reduce heat; cover and simmer for 20 minutes or until carrots are tender. Transfer to a blender or food processor; cover and process until pureed. Return to the pan.

In a skillet, saute the zucchini and chopped onion in oil and butter until tender; add to carrot mixture. Stir in tomatoes. Cover and simmer for 10 minutes or until tomatoes are tender. Stir in milk and parsley; heat through. **Yield:** 2-4 servings.

ITALIAN SAUSAGE AND PEPPERS

Claire Arrico, Portsmouth, Rhode Island

This is a dish my mother used to make. It's easy and convenient, thanks to the purchased spaghetti sauce called for in the recipe.

    2 Italian sausage links, casings removed
    1 small onion, chopped
    1 medium green pepper, cut into 3/4-inch chunks
    1 medium sweet red pepper, cut into 3/4-inch chunks
1-1/4 cups spaghetti sauce
1-1/2 teaspoons sugar
  1/4 teaspoon garlic powder
  1/4 teaspoon onion powder
  1/4 teaspoon dried oregano
  1/4 teaspoon dried parsley flakes
    2 Italian sandwich rolls *or* submarine buns, split

Cut sausage into 3/4-in. pieces. In a skillet, cook sausage and onion over medium heat until sausage is browned; drain. Stir in the peppers, spaghetti sauce, sugar, garlic powder, onion powder, oregano and parsley. Place in a greased 1-qt. baking dish.

Bake, uncovered, at 350° for 50-60 minutes or until sausage and peppers are tender, stirring every 20 minutes. Serve on rolls. **Yield:** 2 servings.

HAMBURGER CROQUETTES
(Pictured at right)

Lee Deneau, Lansing, Michigan

I created this recipe one day after wondering why chicken was often stuffed with ham and cheese but not other meats. I tried it with hamburger and added seasoned bread crumbs for just the right touch.

- 1/2 **pound lean ground beef**
- 1 **thin slice fully cooked ham, halved**
- 2 **slices process American cheese, halved**
- 1/4 **cup seasoned bread crumbs**
- 1 **tablespoon vegetable oil**
- 2 **hamburger buns, split**

Lettuce leaves and red onion and tomato slices, optional

Shape beef into four thin patties. Place a half slice of ham and two half slices of cheese on two patties. Top with remaining patties; pinch edges to seal. Coat both sides of burgers with bread crumbs.

In a skillet, cook burgers in oil for 8-10 minutes or until meat is no longer pink, turning once. Serve on buns with lettuce, onion and tomato if desired. **Yield:** 2 servings.

SKINNY FRIES
(Pictured at right)

Ann Janis, Tucson, Arizona

These fries are "skinny" since they bake to a crisp in the oven, without submerging the potatoes in oil or fat. They're great with a meal or as a snack.

- 2 **medium baking potatoes, peeled and cut into 1/4-inch julienned slices**
- 1 **tablespoon butter, melted**
- 1/4 **teaspoon salt**
- 1/8 **teaspoon pepper**

Place potatoes in a bowl; drizzle with butter and toss to coat. Transfer to a lightly greased 15-in. x 10-in. x 1-in. baking pan.

Bake, uncovered, at 400° for 45 minutes until golden brown, turning once. Sprinkle with salt and pepper. **Yield:** 2 servings.

APPLE CABBAGE TOSS
(Pictured at right)

Mary Skram, Columbia, Missouri

This dish is a favorite of ours because it suits both my husband's and my tastes. We love the touch of sweet flavor with cabbage. The apple adds color, and it's a compatible side dish with ham and either baked or sweet potatoes.

- 3 **cups chopped cabbage**
- 1/2 **cup chopped red onion**
- 1 **large tart apple, chopped**
- 2 **tablespoons butter**
- 1 **tablespoon sugar**

Salt and pepper to taste

In a saucepan, cook cabbage, onion and apple in butter over medium heat for 8-10 minutes. Sprinkle with the sugar, salt and pepper. Serve warm. **Yield:** 2 servings.

PINEAPPLE BANANA SHAKES
(Pictured at right)

Romaine Wetzel, Ronks, Pennsylvania

When I have fruit and milk to use up, any combination of fruit works well in this refreshing shake recipe.

- 1 **can (8 ounces) crushed pineapple, undrained**
- 1 **medium firm banana, quartered**
- 1 **cup buttermilk**
- 1 **tablespoon honey**
- 1/8 **teaspoon coconut extract, optional**

In a food processor or blender, combine all ingredients; cover and process until smooth. Pour into glasses; serve immediately. **Yield:** 2 servings.

SOFT BAKED CUSTARD

Mary Ann Pearce, Sparks, Nevada

The creamy texture of this soft-set custard is so inviting, you could call it comfort food. It has a pleasant vanilla flavor that is complemented by ground nutmeg.

- 1 **egg**
- 1 **cup milk**
- 3 **tablespoons sugar**
- 3/4 **teaspoon vanilla extract**
- 1/8 **teaspoon salt**

Dash ground nutmeg

In a mixing bowl, beat egg. Add the milk, sugar, vanilla and salt; stir well. Pour into two ungreased 6-oz. custard cups. Sprinkle with nutmeg.

Place the custard cups in a baking pan. Fill pan with hot water to a depth of 1 in. Bake, uncovered, at 350° for 35-40 minutes or until a knife inserted near the center comes out clean. **Yield:** 2 servings.

BROILED EGG SALAD SANDWICHES
(Pictured below)

Barbara Suetholz, Racine, Wisconsin

One of my mother's friends gave her this recipe in the late '40s. I grew up eating these sandwiches, and they've been a staple with my own family. Although our children have left home, I still make this dish often for my husband and me to enjoy.

    3 hard-cooked eggs, chopped
　1/4 cup crushed saltines
　1/4 cup chopped celery
    1 tablespoon diced pimientos
　1/2 cup mayonnaise
    2 tablespoons milk
　1/8 teaspoon salt
　1/8 teaspoon garlic salt
　1/8 teaspoon pepper
    2 English muffins, split and toasted

In a bowl, combine the eggs, saltines, celery and pimientos. In another bowl, combine the mayonnaise, milk, salt, garlic salt and pepper; mix well. Stir into the egg mixture.

Spoon about 1/3 cup onto each muffin half; place on an ungreased baking sheet. Broil 4 in. from the heat for 3-4 minutes or until lightly browned. **Yield:** 2 servings.

CHICKEN VEGETABLE SOUP
(Pictured above)

Ruby Williams, Bogalusa, Louisiana

Every grandmother knows that nothing cures a cold better than homemade soup. I find this recipe fits nicely to accommodate my great-grandson and me.

    1 medium onion, chopped
    1 celery rib, chopped
    1 garlic clove, minced
    2 teaspoons vegetable oil
1-1/2 cups chicken broth
    1 cup diced fresh tomatoes
    1 cup cubed cooked chicken
　1/4 teaspoon dried marjoram
　1/4 teaspoon dried thyme
　1/8 teaspoon pepper
    1 bay leaf

In a saucepan, saute the onion, celery and garlic in oil until tender. Stir in the broth, tomatoes, chicken, marjoram, thyme, pepper and bay leaf. Bring to a boil. Reduce heat; cover and simmer for 30 minutes or until heated through. Discard bay leaf. **Yield:** 2 servings.

RASPBERRY-WALNUT SHORTBREAD

Ann Previt, La Grande, Oregon

These buttery fruit-topped shortbread bars are a treat any time of year. They are fancy but not too rich—and a nice change of pace from chocolaty bar cookies.

1-1/4 cups all-purpose flour
1/2 cup sugar
1/2 cup cold butter
TOPPING:
2 eggs, lightly beaten
1/2 cup packed brown sugar
1 teaspoon vanilla extract
2 tablespoons all-purpose flour
1/8 teaspoon salt
1/8 teaspoon baking soda
1 cup chopped walnuts
1/3 cup raspberry jam

In a bowl, combine flour and sugar. Cut in butter until crumbly. Press onto the bottom of a greased 9-in. square baking pan. Bake at 350° for 18-20 minutes or until set and the edges are lightly browned.

Meanwhile, for topping, combine eggs and brown sugar in a mixing bowl. Beat in vanilla. Combine the flour, salt and baking soda; add to egg mixture. Stir in walnuts.

Carefully spread jam over hot crust. Pour egg mixture over jam. Bake 16-20 minutes longer or until browned and set. Cool. Cut into bars. **Yield:** 2 dozen.

■■■■■■■■■■■■■
APPLESAUCE OAT CAKE

Donna Perkins, Mineral Wells, Texas

The spicy aroma of this cake brings back childhood memories of my mother's kitchen. This small cake is just right for a couple of cake lovers.

1-3/4 cups applesauce
1 cup quick-cooking oats
1/2 cup butter-flavored shortening
3/4 cup packed brown sugar
1 egg
1-1/2 cups all-purpose flour
1 teaspoon baking soda
1 teaspoon ground cinnamon
1/2 teaspoon salt
1/2 teaspoon ground cloves
FROSTING:
2 cups confectioners' sugar
2 tablespoons butter, softened
2 tablespoons milk
1/2 teaspoon vanilla extract

In a small saucepan, bring the applesauce to a slow boil. Stir in oats; remove from the heat. Cover and let stand for 20 minutes.

In a mixing bowl, cream shortening and brown sugar. Add egg; mix well. Combine the flour, baking soda, cinnamon, salt and cloves; add to the creamed mixture alternately with applesauce mixture. Pour into a greased 8-in. square baking

pan. Bake at 350° for 40-45 minutes or until a toothpick inserted near the center comes out clean. Cool on a wire rack.

In a mixing bowl, combine the frosting ingredients; beat until smooth. Frost cooled cake. **Yield:** 9 servings.

■■■■■■■■■■■■■
SAUSAGE SQUASH SKILLET
(Pictured below)

Marcia Albury, Severna Park, Maryland

I always thought yellow squash was bland until I prepared it this way. Combined with Italian sausage, it makes a delicious main dish.

1/2 pound bulk Italian sausage
1/4 cup chopped onion
1 medium yellow summer squash, halved and sliced
1/4 cup chicken broth
Salt and pepper to taste
1/3 cup seasoned salad croutons

In a skillet over medium heat, cook sausage and onion until the meat is no longer pink; drain. Add the squash; cook for 3-4 minutes or until tender. Stir in the broth, salt and pepper. Cook 2 minutes longer or until heated through. Sprinkle with croutons. **Yield:** 2 servings.

Meals in Minutes

These tasty yet time-saving recipes make mealtime a snap—all in 30 minutes or less!

Shorten Prep Time Without Skimping On Flavor

TO FIX square meals for her circle of family and friends, Stephanie Moon has learned to cut a few corners, except where flavor is concerned.

"As a Navy wife, mother and manager of a coffee shop, I'm always on the go," Stephanie says from Nampa, Idaho. Cooks with heavy schedules will find Stephanie's recipes are super speedy.

"Using precooked poultry, frozen broccoli and a fuss-free sauce, I can quickly whip up Turkey Divan," she says. "Garlic Buttered Pasta goes nicely with any entree. Guests always leave a spot for it on their plates. It's great hot or served cold with fresh herbs from my garden."

When it comes to the ease of her dessert, the proof is in the pudding. "My yummy Mocha Parfaits are popular with adults and kids alike," she shares.

TURKEY DIVAN

    2 packages (10 ounces *each*) frozen
      broccoli spears
1/4 cup butter
1/4 cup all-purpose flour
    2 teaspoons chicken bouillon granules
    2 cups milk
3/4 pound sliced cooked turkey breast
1/4 cup grated Parmesan cheese

In a saucepan, cook broccoli until crisp-tender. Meanwhile, in another saucepan, melt butter; stir in flour and bouillon until smooth. Gradually add milk. Cook; stir for 2 minutes or until thickened.

Drain broccoli; place in a greased 13-in. x 9-in. x 2-in. baking dish. Top with half of the sauce and all of the turkey. Spoon remaining sauce over the top. Sprinkle with cheese. Broil 4-6 in. from the heat for 3-4 minutes or until golden brown and edges are bubbly. **Yield:** 4 servings.

GARLIC-BUTTERED PASTA

    2 cups uncooked small pasta shells
    3 to 4 garlic cloves, minced
1/2 cup butter
1/4 cup grated Parmesan cheese
    2 tablespoons minced fresh parsley
1/4 teaspoon salt
1/8 teaspoon pepper

Cook pasta according to package directions. Meanwhile, in a large saucepan, saute garlic in butter. Remove from heat. Drain pasta; add to garlic butter. Stir in cheese, parsley, salt and pepper; toss to coat. **Yield:** 4 servings.

MOCHA PARFAITS

(Not pictured)

1-3/4 cups cold milk, *divided*
    1 teaspoon instant coffee granules
    1 package (8 ounces) cream cheese,
      softened
    1 package (3.9 ounces) instant chocolate
      pudding mix
    1 carton (8 ounces) frozen whipped
      topping, thawed
    8 cream-filled chocolate sandwich
      cookies, crushed
Additional cream-filled chocolate sandwich
    cookies, optional

In a microwave-safe dish, heat 1/4 cup milk and coffee granules for about 30 seconds; stir until coffee is dissolved. Add remaining milk; mix well. In a small mixing bowl, beat the cream cheese, pudding mix and milk mixture until thickened.

In parfait glasses, layer half of the pudding mixture, whipped topping and crushed cookies. Repeat layers. Garnish with whole cookies if desired. **Yield:** 4-6 servings.

Quick Meal Runs Long on Taste

RUNNING AROUND her neighborhood in Naples, Florida is one of Beth Brown's favorite pastimes. But when it comes to mealtime, she takes steps to sit down with her family.

"Besides running for exercise, I'm always on the go as a wife, mother and real estate agent," Beth reports. "That's why I like fast meals that leave me time to join my family—husband Jonathan and our kids, Josh, Jeremy, Jessica and Julia."

Luckily, Beth's on the fast track when it comes to putting together deliciously speedy recipes, such as the ones featured here.

"I usually prepare Mustard Tarragon Chicken in the morning, refrigerate it the rest of the day and then just pop it into the oven right before mealtime," she advises.

"If you have cheese fans in your family, add Parmesan to the bread crumbs before coating the chicken," Beth suggests. "I've used this coating on turkey and pork chops, and both turned out moist and tasty."

"Colorful Bean Salad is a mainstay, both for family meals and neighborhood potlucks. People rave about the cumin dressing with its zesty flavor. The salad tastes even better when made ahead and marinated in the fridge overnight."

To make Beth's salad even more interesting, vary the types of beans you use. She suggests including butter beans or green beans and substituting chives for the green onions.

As a snack or as a dessert, Beth's Fudgy No-Bake Cookies earn top marks, too. "Peanut butter and chocolate are a perfect combination," she notes. "My cookie recipe can be changed to suit your sweet tooth," says Beth. "Try adding almond or mint extract. These cookies make a fun garnish for ice cream, too."

MUSTARD TARRAGON CHICKEN

1/2 cup butter, melted
1/2 teaspoon ground mustard
1/2 teaspoon garlic salt
3/4 cup dry bread crumbs
1/4 to 1/2 teaspoon dried tarragon
1/4 teaspoon pepper
6 boneless skinless chicken breast halves

In a shallow bowl, combine the butter, mustard and garlic salt. In another shallow bowl, combine the bread crumbs, tarragon and pepper.

Dip chicken into butter mixture, then coat with crumb mixture. Place in an ungreased 13-in. x 9-in. x 2-in. baking dish.

Bake, uncovered, at 375° for 20-25 minutes or until the chicken juices run clear. **Yield:** 6 servings.

COLORFUL BEAN SALAD

3 tablespoons olive oil
3 tablespoons red wine vinegar
1/2 teaspoon garlic powder
1/2 teaspoon ground cumin
1/4 teaspoon salt
1/4 teaspoon pepper
1 can (16 ounces) kidney beans, rinsed and drained
1 can (15 ounces) black beans, rinsed and drained
1 can (11 ounces) Mexicorn, drained
1/4 cup thinly sliced green onions

In a bowl, combine the oil, vinegar, garlic powder, cumin, salt and pepper; mix well.

Add the beans, corn and onions; stir to coat. Cover and refrigerate until serving. **Yield:** 6 servings.

FUDGY NO-BAKE COOKIES
(Not pictured)

1 cup sugar
2 tablespoons baking cocoa
1/4 cup butter
1/4 cup milk
1 cup quick-cooking oats
1/4 cup flaked coconut
2 tablespoons peanut butter
1/2 teaspoon vanilla extract

In a saucepan, combine sugar and cocoa; add butter and milk. Cook and stir over medium heat until mixture comes to a boil; boil for 1 minute.

Remove from the heat; stir in the oats, coconut, peanut butter and vanilla. Let stand until the mixture mounds when dropped by tablespoonfuls onto waxed paper. Cool. **Yield:** 1 dozen.

Reap Benefits With Make-Ahead Menu Options

IF YOU CAN fix a fast meal at a moment's notice, you have the makings of a farm wife, as Rose Purrington of Windom, Minnesota attests.

"When we're busy, dinner can be any time between 6 p.m. and 3 in the morning," she reports from the soybean and corn farm she runs with her husband, Doug.

"My shopping list usually includes tires, plugs and tractor parts in one column and ingredients for speedy meals in the other," shares Rose.

Luckily, Rose is outstanding in her field when it comes to agriculture and dreaming up family-pleasing menus such as the one featured here.

"The mouth-watering mix of ground beef, baked beans and barbecue sauce in Bean and Beef Skillet is a mainstay for us," she notes. "Often, I'll brown the meat with the barbecue sauce and freeze it in a resealable bag. Later, I thaw it, add the beans, cook and serve.

"My favorite way of eating this skillet dish is scooping it up with tortilla chips. Or you could crumble corn chips over the top," Rose shares. "You might even mix the meat and beans with taco sauce, spoon it onto tortillas and roll them up like a burrito.

"My Tangy Cabbage Slaw is always in demand at home and for potluck functions. People enjoy the crunchy texture and the sweet-and-sour zip. Plus, it can easily be made ahead of time."

To give the cabbage salad a different twist, use beef ramen noodles and toss in some sesame or sunflower seeds.

Her comfortingly creamy dessert is literally "kid stuff", Rose confirms. "Our daughters, Erin and Shannon, now grown, have always loved these make-your-own Pudding Parfaits. Spooning through layers of pudding, pie filling and granola is a fun way to end a meal.

"Try chocolate or butterscotch pudding for the parfaits," Rose advises. "Instead of granola, you can substitute cookie crumbs or nuts. Fresh fruit could replace the pie filling."

In her time off from chores, Rose is cultivating a career as a substitute teacher. "I'm also a collector of stamps, rocks, angels, Depression glass, Santas..." she lists, "and quick recipes for farmer-filling food, of course."

BEAN AND BEEF SKILLET

1 pound ground beef
1 medium onion, chopped
1 can (28 ounces) baked beans
1/4 cup barbecue sauce or ketchup
1 cup (4 ounces) shredded cheddar cheese

In a large skillet, cook the ground beef and onion over medium heat until the meat is no longer pink; drain.

Stir in the baked beans and barbecue sauce; heat through. Sprinkle with cheddar cheese; cover and cook on low until the cheese is melted. **Yield:** 4 servings.

TANGY CABBAGE SLAW

1 package (3 ounces) chicken ramen noodles
3-3/4 cups coleslaw mix
1/3 cup slivered almonds
3 tablespoons sliced green onions
1/2 cup vegetable oil
1/3 cup white wine vinegar
3 tablespoons sugar

In a large bowl, break noodles into small pieces; set seasoning packet aside. Add the coleslaw mix, almonds and onions.

In a small bowl, combine the oil, vinegar, sugar and contents of seasoning packet. Pour over the coleslaw mixture and toss to coat; serve immediately. Refrigerate any leftovers. **Yield:** 4-6 servings.

PUDDING PARFAITS

2 cups cold milk
1 package (3.4 ounces) instant vanilla pudding mix
1 can (21 ounces) cherry pie filling
1 cup granola cereal
Whipped topping, optional

In a mixing bowl, beat milk and pudding mix on low speed for 2 minutes or until thickened. Refrigerate for 10 minutes.

Spoon half of the pudding into four parfait glasses. Top each with 3 tablespoons pie filling and 2 tablespoons granola. Repeat layers. Garnish with whipped topping if desired. **Yield:** 4 servings.

Round Up a Quick and Tasty Meal

SUPPERTIME often finds Florine Bruns with a whole herd of hungry mouths to feed. So it's no wonder this Texas ranch wife and grandmother has a knack for keeping food moving.

"My husband, Alton, and I raise cattle and a few sheep and goats," she notes from their spread near rural Fredericksburg. "After hours spent penning and feeding the livestock, we've worked up appetites, too—for something that's tasty, nutritious and quick."

Luckily, Florine has corralled flavorful no-fuss fare including the recipes featured here. This complete meal can be on the table in just half an hour.

"My crusty Creole Salmon Fillets bake up moist and golden brown," she says. "Our grown daughters and grandsons like their food on the spicy side, so I knew Creole seasoning would make this entree a family favorite.

"Feel free to season the salmon with your favorite herbs and spices. A sprinkle of paprika works nicely," Florine suggests.

"Fresh lemon gives it a tasty twist. Or try a touch of tartar sauce or melted garlic butter."

Being in a pickle with prolific cucumbers one summer inspired Florine's refreshing Tomato Cucumber Salad. "This yummy medley of vegetables is a cool complement to zesty dishes like my fish, and also barbecued meats and poultry," she shares.

To add color and crunch to the salad, toss in bell pepper strips and croutons just before serving.

A homemade vinaigrette dressing will give the side dish zip and can be prepared ahead.

For dessert, the convenience of canned fruit is just peachy, Florine suggests. "Folks who aren't fond of rich treats prefer my pretty and refreshing Mixed Fruit Cups. A dollop of real whipped cream and a cherry on top make them look and taste extra-special.

"You might like to serve these cups as a sweet breakfast side. Or use the recipe to top off an angel food trifle.

"Our part of Texas is famous for its juicy peaches, so I use fresh fruit when I can," Florine says. "For a switch, try dressing up the dessert with frozen whipped topping and a sprinkle of nutmeg or a scoop of ice cream."

In her free time, Florine enjoys performing with a local church chorus, The Sunshine Singers, in concerts all around the community. That sounds natural for a busy country cook who always keeps things humming in the kitchen!

CREOLE SALMON FILLETS

  4 teaspoons Creole seasoning
  2 garlic cloves, minced
  2 teaspoons pepper
  4 salmon fillets (6 ounces *each*)
1/4 cup minced fresh parsley

In a large resealable plastic bag, combine the creole seasoning, garlic and pepper. Add the salmon and shake to coat.

Place salmon on a broiler pan or baking sheet. Broil 6 in. from the heat for 10-14 minutes or until fish flakes easily with a fork. Sprinkle with parsley. **Yield:** 4 servings.

TOMATO CUCUMBER SALAD

  2 medium cucumbers, cut into 1/4-inch slices
  1 large tomato, cut into wedges
  1 small red onion, cut into thin strips
1/4 cup creamy Italian, ranch *or* salad dressing of your choice

In a bowl, combine the cucumbers, tomato and onion. Add the dressing and toss to coat. **Yield:** 4 servings.

MIXED FRUIT CUPS

  1 can (15-1/4 ounces) sliced peaches, drained
  1 can (15 ounces) fruit cocktail, drained
Whipped cream

Spoon the peaches and fruit cocktail into four individual dishes. Top with the whipped cream. **Yield:** 4 servings.

FAST PUNCH

Pour leftover juice from canned fruit into a container and freeze. Thaw later for an easy-to-make punch.

Serve Up Dinner Without Cutting Into Your Time

MAKING SURE her fast-paced family is well-fed can be a challenge for Patricia Richardson of Verona, Ontario.

"With two active youngsters, a full-time job and a home business I run with my husband, Greg, it's hard enough keeping track of what day it is, let alone what we're having for supper," Patricia says with a chuckle.

"But instead of settling for frozen dinners or fast food, I rely on speedy recipes that are wholesome, tasty and easy enough for the children to help me prepare."

Kid-friendly dishes, such as those Patricia shares here, are a quick fix if you're in a mealtime pinch.

"My Barbecued Chicken Pizza starts with a prepared bread shell and barbecue sauce, plus leftover cooked chicken. I simply assemble and bake," she advises. "Daughter Haley loves creating smiling pizza 'faces' with shredded cheese and fresh veggie toppings.

"Often, I cut the pizza into small bite-size pieces and serve it as an appetizer at parties or potluck dinners," Patricia says. "Thick flat bread can be used for a crust, and round steak can replace the chicken.

"Pecans and canned mandarin oranges give Pecan Mandarin Salad the color, crunch and sweetness needed to convince the children to eat their greens. Our young son, Cole, has more than enough energy to shake up the refreshing dressing for me."

Patricia's salad can be easily drizzled with a bottled Italian dressing to make it even speedier. Sesame seeds and mini marshmallows can be tossed into the mix, too.

The siblings also like to help Patricia make dessert. "One gets busy with the melon baller while the other scoops out the whipped cream," she notes. "We enjoy Gingered Melon for brunch and as an after-school snack.

"For get-togethers, let guests spoon their melon from a large serving bowl and put on their own topping," she recommends. "Combine the fruit with ice cream or frozen yogurt and ginger ale to make a melon float."

BARBECUED CHICKEN PIZZA

    1 prebaked Italian bread shell crust
      (14 ounces)
  2/3 cup honey garlic barbecue sauce
    1 small red onion, chopped
    1 cup cubed cooked chicken
    2 cups (8 ounces) shredded mozzarella
      cheese

Place the crust on a pizza pan. Spread with barbecue sauce; sprinkle with onion, chicken and cheese. Bake at 350° for 10 minutes or until cheese is melted. **Yield:** 4 servings.

PECAN MANDARIN SALAD

2-1/2 cups torn romaine
    1 can (11 ounces) mandarin oranges,
      drained
  1/3 cup sliced cucumber
  1/4 cup coarsely chopped pecans, toasted
  1/4 cup evaporated milk
    2 tablespoons sugar
    1 tablespoon red wine vinegar
  1/8 teaspoon pepper

In a bowl, combine the romaine, oranges, cucumber and pecans.

In a jar with a tight-fitting lid, combine the milk, sugar, vinegar and pepper; shake well. Pour over the salad and toss to coat. **Yield:** 4 servings.

GINGERED MELON

  1/2 medium honeydew, cut into 1-inch
      cubes
  1/4 cup orange juice
1-1/2 teaspoons ground ginger
  1/2 to 1 cup whipped cream
  1/4 cup fresh *or* frozen unsweetened
      raspberries

In a bowl, combine the melon, orange juice and ginger; refrigerate for 5-10 minutes. Spoon into tall dessert glasses or bowls. Top with whipped cream and raspberries. **Yield:** 4 servings.

MELON STORAGE

Store cut melon in the refrigerator, sealed in plastic wrap, for up to 3 days.

Cut melon absorbs other food odors easily, so make sure the wrapping is airtight.

You Can Count On This Simple, Satisfying Supper

GOOD NEWS travels fast for Karalee Reainke of Omaha, Nebraska. And, with a house and a young child to care for, so does she…particularly around mealtime.

"It's not unusual for me to be chasing my son, Jonathan, one minute and working on my home-based computer job the next, before heading to a church meeting with my husband, Tony."

Happily, streamlined recipes such as the ones featured here help Karalee get cooking. "The simple sauce on my Angel Hair Alfredo is delicious reheated," she advises. "In fact, I often keep a couple servings in the freezer.

"To make my entree heartier, I sometimes add grilled chicken, shrimp or steamed vegetables," Karalee says.

"My Creamy Italian Salad dressing calls for on-hand ingredients and complements any kind of greens—from pre-bagged salad to fresh lettuce from our garden. What's more, it stays tasty for several days in the refrigerator." To pep up the dressing, she suggests adding parsley, black pepper or blue cheese.

By using pudding mix, Karalee can prepare picture-perfect Chocolate Mint Parfaits in an instant. "This minty chocolate dessert tastes so light and refreshing, especially after my zesty noodle dish," she notes.

"For fun, you can add some tempting finishing touches to the dessert parfaits," she says. "Top them with shaved chocolate, nuts or crumbled cookies. Or you can substitute vanilla or banana pudding."

ANGEL HAIR ALFREDO

8 to 12 ounces angel hair pasta
2 garlic cloves, minced
2 tablespoons olive oil
2 tablespoons all-purpose flour
1 tablespoon cornstarch
1/4 teaspoon garlic salt
1/4 teaspoon pepper
1/4 teaspoon dried basil
1-1/2 cups milk
4 ounces cream cheese, cubed

1/4 cup grated Parmesan cheese
1/3 to 1/2 cup diced fully cooked ham, optional

Cook pasta according to package directions. Meanwhile, in a large skillet, saute garlic in oil until lightly browned. Stir in the flour, cornstarch, garlic salt, pepper and basil until blended. Gradually stir in milk.

Bring to a boil; cook and stir for 2 minutes or until thickened. Reduce heat; whisk in cream cheese and Parmesan cheese until smooth. Add ham if desired; heat through. Drain pasta; add to sauce and toss to coat. **Yield:** 4-6 servings.

CREAMY ITALIAN SALAD

4 to 6 cups mixed salad greens
Sliced plum tomatoes *or* halved cherry tomatoes
1/4 cup mayonnaise
1 tablespoon milk
1 tablespoon cider vinegar
1/2 teaspoon dried oregano
1/2 teaspoon dried basil
1/4 teaspoon sugar
1/8 teaspoon garlic powder
1/8 teaspoon garlic salt
Pepper to taste

Divide greens and tomatoes among salad plates. In a jar with a tight-fitting lid, combine the remaining ingredients; shake well. Drizzle over salads. **Yield:** 4-6 servings.

CHOCOLATE MINT PARFAITS

2 cups plus 1 tablespoon cold milk, *divided*
1 package (3.9 ounces) instant chocolate pudding mix
4 ounces cream cheese, softened
1 tablespoon sugar
1/4 teaspoon peppermint extract
1 cup whipped topping
4 to 6 mint Andes candies, optional

In a bowl, whisk 2 cups milk and pudding mix for 2 minutes; set aside. In a small mixing bowl, beat cream cheese, sugar, extract and remaining milk. Fold in whipped topping.

In parfait or dessert glasses, layer the pudding and cream cheese mixtures. Garnish with mint candies if desired. **Yield:** 4-6 servings.

The Best of Country Cooking 2004

Our Most Memorable Meals

Home-cooked meals help bring family together
for old-fashioned, sit-down dinners.

Dish Up a Delicious Homemade Meal

DEEP-DISH CHICKEN POTPIE

Bonnie Jean Lintick, Kathyrn, Alberta

I adapted this recipe from a cookbook that I have had for many years. It's an excellent way to use up left-over chicken.

    2 cups all-purpose flour
    1/4 teaspoon salt
    2/3 cup cold butter
    1/4 cup cold water
FILLING:
 2-1/2 cups cubed cooked chicken
    2 cups fresh or frozen peas
    2 medium potatoes, peeled and cubed
    3 medium carrots, thinly sliced
    2 celery ribs, finely chopped
    1/4 cup finely chopped onion
    3 tablespoons butter
    3 tablespoons all-purpose flour
    1 to 2 tablespoons chicken bouillon
      granules
 1-1/2 teaspoons dried tarragon
Pepper to taste
    1 cup milk
    1/2 cup chicken broth
Additional milk

In a bowl, combine flour and salt; cut in butter until crumbly. Gradually add water, tossing with a fork until dough forms a ball. Set aside a third of the dough. Roll out remaining dough to fit a 2-1/2-qt. baking dish. Transfer pastry to baking dish. Trim pastry even with edge; set aside.

For filling, in a bowl, combine the chicken, peas, potatoes, carrots, celery and onion; set aside. In a saucepan, melt butter. Stir in flour, bouillon,

tarragon and pepper until smooth. Gradually stir in the milk and broth. Bring to a boil; cook and stir for 2 minutes or until thickened. Stir into chicken mixture; spoon into crust.

Roll out reserved dough to fit top of pie. Make cutouts in pastry. Place over filling; trim, seal and flute edges. Brush additional milk over pastry. Bake at 375° for 50-60 minutes or until the crust is golden brown and filling is bubbly. **Yield:** 6 servings.

GINGER PEAR GELATIN

Sunnye Tiedemann, Bartlesville, Oklahoma

I love to cook and experiment with recipes, and I came up with this one after trying different combinations of fruits. The tangy taste is nice and refreshing.

    1 package (3 ounces) lemon gelatin
    1 cup boiling water
    1 cup chilled ginger ale
    1 can (15-1/4 ounces) pear halves,
      drained and cubed
    1 cup halved green grapes

In a bowl, dissolve gelatin in boiling water. Stir in ginger ale. Cover and refrigerate until partially set. Stir in pears and grapes. Pour into a serving bowl. Chill until set. **Yield:** 6 servings.

FRUIT COOLER

Frann Clark, DeRidder, Louisiana

I especially enjoy this great pick-me-up drink after I have spent hours working out in the yard.

    2 cups orange juice
    1 cup pineapple juice
 1-1/2 cups fresh strawberries
    1/4 cup confectioners' sugar
    1 cup chilled carbonated water

In a blender, combine the juices, strawberries and sugar. Cover and process until smooth. Transfer to a pitcher; stir in water. Serve on ice. **Yield:** 6 servings.

ORANGE CHIFFON CAKE

Ann Pitt, Mountainside, New Jersey

This cake recipe was given to me by my sister-in-law many years ago. It's light in texture, compatible with any meal and makes a beautiful presentation.

    2 cups all-purpose flour
1-1/2 cups sugar
    3 teaspoons baking powder
1/4 teaspoon salt
    7 eggs, *separated*
1/2 cup orange juice
1/2 cup vegetable oil
1/4 cup water
    2 teaspoons vanilla extract
    1 tablespoon grated orange peel
    2 teaspoons grated lemon peel
1/2 teaspoon cream of tartar
ICING:
1/2 cup confectioners' sugar

    2 tablespoons shortening
    1 tablespoon butter, softened
    1 can (8 ounces) crushed pineapple, well
      drained

Sift the flour, sugar, baking powder and salt into a large bowl; make a well in the center. In another bowl, beat egg yolks until thick and lemon-colored. Beat in the orange juice, oil, water, vanilla, and orange and lemon peels. Pour into well in dry ingredients; beat with a wooden spoon until smooth.

In a mixing bowl, beat egg whites on medium speed until foamy. Add cream of tartar; beat until stiff peaks form. Gradually fold into batter.

Transfer to an ungreased 10-in. tube pan. Bake at 325° for 55-60 minutes or until cake springs back when lightly touched. Immediately invert cake; cool completely. Loosen cake from sides of pan; remove cake and place on a serving platter.

Combine the confectioners' sugar, shortening and butter until smooth. Spread over top of cake. Spoon pineapple over icing. **Yield:** 12 servings.

Flavorful Fare Is Sure to Satisfy Your Family

SLOW-COOKED CHERRY PORK CHOPS

Mildred Sherrer, Bay City, Texas

I mixed and matched several recipes to come up with this one. I'm always happy to adapt recipes for my slow cooker. It's so easy to prepare a meal that way.

  6 bone-in pork loin chops (3/4 inch thick)
1/8 teaspoon salt
Dash pepper
  1 cup canned cherry pie filling
  2 teaspoons lemon juice
1/2 teaspoon chicken bouillon granules
1/8 teaspoon ground mace

In a skillet coated with nonstick cooking spray, brown the pork chops over medium heat on both sides. Season with salt and pepper.

In a slow cooker, combine pie filling, lemon juice, bouillon and mace. Add pork chops. Cover and cook on low for 3-4 hours or until meat is no longer pink. **Yield:** 6 servings.

APPLE MASHED POTATOES

Rebecca Page, Pensacola, Florida

I love potatoes…especially mashed. When I came up with this combination, it was declared a winner. I serve this as a side dish when I have pork as an entree, but it's great with any meat.

  4 medium potatoes, peeled and cubed
  2 medium tart apples, peeled and quartered
1/2 teaspoon salt
  4 bacon strips, diced
  1 small onion, quartered and thinly sliced
1/4 cup butter
  1 teaspoon cider vinegar
1/2 teaspoon sugar
Dash ground nutmeg

Place the potatoes, apples and salt in a large saucepan; add enough water to cover. Bring to a boil; cover and cook for 12 minutes or until tender. Meanwhile, in a small skillet, cook bacon over medium heat until crisp. Remove to paper towels; drain, reserving 1 teaspoon drippings. In the drippings, saute onion until tender.

Drain the potatoes and apples. Add the butter, vinegar and sugar; mash until smooth. Top with onion, bacon and nutmeg. **Yield:** 4-6 servings.

MARJORAM GREEN BEANS

Charlene Griffin, Minocqua, Wisconsin

This easy-to-do vegetable dish becomes memorable with the addition of marjoram. The taste is subtle, yet distinctive. I like to fix beans this way for special dinners, since the bright green is so pretty on the plate.

1-1/2 pounds fresh green beans, cut into 1-inch pieces
3/4 cup water
  3 tablespoons butter
1/2 teaspoon salt
1/4 teaspoon pepper
1/8 to 1/4 teaspoon dried marjoram

Place the beans and water in a large saucepan; bring to a boil. Reduce heat; cover and cook for 8-10 minutes or until crisp-tender. Drain. Add the butter, salt, pepper and marjoram; stir until butter is melted. **Yield:** 6-8 servings.

CHOCO-SCOTCH MARBLE CAKE

Pam Giammattei, Valatie, New York

Teaming chocolate with butterscotch for a marble cake makes it more flavorful and colorful than the usual chocolate-vanilla combination. This rich family favorite is very moist and keeps well.

  1 package (18-1/4 ounces) yellow cake mix
  1 package (3.4 ounces) instant butterscotch pudding mix
  4 eggs
  1 cup (8 ounces) sour cream
1/3 cup vegetable oil
1/2 cup butterscotch chips
  1 square (1 ounce) unsweetened chocolate, melted
FROSTING:
1-1/2 cups butterscotch chips, melted
  1 square (1 ounce) unsweetened chocolate, melted
  5 to 6 tablespoons half-and-half cream
  2 tablespoons finely chopped pecans

In a large mixing bowl, combine cake mix, pudding mix, eggs, sour cream and oil; beat on low

speed for 2 minutes. Divide batter in half; stir butterscotch chips into half and chocolate into the other half. Spoon half of the butterscotch batter in a greased 10-in. fluted tube pan; top with half of the chocolate batter. Repeat layers. Cut through batter with a knife to swirl.

Bake at 350° for 40-45 minutes or until a toothpick inserted near the center comes out clean.

Cool for 10 minutes before removing from pan to a wire rack to cool completely.

For frosting, combine butterscotch chips and chocolate in a small mixing bowl. Beat in enough cream until the frosting is smooth and reaches desired spreading consistency. Spread over top of cake. Sprinkle with pecans. **Yield:** 12-16 servings.

Blend Together Menu Memories This Holiday Season

NEW ENGLAND SALMON PIE

Jeanne Uttley, Salem, New Hampshire

My mom always made salmon pie on Christmas Eve. Now I bake it for the holidays and other get-togethers during the year. It takes little time to prepare and makes a satisfying meal with a salad on the side.

3-1/2 cups warm mashed potatoes (prepared
      without milk and butter)
  1 medium onion, finely chopped
1/3 cup milk
1/2 teaspoon celery seed
1/2 teaspoon garlic powder
1/2 teaspoon salt
1/4 teaspoon white pepper
  1 can (14-3/4 ounces) salmon, drained,
      bones and skin removed
  2 tablespoons minced fresh parsley
Pastry for double-crust pie (9 inches)
  1 egg
  1 tablespoon water

In a bowl, combine the potatoes, onion, milk, celery seed, garlic powder, salt and pepper. Stir in salmon and parsley. Line a 9-in. pie plate with bottom pastry; trim even with edges. Spread salmon mixture into crust.

Roll out remaining pastry to fit top of pie; place over filling. Trim, seal and flute edges. Cut slits in top. Beat egg and water; brush over pastry. Bake at 350° for 40-45 minutes or until crust is golden. Refrigerate leftovers. **Yield:** 6-8 servings.

RUBY-RED BEET SALAD

Toni Talbott, Fairbanks, Alaska

Adapted from a recipe that I've had for about 30 years, this salad was a big hit when I served it to my future in-laws.

1 package (3 ounces) cherry gelatin
1 package (3 ounces) raspberry gelatin
1 package (3 ounces) strawberry gelatin
4 cups boiling water
1 can (20 ounces) crushed pineapple
  1 can (15 ounces) diced beets, drained
DRESSING:
  1/2 cup mayonnaise
  1/2 cup sour cream
    3 tablespoons *each* chopped celery, green
      pepper and chives
Leaf lettuce, optional

In a large bowl, combine the gelatins; add boiling water and stir to dissolve. Drain pineapple, reserving the juice; set pineapple aside. Stir juice into gelatin. Refrigerate until slightly thickened. Stir in beets and pineapple. Pour into a 13-in. x 9-in. x 2-in. dish. Refrigerate until firm.

For dressing, combine the mayonnaise, sour cream, celery, green pepper and chives in a small bowl. Cut gelatin into squares; serve on lettuce-lined salad plates if desired. Dollop with dressing. **Yield:** 12-15 servings.

MUSHROOM BROCCOLI MEDLEY

Edie Draper, Pensacola Beach, Florida

This side dish has a wonderful blend of flavors that goes great with any entree. The colorful combination looks festive during the holidays.

6 bacon strips, cut into 1/2-inch pieces
1 cup sliced fresh mushrooms
1/2 cup chopped green onions
1/4 cup chicken broth
1/4 teaspoon salt, optional
1/8 teaspoon pepper
4 cups broccoli florets

In a skillet, cook bacon over medium heat until crisp. Remove to paper towels. Drain, reserving 2 tablespoons drippings. Saute mushrooms and onions in the drippings for 2-3 minutes or until tender. Add broth, salt if desired and pepper; bring to a boil. Reduce heat; simmer, uncovered, for 3-4 minutes.

Meanwhile, in a saucepan, bring broccoli and 1 in. of water to a boil. Reduce heat; cover and simmer for 3-5 minutes or until crisp-tender. Drain. Add broccoli and bacon to mushroom mixture; toss to coat. **Yield:** 6 servings.

MOLASSES CUTOUTS

Sue Bartlett, Berlin, Wisconsin

Making these soft, chewy cookies with a rich flavor has been a family tradition since my children were small. At Christmastime, I shape the dough into gingerbread men with tasty raisin eyes and buttons.

1 cup butter, softened
1 cup sugar
2 eggs
1 cup molasses
1/2 cup cold water
5-1/2 cups all-purpose flour
4 teaspoons baking soda
1 teaspoon salt
1 teaspoon ground cinnamon
1 teaspoon ground ginger
FROSTING:
4 cups confectioners' sugar
1/4 cup butter, softened
1 teaspoon ground ginger
1/2 teaspoon salt
1/2 teaspoon ground cinnamon
3 to 4 tablespoons boiling water

M&M baking bits *or* other candies

In a mixing bowl, cream butter and sugar. Add eggs, one at a time, beating well after each addition. Beat in molasses and water. Combine the flour, baking soda, salt, cinnamon and ginger; gradually add to creamed mixture. Cover and refrigerate for 4 hours or until easy to handle.

On a lightly floured surface, roll out dough to 1/8-in. thickness. Cut with a 5-in. gingerbread man cutter. Place 1 in. apart on ungreased baking sheets. Bake at 375° for 6-8 minutes or until edges are golden brown. Remove to wire racks to cool.

For frosting, in a mixing bowl, combine the confectioners' sugar, butter, ginger, salt, cinnamon and enough water to achieve spreading consistency. Frost and decorate cookies as desired. **Yield:** about 3 dozen.

Flavorful Favorites Your Family Will Love

OVEN CHICKEN STEW

Phyllis Sheeley, Altona, Illinois

I grew up with this entree. It couldn't be easier to prepare, and it turns out delicious every time.

    1 broiler/fryer chicken (3 pounds), cut up
    1 cup chicken broth
    1 cup water
    2 medium carrots, sliced
    2 medium onions, chopped
    2 celery ribs, sliced
    2 teaspoons salt
  1/2 teaspoon pepper
  1/2 teaspoon dried basil

Place the chicken, broth and water in a Dutch oven or 3-qt. baking dish. Top with carrots, onions and celery; sprinkle with salt, pepper and basil.

Cover and bake at 350° for 1-1/2 to 2 hours or until chicken juices run clear. **Yield:** 6 servings.

SWEET POTATO CASSEROLE

Verona Wilder, Marble Hill, Missouri

This is my favorite sweet potato recipe. I got it years ago and added the cinnamon and cardamon.

  1-1/2 pounds sweet potatoes, peeled and
        quartered
    1/2 cup sugar
    1/4 cup butter, melted
    1/2 cup sweetened condensed milk
      3 eggs, lightly beaten
    1/2 teaspoon ground cinnamon
    1/4 to 1/2 teaspoon ground cardamom
  Dash lemon juice

Place the sweet potatoes in a large saucepan or Dutch oven; cover with water. Bring to a boil; cook for 20-25 minutes or until tender. Drain; cool slightly and mash.

Add the sugar, butter, milk, eggs, cinnamon, cardamom and lemon juice. Transfer to a greased 1-1/2-qt. baking dish. Cover and bake at 350° for 45-50 minutes or until set. **Yield:** 4-6 servings.

GREEN BEANS WITH ZUCCHINI

Gladys DeBoer, Castleford, Idaho

This tasty combination appears on my table often, especially when zucchini is so abundant.

    4 cups cut green beans (1-inch pieces)
    1 small onion, diced
  1/4 cup butter
    2 small zucchini, cut into 1/4-inch slices
    4 bacon strips, cooked and crumbled
  Salt and pepper to taste

Place beans in a saucepan and cover with water. Bring to a boil; cook, uncovered, for 8-10 minutes or until crisp-tender; drain. In a large skillet, saute onion in butter for 3 minutes. Add the zucchini; cook for 4 minutes. Stir in the bacon, beans, salt and pepper; heat through. **Yield:** 6 servings.

PUMPKIN BREAD RING

Theresa Stewart, New Oxford, Pennsylvania

I've been making this moist bread for years. It looks so pretty on the table.

    1/4 cup butter, softened
      1 cup sugar
      1 cup packed brown sugar
      4 eggs
      1 can (15 ounces) solid-pack pumpkin
      3 cups biscuit/baking mix
      2 teaspoons ground cinnamon
    1/2 teaspoon ground ginger
    1/4 teaspoon ground cloves
    1/4 teaspoon ground nutmeg
    1/4 cup milk
  GLAZE:
    1/3 cup butter
      2 cups confectioners' sugar
  1-1/2 teaspoons vanilla extract
      4 to 6 tablespoons water

In a mixing bowl, cream butter and sugars. Add the eggs, one at a time, beating well after each addition. Add pumpkin; mix well. Combine the biscuit mix, cinnamon, ginger, cloves and nutmeg; add to the creamed mixture alternately with milk. Pour into a greased 10-in. fluted tube pan.

Bake at 350° for 55-60 minutes or until a toothpick comes out clean. Cool for 10 minutes before removing from pan to wire rack.

For glaze, in a saucepan, cook and stir butter over medium heat for 6-7 minutes or until golden brown. Pour into a mixing bowl; beat in confectioners' sugar, vanilla and enough water to achieve drizzling consistency. Drizzle over cooled bread. **Yield:** 12-16 servings.

Great Summer Standbys Taste Good Year-Round

▪▪▪▪▪▪▪▪▪▪▪▪
TASTY SLOPPY JOES

Pauline Schrock, Sullivan, Illinois

These sandwiches have been a hit with my family from the first time I served them years ago. They make a quick hearty meal along with soup or a salad. I like to make a large batch and freeze the leftovers.

1-1/2 pounds lean ground beef
    1 cup milk
  3/4 cup quick-cooking oats
    1 medium onion, chopped
    1 tablespoon Worcestershire sauce
1-1/2 teaspoons salt
  1/4 teaspoon pepper
    1 cup ketchup
  1/2 cup water
    3 tablespoons white vinegar
    2 tablespoons sugar
  10 sandwich buns, split

In a large skillet over medium heat, cook the beef, milk, oats, onion, Worcestershire sauce, salt and pepper until meat is no longer pink. Transfer to an ungreased 8-in. square baking dish. Combine the ketchup, water, vinegar and sugar; pour over meat mixture. Bake, uncovered, at 350° for 45 minutes, stirring every 15 minutes. Spoon about 1/2 cup into each bun. **Yield:** 10 servings.

▪▪▪▪▪▪▪▪▪▪▪▪
CHEDDAR MUSHROOM MACARONI

Barbara Williams, Shady Dale, Georgia

This is my favorite dish to bring to church dinners, and whenever we have a carry-in at work, I'm asked to make it. I discovered the recipe several years ago. The rich creamy taste keeps it on my list of favorites. My husband even loves it cold!

    4 cups (16 ounces) shredded cheddar
      cheese
    1 can (10-3/4 ounces) condensed cream
      of mushroom soup, undiluted
    1 cup mayonnaise*
    1 can (7 ounces) mushroom stems and
      pieces, drained

    1 medium onion, finely chopped
    1 jar (2 ounces) diced pimientos, drained
    4 cups cooked elbow macaroni
    1 garlic clove, minced, optional

In a large bowl, combine the first six ingredients; mix well. Stir in macaroni and garlic if desired. Transfer to a greased 2-1/2-qt. baking dish. Cover; bake at 325° for 30 minutes or until heated through and cheese is melted. **Yield:** 6-8 servings.

*Editor's Note: Reduced-fat or fat-free mayonnaise is not recommended for this recipe.

▪▪▪▪▪▪▪▪▪▪▪▪
BASIL DILL COLESLAW

June Cappetto, Seattle, Washington

I was introduced to basil when I married into an Italian family. I loved the aromatic fragrance and flavor of the herb and began to use it in everything. Basil and dill add a unique touch to this cabbage slaw.

    6 cups shredded cabbage
    3 to 4 tablespoons chopped fresh basil
      or 1 tablespoon dried basil
    3 tablespoons snipped fresh dill *or* 1
      tablespoon dill weed
DRESSING:
  1/2 cup mayonnaise
    3 tablespoons sugar
    2 tablespoons cider vinegar
    2 tablespoons half-and-half cream
    1 teaspoon coarsely ground pepper

In a serving bowl, combine the cabbage, basil and dill. In a small bowl, combine dressing ingredients until blended. Pour over cabbage mixture and toss to coat. Cover and refrigerate until serving. **Yield:** 6-8 servings.

▪▪▪▪▪▪▪▪▪▪▪▪
WHITE CHOCOLATE CHIP HAZELNUT COOKIES

Denise DeJong, Pittsburgh, Pennsylvania

This is a cookie you will want to make again and again. I like to take it to church get-togethers and family reunions. It's very delicious...crispy on the outside and chewy on the inside.

1-1/4 cups whole hazelnuts, toasted, *divided*
    9 tablespoons butter, softened, *divided*
  1/2 cup sugar
  1/2 cup packed brown sugar
    1 egg
    1 teaspoon vanilla extract
1-1/2 cups all-purpose flour
  1/2 teaspoon baking soda

1/2 teaspoon salt
1 cup white *or* vanilla chips

Coarsely chop 1/2 cup hazelnuts; set aside. Melt 2 tablespoons butter. In a food processor, combine melted butter and remaining hazelnuts. Cover and process until the mixture forms a crumbly paste; set aside.

In a mixing bowl, cream the remaining butter. Beat in the sugars. Add egg and vanilla; beat until light and fluffy. Beat in ground hazelnut mixture until blended. Combine the flour, baking soda and salt; add to batter and mix just until combined. Stir in chips and chopped hazelnuts.

Drop by rounded tablespoonfuls 2 in. apart onto greased baking sheets. Bake at 350° for 10-12 minutes or until lightly browned. Remove to wire racks to cool. **Yield:** 3 dozen.

Reel in a New Family Favorite Supper

▰▰▰▰▰▰▰▰▰▰▰▰
SPANISH CORN WITH FISH STICKS

Roberta Nelson, Portland, Oregon

This tasty casserole is a family favorite and is my old standby for social functions. It's easy to assemble and economical, too.

- 1/4 cup chopped onion
- 1/4 cup chopped green pepper
- 1/4 cup butter
- 1/4 cup all-purpose flour
- 1-1/2 teaspoons salt
- 1/4 teaspoon pepper
- 2 teaspoons sugar
- 2 cans (14-1/2 ounces *each*) stewed tomatoes
- 2 packages (10 ounces *each*) frozen corn, partially thawed
- 2 packages (12 ounces *each*) frozen fish sticks

In a skillet, saute the onion and green pepper in butter until tender. Stir in the flour, salt, pepper and sugar until blended. Add tomatoes; bring to a boil. Reduce heat; simmer, uncovered, for 3-5 minutes or until thickened, stirring occasionally. Stir in corn.

Transfer to two greased 11-in. x 7-in. x 2-in. baking dishes. Cover and bake at 350° for 25 minutes. Uncover; arrange fish sticks over the top. Bake 15 minutes longer or until fish sticks are heated through. **Yield:** 8-10 servings.

▰▰▰▰▰▰▰▰▰▰▰▰
RAISIN BROCCOLI SALAD

Pat Faircloth, Lillington, North Carolina

Years ago, I needed a colorful dish for my menu and created this salad. I experimented with the dressing until the combination was a success. This is a great make-ahead salad.

- 4 cups broccoli florets
- 1 cup chopped green pepper
- 1 cup sliced carrots
- 1 cup raisins
- 1 cup chopped walnuts

- 1 medium onion, chopped
- 1 cup mayonnaise
- 1/2 cup sugar
- 1/4 cup white vinegar

In a large serving bowl, combine the first six ingredients. In a small bowl, combine the mayonnaise, sugar and vinegar until smooth. Pour over vegetable mixture and toss to coat. Cover and refrigerate for at least 1 hour or until serving. **Yield:** 12 servings.

▰▰▰▰▰▰▰▰▰▰▰▰
PUDDING-TOPPED FRUIT SALAD

Michelle Masciarelli, Torrington, Connecticut

My sister shared this recipe with me. She served the fruit in wine goblets, topped with the pudding. For large groups, serve it in a big salad bowl. Either way, it's refreshing and delicious.

- 1 can (20 ounces) pineapple chunks
- 1 can (8 ounces) crushed pineapple, undrained
- 1 cup (8 ounces) sour cream
- 1 package (3.4 ounces) instant vanilla pudding mix
- 2 medium ripe bananas, sliced
- 2 cups fresh *or* frozen blueberries, thawed
- 2 medium ripe peaches, peeled and sliced
- 2 cups sliced fresh strawberries
- 1 cup seedless green grapes
- 1 cup seedless red grapes

Fresh mint, optional

Drain pineapple chunks, reserving juice; refrigerate pineapple. Add water to juice if necessary to measure 3/4 cup. In a bowl, combine the juice, crushed pineapple, sour cream and pudding mix until blended. Cover and refrigerate for at least 3 hours.

In a large bowl, combine the bananas, blueberries, peaches, strawberries, grapes and pineapple chunks. Spread pudding mixture over the top. Garnish with mint if desired. **Yield:** 12-14 servings.

▰▰▰▰▰▰▰▰▰▰▰▰
LEMON GRAHAM SQUARES

Janis Plourde, Smooth Rock Falls, Ontario

My Aunt Jackie brought these lemon bars to every family gathering. They're my favorite lemon dessert. The crispy top and bottom give them a nice texture.

- 1 can (14 ounces) sweetened condensed milk
- 1/2 cup lemon juice
- 1-1/2 cups graham cracker crumbs (about 24 squares)

3/4 cup all-purpose flour
1/3 cup packed brown sugar
1/2 teaspoon baking powder
Pinch salt
1/2 cup butter, melted

In a bowl, combine the milk and lemon juice; mix well and set aside. In another bowl, combine the cracker crumbs, flour, brown sugar, baking powder and salt. Stir in butter until crumbly.

Press half of the crumb mixture into a greased 9-in. square baking dish. Pour lemon mixture over crust; sprinkle with remaining crumbs. Bake at 375° for 20-25 minutes or until lightly browned. Cool on a wire rack. **Yield:** 3 dozen.

General Recipe Index

A

APPETIZERS & SNACKS
Asparagus Cheese Bundles, 67
Calico Cheese Dip, 11
Cheese Spread Pinecone, 8
✓Cheesy Bean Dip, 10
Chunky Black Bean Salsa, 8
Deviled Crab Dip, 5
Hearty Nacho Dip, 6
Molded Shrimp Spread, 7
Mustard Vegetable Dip, 134
Paddy's Reuben Dip, 9
Parmesan Chicken Wings, 10
Peanut Butter Fruit Dip, 134
St. Patrick's Day Popcorn, 9
Strawberry Fruit Dip, 8
Vegetable Pizza, 5

APPLES
Apple Bundt Cake, 102
Apple Cabbage Toss, 144
Apple Fruit Bread, 77
Apple Mashed Potatoes, 162
Applesauce Oat Cake, 147
Butternut Apple Crisp, 118
Citrus Apple Pie, 119
Cran-Apple Cobbler, 102
Peanut Apple Salad, 56
Rhubarb Apple Pie, 101
Saucy Spiced Apple Pie, 96
Walnut Apple Pie, 121
Winter Fruit Chutney, 69

ASPARAGUS
Asparagus Cheese Bundles, 67
Chicken and Asparagus Bake, 26

B

BANANAS
Honey-Baked Bananas, 133
Pineapple Banana Shakes, 144
Yuletide Banana Bread, 82

BARS & BROWNIES
Chocolate Cheese Layered Bars, 85
Chocolate Maple Bars, 87
Coconut Chip Nut Bars, 90
Double Chip Cheesecake Bars, 93
Lemon Graham Squares, 170
Pecan Pie Bars, 92
Quick Brownies, 91
Raspberry-Walnut Shortbread, 146
Strawberry Yogurt Crunch, 115
✓Triple-Chocolate Brownie
  Squares, 89

BEANS & LENTILS
Bean and Beef Skillet, 153
✓Black Bean Soup, 59
✓Cheesy Bean Dip, 10
Chunky Black Bean Salsa, 8
Colorful Bean Salad, 150
Four-Bean Supreme, 73
✓Garbanzo Beans 'n' Rice, 72
Green Beans with Carrots, 126
Green Beans with Zucchini, 166
Hearty Nacho Dip, 6
Lentil Chicken Salad, 60
Marjoram Green Beans, 162
Mexican Bean Barley Soup, 56
✓Pasta Bean Soup, 52
Three-Bean Barley Salad, 59
Turkey Bean Chili, 56

BEEF & CORNED BEEF
(also see Ground Beef)
Beef 'n' Potato Pie, 45
Coffee Marinated Steak, 42
Cranberry-Mushroom Beef
  Brisket, 38
Italian Pot Roast, 28

Italian Swiss Steak, 23
Mexican Beef and Mushrooms, 22
New England Boiled Dinner, 31
Oven Beef Stew, 135
Paddy's Reuben Dip, 9
Pepper Steak, 47
Pineapple Beef Stir-Fry, 40
Pinwheel Flank Steaks, 13
Round Steak with Dumplings, 13
Spiced Pot Roast, 27
✓Steak Fajitas, 41
✓Stuffed Flank Steak, 36
Teriyaki Sirloin Steak, 19

BEVERAGES
Cranberry Cooler, 133
Cranberry-Orange Shake, 11
Cranberry Slush, 10
Fruit Cooler, 160
Hot Spiced Punch, 9
Orange Mint Coffee, 128
Peppermint Chocolate Malt, 6
Pineapple Banana Shakes, 144
Rhubarb Slush Punch, 5
Strawberry Cooler, 11
Strawberry Shakes, 9
Thick Fruit Whip, 6

BLUE-RIBBON RECIPES
Appetizers & Beverages
  Asparagus Cheese Bundles, 67
  Cranberry Slush, 10
  Deviled Crab Dip, 5
  Rhubarb Slush Punch, 5

Breads, Rolls & Muffins
  Brown Sugar Oat Muffins, 76
  Dill Seed Braid, 75
  Rhubarb Sticky Buns, 76
  Rhubarb Streusel Muffins, 75
  Whole Wheat Bread, 83

Cakes, Pies & Desserts
  Apple Bundt Cake, 102

C

✓*Recipe includes Nutritional Analysis*
and Diabetic Exchanges

*✓Recipe includes Nutritional Analysis
and Diabetic Exchanges*

D

DESSERTS (*also see specific kinds*)
Black Forest Trifle, 104
Blueberry Buckle, 119
Caramel Rice Dessert, 98
Cool Strawberry Cream, 113
Fruit Kuchen, 105
Honey-Baked Bananas, 133
Microwave Rhubarb Sauce, 100
Pineapple-Rhubarb Streusel
  Dessert, 101
Plum Kuchen, 110
Raspberry Tarts, 141
Rhubarb Cloud, 100
Soft Baked Custard, 144
Strawberry-Lemon Cream
  Puffs, 104
Strawberry Rhubarb Dumplings, 100
Strawberry Trifle, 109
Strawberry Yogurt Crunch, 115
✓Tropical Pineapple Dessert, 107
Watermelon Gelatin Dessert, 112

E

EGGS
Broccoli Sausage Breakfast Bake, 41
Broiled Egg Salad Sandwiches, 146
Fantastic Flan Pie, 120
Gouda Spinach Quiche, 27
Shake and Scramble, 133
Soft Baked Custard, 144
Spinach Egg Croissants, 44
Strawberry Bliss Omelet, 18

F

FISH & SEAFOOD
Citrus Grilled Salmon, 24
Clam Chowder, 49
Creole Salmon Fillets, 154
Curried Shrimp Salad, 57
Fish Fillets Italiano, 136
Garlic Shrimp Spaghetti, 34
Molded Shrimp Spread, 7
New England Salmon Pie, 164
Pecan-Crusted Salmon, 130
Shrimp Creole, 134
Shrimp Fried Rice, 36
Spanish Corn with Fish Sticks, 170
Stuffed Walleye, 26
Tasty Tuna Melts, 43

FRUIT (*also see specific kinds*)
Apple Fruit Bread, 77
Four-Fruit Salad, 57
Fruit 'n' Nut Rings, 83
Fruit Cooler, 160
Fruit-Filled White Cake, 122
Fruit Kuchen, 105
Fruit-Stuffed Chicken, 128
✓Fruity Greek Salad, 60
Fruity Tortellini Salad, 51
Gingered Melon, 157
Greens 'n' Fruit Salad, 55
Mixed Fruit Cups, 154
Peanut Butter Fruit Dip, 134
Pudding-Topped Fruit Salad, 170
Thick Fruit Whip, 6
Tropical Coleslaw, 61
Tropical Fruit Slush, 54
Watermelon Gelatin Dessert, 112
Winter Fruit Chutney, 69

G

**GRILLED & BROILED
RECIPES**
Barbecued Chicken, 39
Broiled Egg Salad Sandwiches, 146
Chicken Parmesan, 141
Citrus Grilled Salmon, 24
Coffee Marinated Steak, 42
Creole Salmon Fillets, 154
✓Grilled Breaded Chicken, 24
Grilled Pineapple Pork Chops, 15
✓Grilled Turkey Sandwiches, 29
Grilled Veggie Mix, 64

Maple Ham Steak, 47
Marinated Pork Chops, 18
Marinated Turkey Tenderloins, 32
Oriental Pork Burgers, 23
Pinwheel Flank Steaks, 13
Teriyaki Sirloin Steak, 19
Turkey Divan, 149

GROUND BEEF
Bean and Beef Skillet, 153
Beefy Mushroom Meatballs, 43
Cabbage Bundles with Kraut, 25
Cheeseburger Pepper Cups, 14
Cranberry Meat Loaf, 24
Giant Meatball Sub, 29
Hamburger Croquettes, 144
Hamburger Mac Skillet, 130
Meaty Macaroni Bake, 44
Onion Meatball Stew, 37
Pizza Rice Casserole, 45
Pumpkin Burgers, 42
Sloppy Joe Pizza, 26
Southwestern Rice Bake, 64
Tasty Sloppy Joes, 168
✓Wagon Wheel Casserole, 25

H

HAM & BACON
Biscuit-Topped Creamed
  Ham, 16
Colorful Vegetable Medley, 63
Cowpoke Corn Bread Salad, 53
Cranberry Meat Loaf, 24
Easter Ham, 34
Gouda Spinach Quiche, 27
Ham and Swiss Braid, 30
Maple Ham Steak, 47
Marmalade-Glazed Ham Loaf, 17
No-Fuss Ham Patties, 31
Straw and Hay, 18

I

**ICE CREAM &
FROZEN YOGURT**
Blueberry Ice Cream Topping, 112

Chocolate Malted Ice Cream, 108
Cranberry-Orange Shake, 11
Frozen Chocolate Mint Pie, 99
Peanut Ice Cream Pie, 116
✓Rhubarb Frozen Yogurt, 105
White Chocolate Cones, 123

L

LEMON & LIME
Lemon Graham Squares, 170
Lemon Surprise Cheesecake, 109
Strawberry-Lemon Cream Puffs, 104
White Chocolate Lime Mousse
  Cake, 121

M

MEAT LOAVES & MEATBALLS
Beefy Mushroom Meatballs, 43
Cranberry Meat Loaf, 24
Giant Meatball Sub, 29
Marmalade-Glazed Ham Loaf, 17
Onion Meatball Stew, 37
Turkey Meat Loaf, 138
Turkey Meatballs in Garlic
  Sauce, 135

MEAT PIES & PIZZAS
Barbecued Chicken Pizza, 157
Beef 'n' Potato Pie, 45
Chicago-Style Deep-Dish Pizza, 40
Deep-Dish Chicken Potpie, 160
Gouda Spinach Quiche, 27
New England Salmon Pie, 164
Sloppy Joe Pizza, 26
Stuffed-to-the-Gills Pizza, 28
Three-Cheese Pesto Pizza, 37
Upside-Down Meatless Pizza, 35
Vegetable Pizza, 5

MICROWAVE RECIPES
Cranberry Pecan Clusters, 89
Easy Tex-Mex Rice, 69
Homemade Cocoa Pudding, 110
Microwave Rhubarb Sauce, 100

White Chocolate Cones, 123

MINT
Chocolate Mint Parfaits, 158
Frozen Chocolate Mint Pie, 99
Orange Mint Coffee, 128
Peppermint Chocolate Malt, 6

MUFFINS
Brown Sugar Oat Muffins, 76
Orange Raisin Muffins, 79
Rhubarb Streusel Muffins, 75
Whole Wheat Muffins, 78

MUSHROOMS
Beefy Mushroom Meatballs, 43
Cheddar Mushroom Macaroni, 168
Cranberry-Mushroom Beef
  Brisket, 38
Mexican Beef and Mushrooms, 22
Mushroom Broccoli Medley, 164

N

NUTS & PEANUT BUTTER
Almond Chicken Stir-Fry, 38
Almond Cranberry Sauce, 110
Almond Fudge, 90
Cheese Spread Pinecone, 8
Coconut Chip Nut Bars, 90
Cranberry Pecan Clusters, 89
Cranberry Walnut White Fudge, 85
Filbertines, 93
Fruit 'n' Nut Rings, 83
Peanut Apple Salad, 56
Peanut Butter Fruit Dip, 134
Peanut Chicken Salad, 49
Peanut Chicken Stir-Fry, 35
Peanut Ice Cream Pie, 116
Pecan-Crusted Salmon, 130
Pecan Mandarin Salad, 157
Pecan Pie Bars, 92
Raspberry-Walnut Shortbread, 146
Walnut Apple Pie, 121
Walnut Cookie Strips, 125
Walnut Sandwich Cookies, 87
Walnut Sweet Potato Bake, 71

White Chocolate Chip Hazelnut
  Cookies, 168
Wild Rice Pecan Waffles, 78

O

OATS
Applesauce Oat Cake, 147
Brown Sugar Oat Muffins, 76
Coconut Oatmeal Crispies, 91

ONIONS
Cranberry Rice with Caramelized
  Onions, 65
Onion Meatball Stew, 37
Onion Pie, 30

ORANGE
Citrus Apple Pie, 119
Citrus Grilled Salmon, 24
✓Cranberry Orange Bread, 82
Cranberry-Orange Shake, 11
Mandarin Chicken Salad, 60
Orange Chiffon Cake, 161
Orange Chocolate Mousse, 136
Orange Mint Coffee, 128
Orange Raisin Muffins, 79
Orange Sauced Pork Chops, 46
Pecan Mandarin Salad, 157

OVEN ENTREES (also see
Casseroles; Meat Loaves & Meatballs;
Meat Pies & Pizzas; Microwave
Recipes)
Apricot-Glazed Chicken, 125
April Fools' Cake, 44
Biscuit-Topped Creamed Ham, 16
Cheeseburger Pepper Cups, 14
Chicken with Cheese Sauce, 19
Chicken with Cranberry
  Stuffing, 14
Cranberry-Mushroom Beef
  Brisket, 38

✓*Recipe includes Nutritional Analysis
and Diabetic Exchanges*

P

*✓Recipe includes Nutritional Analysis
and Diabetic Exchanges*

Alphabetical Recipe Index

✓*Recipe includes Nutritional Analysis
and Diabetic Exchanges*

Biscuit-Topped Creamed Ham, 16
✓Black Bean Soup, 59
Black Forest Trifle, 104
Blue Cheese Pear Salad, 60
Blueberry Buckle, 119
Blueberry Ice Cream Topping, 112
Broccoli Sausage Breakfast Bake, 41
Broiled Egg Salad Sandwiches, 146
✓Brown Sugar Angel Food
   Cake, 111
Brown Sugar Oat Muffins, 76
Bus Trip Cookies, 92
Butternut Apple Crisp, 118
Butterscotch Fudge, 93

C

Cabbage Bundles with Kraut, 25
Calico Cheese Dip, 11
Caramel Rice Dessert, 98
Carrot Zucchini Soup, 143
Cheddar Mushroom Macaroni, 168
Cheese Spread Pinecone, 8
Cheeseburger Pepper Cups, 14
Cheesy Baked Potatoes, 126
✓Cheesy Bean Dip, 10
Cheesy BLT Salad, 136
Cheesy Spanish Rice, 131
Cheesy Vegetable Medley, 72
Cheesy Zucchini Rice Casserole, 70
Cherry Crunch Cookies, 92
Cherry Pear Conserve, 71
Chicago-Style Deep-Dish Pizza, 40
Chicken and Asparagus Bake, 26
Chicken Parmesan, 141
Chicken Vegetable Soup, 146
Chicken with Cheese Sauce, 19
Chicken with Cranberry
   Stuffing, 14
Choco-Scotch Marble Cake, 162
Chocolate 'n' Toffee Rice
   Pudding, 116
Chocolate Cake with Fudge
   Sauce, 106
Chocolate Caramel Pears, 96
Chocolate-Caramel Supreme
   Pie, 95

Chocolate Cheese Layered Bars, 85
Chocolate Easter Eggs, 88
Chocolate Malted Ice Cream, 108
Chocolate Maple Bars, 87
Chocolate Mint Parfaits, 158
✓Chocolate Snack Cake, 105
Chocolate Strawberry Torte, 113
Chocolate Truffle Pie, 103
Chops with Corn Salsa, 46
Chunky Black Bean Salsa, 8
Chunky Chicken Rice Soup, 61
Citrus Apple Pie, 119
Citrus Grilled Salmon, 24
Clam Chowder, 49
Cobble Bread, 79
Coconut Chip Nut Bars, 90
Coconut Oatmeal Crispies, 91
Coffee Marinated Steak, 42
Colorful Bean Salad, 150
Colorful Vegetable Medley, 63
Cool 'n' Creamy Chocolate Pie, 103
Cool Strawberry Cream, 113
Corn Rice Medley, 125
Cowpoke Corn Bread Salad, 53
Cran-Apple Cobbler, 102
✓Cran-Raspberry Relish, 65
Cranberry-Carrot Layer Cake, 118
Cranberry Chip Cookies, 86
Cranberry Cooler, 133
Cranberry Meat Loaf, 24
Cranberry-Mushroom Beef
   Brisket, 38
✓Cranberry Orange Bread, 82
Cranberry-Orange Shake, 11
Cranberry Pecan Clusters, 89
Cranberry Raisin Pie, 123
Cranberry Rice with Caramelized
   Onions, 65
Cranberry Slush, 10
Cranberry Syrup, 73
Cranberry Tossed Salad, 54
Cranberry Walnut White Fudge, 85
Cream Cheese Corn Bake, 134
Creamy Italian Salad, 158
Creamy Potato Casserole, 67
Creamy Rhubarb Crepes, 122

Creole Salmon Fillets, 154
Crumb-Topped Cauliflower, 142
Crunchy Cabbage Salad, 56
Crustless New York
   Cheesecake, 111
Curried Chicken Barley Salad, 52
Curried Rice Salad, 55
Curried Shrimp Salad, 57

D

Deep-Dish Chicken Potpie, 160
Deviled Crab Dip, 5
Dill Seed Braid, 75
Double Chip Cheesecake Bars, 93

E

Easter Ham, 34
Easy Chicken Enchiladas, 17
Easy Tex-Mex Rice, 69
Eggplant Parmesan, 142

F

Fancy Joes, 32
Fantastic Flan Pie, 120
Favorite Chocolate Sheet
   Cake, 97
Filbertines, 93
Fish Fillets Italiano, 136
Four-Bean Supreme, 73
Four-Fruit Salad, 57
French Peas, 67
Fried Green Tomatoes, 63
Frozen Chocolate Mint Pie, 99
Fruit 'n' Nut Rings, 83
Fruit Cooler, 160
Fruit-Filled White Cake, 122
Fruit Kuchen, 105
Fruit-Stuffed Chicken, 128
✓Fruity Greek Salad, 60
Fruity Tortellini Salad, 51
Fudgy No-Bake Cookies, 150

G

✓Garbanzo Beans 'n' Rice, 72
Garlic-Buttered Pasta, 149
Garlic-Herbed Mashed Potatoes, 71

✓ *Recipe includes Nutritional Analysis
and Diabetic Exchanges*

R

Radish Cucumber Salad, 143
Raisin Broccoli Salad, 170
Raspberry Breeze Pie, 107
Raspberry Ribbon Pie, 115
Raspberry Tarts, 141
Raspberry-Walnut
    Shortbread, 146
Rhubarb Apple Pie, 101
Rhubarb Bread Pudding, 106
Rhubarb Chutney, 66
Rhubarb Cloud, 100
Rhubarb-Filled Cookies, 86
✓Rhubarb Frozen Yogurt, 105
Rhubarb Jelly-Roll Cake, 98
Rhubarb Slush Punch, 5
Rhubarb Sticky Buns, 76
Rhubarb Streusel Muffins, 75
Rich and Creamy Potato
    Bake, 63
Rich Chocolate Cake, 95
Round Steak with Dumplings, 13
Ruby-Red Beet Salad, 164

S

Salad with Cran-Raspberry
    Dressing, 50
Saucy Pork Chops, 127
Saucy Spiced Apple Pie, 96
Sausage Squash Skillet, 147
Savory Summer Squash, 141
Shake and Scramble, 133
Shamrock Cookies, 90
Shrimp Creole, 134
Shrimp Fried Rice, 36
Skillet Chicken and
    Vegetables, 33
Skinny Fries, 144
Sloppy Joe Pizza, 26
Slow-Cooked Cherry Pork
    Chops, 162
✓Slow-Cooked Pork Roast, 32
Soft Baked Custard, 144
Southern Scrapple, 34
Southwestern Rice Bake, 64

Southwestern Veggie Salad, 58
Spanish Corn with Fish Sticks, 170
Spiced Pot Roast, 27
✓Spiced Rhubarb Soup, 50
Spicy Chicken Rice Soup, 58
Spicy Pumpkin Bread, 76
Spinach Cheddar Bake, 130
Spinach Egg Croissants, 44
St. Patrick's Day Popcorn, 9
✓Steak Fajitas, 41
Stewed Tomatoes with
    Dumplings, 138
Straw and Hay, 18
Strawberry Bliss Omelet, 18
Strawberry Coffee Cake, 77
Strawberry Cooler, 11
Strawberry Fruit Dip, 8
Strawberry-Lemon Cream
    Puffs, 104
Strawberry Rhubarb
    Dumplings, 100
Strawberry Shakes, 9
Strawberry Spinach Salad, 49
Strawberry Trifle, 109
Strawberry Yogurt Crunch, 115
✓Stuffed Flank Steak, 36
Stuffed-to-the-Gills Pizza, 28
Stuffed Walleye, 26
Stuffed Zucchini, 73
Sweet 'n' Sour Tossed Salad, 59
Sweet Potato Casserole, 166
Sweet Potato Pear Bake, 68

T

Tangy Cabbage Slaw, 153
Tangy Cucumber Gelatin, 127
Tasty Sloppy Joes, 168
Tasty Tuna Melts, 43
Teapot Cranberry Relish, 63
Tender Potato Rolls, 78
Teriyaki Sirloin Steak, 19
Thanksgiving Sandwiches, 17
Thick Fruit Whip, 6
Three-Bean Barley Salad, 59
Three-Cheese Pesto Pizza, 37
Tomato Barley Salad, 58

Tomato Cucumber Salad, 154
Tomato Soup with a Twist, 126
✓Tricolor Pepper Pasta, 65
✓Triple-Chocolate Brownie
    Squares, 89
Tropical Cake, 117
Tropical Coleslaw, 61
Tropical Fruit Slush, 54
✓Tropical Pineapple Dessert, 107
Turkey Bean Chili, 56
✓Turkey Chili, 51
Turkey Divan, 149
Turkey Meat Loaf, 138
Turkey Meatballs in Garlic
    Sauce, 135

U

Upside-Down Meatless Pizza, 35

V

Vegetable Pizza, 5
Vegetable Rice Skillet, 68

W

✓Wagon Wheel Casserole, 25
Walnut Apple Pie, 121
Walnut Cookie Strips, 125
Walnut Sandwich Cookies, 87
Walnut Sweet Potato Bake, 71
Watermelon Gelatin
    Dessert, 112
West Tennessee Corn Bread, 141
White Chocolate Chip Hazelnut
    Cookies, 168
White Chocolate Cones, 123
White Chocolate Lime Mousse
    Cake, 121
Whole Wheat Bread, 83
Whole Wheat Muffins, 78
Wild Rice Pecan Waffles, 78
Winter Fruit Chutney, 69
Winter Squash Soup, 53

Y

Yuletide Banana Bread, 82